Territorial politics
and health policy

DEVOLUTION series
series editor Charlie Jeffrey

Devolution has established new political institutions in Scotland, Wales, Northern Ireland, London and the other English regions since 1997. These devolution reforms have far-reaching implications for the politics, policy and society of the UK. Radical institutional change, combined with a fuller capacity to express the UK's distinctive territorial identities, is reshaping the way the UK is governed and opening up new directions of public policy. These are the biggest changes to UK politics for at least 150 years.

The *Devolution* series brings together the best research in the UK on devolution and its implications. It draws together the best analysis from the Economic and Social Research Council's research programme on Devolution and Constitutional Change. The series will have three central themes, each a vital component in understanding the changes devolution has set in train.

1 **Delivering public policy after devolution, diverging from Westminster**. Does devolution result in the provision of different standards of public service in health or education, or in widening economic disparities from one part of the UK to another? If so, does it matter?

2 **The political institutions of devolution**. How well do the new devolved institutions work? How effectively are devolved and UK-level matters coordinated? How have political organisations which have traditionally operated UK-wide – political parties, interest groups – responded to multi-level politics?

3 **Public attitudes, devolution and national identity**. How do people in different parts of the UK assess the performance of the new devolved institutions? Do people identify themselves differently as a result of devolution? Does a common sense of Britishness still unite people from different parts of the UK?

Territorial politics and health policy

UK health policy in comparative perspective

Scott L. Greer

Manchester University Press

Manchester and New York

distributed exclusively in the USA by Palgrave

Published by Manchester University Press
Oxford Road, Manchester M13 9NR, UK
and Room 400, 175 Fifth Avenue, New York, NY 10010, USA
www.manchesteruniversitypress.co.uk

Distributed exclusively in the USA by
Palgrave, 175 Fifth Avenue, New York NY 10010, USA

Distributed exclusively in Canada by
UBC Press, University of British Columbia, 2029 West Mall,
Vancouver, BC, Canada V6T 1Z2

British Library Cataloguing-in-Publication Data
A catalogue record for this book is available from the British Library

Library of Congress Cataloging-in-Publication Data
A catalog record for this book is available from the Library of Congress

ISBN 13: 978 0 7190 6951 2

First published in hardback 2004 by Manchester University Press
This paperback edition first published 2009

Printed by Lightning Source

Contents

Figures and tables

Figures

Tables

Acknowledgments

This book, like most other works of social science, is a product of years of conversations and a great deal of help from many different people. It is, above all, a product of the Constitution Unit at the School of Public Policy of University College London and it is to the Unit, its director Robert Hazell, and my colleagues there that I owe most of the thanks – for help, companionship, and experience of almost the only truly successful interdisciplinary organisation I have ever seen. Special thanks to our administrators Matthew Butt and Helen Daines, who work wonders, and to their predecessors Rebecca Blackwell and Gareth Lewis. Equal thanks to the heroic research assistants Guy Lodge, who organised interviews on two continents, read texts, telephoned incessantly, and found a great deal of information nobody collects, and Cath Flew, who did a great deal in a short time. Robert Hazell's help has been invaluable. Without their help I cannot imagine this book. Emma Wild produced the tables, Matthew Butt created the figures, Alex Westlake found facts, Lucinda Maer did a valuable comparison of health plans at the start of the study, and everybody at the Unit answered lots of my questions.

Robert Cox, Mark Exworthy, Robert Fannion, William Hazleton, Rudolf Klein, Margitta Mätzke, Chris Nottingham, Alan Trench, and Robin Wilson all read sections or attempts and made valuable comments. Charlie Jeffery and Robert Hazell also read drafts of the whole volume and offered valuable guidance. Where the description of the research methods in Chapter 1 refers to seeking help from experts as an intrinsic part of the study, it means particular people whose generosity and expertise was invaluable and is much appreciated: Robin Wilson and Rick Wilford in Northern Ireland, who helped guide me through that complex place; James Mitchell, Chris Nottingham, and Kevin Woods in Scotland; Kevin Morgan, John Wyn Owen and Richard Wyn Jones in Wales; and Mark Sandford and John Tomaney in England. When I started work in 2001 I enjoyed the opportunity to work with and build on the research of Paul Jervis and William Plowden. In Canada, Keith Banting, Harvey Lazar, Tom McIntosh, Rachel Simeon, Richard Simeon, and Ron Watts took the time to give me a crash course in their country's politics, and the Institute of Intergovernmental Relations at Queens University was very helpful to a passing researcher. In Catalonia, Joan Subirats and Raquel Gallego at the Autonomous University of Barcelona have been helpful for years. David McCrone at the University of Edinburgh was a host and commentator in Edinburgh just before devolution. And thanks to Tony Mason at Manchester University Press and the series editor, Charlie Jeffery, for accepting the book and being very supportive and helpful all along.

Many long conversations with Margitta Mätzke and Alan Trench over the years shaped my thinking about the UK and comparative politics and saved me from innumerable silly ideas. The Devolution and Health project was originally the idea of John Wyn Owen and the Nuffield Trust, and has also received generous funding from the Leverhulme Trust under its Nations and Regions programme. I thank them for the support that made this study possible. Some of the research on Scotland and Catalonia draws upon various projects between 1997 and 2001 funded by the Council for European Studies and the Social Science Research Council (New York).

Over three years the arguments in this book evolved through presentations to various conferences and seminars, including those organised by the American Political Science Association, the British Politics Group, the Health Foundation, the Judge Institute of Cambridge University, the Law and Society Association, the NHS Confederation, the Nuffield Trust, the University of Oklahoma, the Political Studies Association, Queens University School of Policy Studies, the Royal College of Nursing, the Society for the Advancement of Socioeconomics, and the University of Edinburgh College of Medicine. I thank these audiences and organisations for the time, opportunity to try out ideas, and comments.

Thanks go to the many people who gave time from busy schedules to speak to me. It is common but entirely true to say that without their time, insights, and help in understanding their work and their societies this book could not have happened. A qualitative researcher's greatest debts must be to the people who give their time and thoughts for the small reward of informing academic study.

None of the people I thank are to blame for errors of fact or interpretation; these are mine alone. But special thanks to the people who shared their contacts and put in hours tutoring me, but who, in their highly political environments, would rather not be named.

Finally, I dedicate this book to my mother, Ann L. Greer, for all the reasons one dedicates a book to one's mother, and also because it is from watching her do research on health and the UK, and having long conversations about the topic, that I can write this book at all.

Note on terminology

The UK's asymmetric devolution extends to language. There is no agreed language to discuss either devolution or Northern Ireland. Almost any word given plausibility by regular use also has a meaning attached that will make it offensive to somebody.

I refer to the devolved areas as regions. This is in keeping with international terminology and implies no offence. *Regions* are meso-level political formations that might or might not pertain to a nation, just as states are political formations that might or might not correspond to nations. Their elected bodies (the Northern Ireland Assembly, National Assembly for Wales, and Scottish Parliament) also have no common word in UK usage since only Scotland and Westminster have Parliaments. Nevertheless *legislature* is more appropriate than any other term. The executives in these bodies also lack a common term that groups them together or distinguishes them from the civil service (or, in the case of Wales, other parties). I refer to the *governments*, meaning the common understanding of the small group of politicians in command of the permanent executive apparatus and, generally, a majority in the legislature. To do otherwise obscures who is doing what, since the Scottish Executive (civil service) is not the Scottish Executive (politicians) and the National Assembly for Wales' acrobatic efforts to turn itself into a conventional parliament have got far enough to make a group identifiable as a government (calling itself the Welsh Assembly Government).

Northern Ireland creates a yet more controversial set of problems. The Department of Health, Social Services, and Public Safety could not find any universally acceptable term for the place and so devolved health documents from Northern Ireland refer to it as 'here'. I refer to it as *Northern Ireland* since that is the most common international term and indulgence can only go so far. I try to use *Nationalist* and *Unionist* unless referring to an explicit group that calls itself something else. Religion explains much, but not enough, of the conflict, since the relationship between religion and politics is not quite total and more religious essentialism is the last thing Northern Ireland needs. Otherwise I try to cleave to the groups' own self-descriptions and the inhabitants' usual name for a place.

When CHAI began work in 2004, it called itself The Healthcare Commission.

1

Laboratories of democracy?

The birth of the Scottish Parliament, Northern Ireland Assembly, and National Assembly for Wales in the summer of 1999 was a momentous and long-debated event in the history of the United Kingdom and its nations and yet another step in the global rise of regional government.[1] Jubilant advocates of self-government for Northern Ireland, Scotland, and Wales spoke with a widely shared conviction that the new, devolved governments promised a new day for new politics and old nations. But just what the new governments could and would do was less clear. It is often said that in an epoch of 'globalisation' the decreasing importance of politics is as characteristic as the proliferation of new tiers of government.

And there was real reason to expect that the practical consequences, the meaningful policy divergence, would be minimal. All the pressures for convergence from global forces, Europeanisation, and the shared problems of mature welfare states should, in many scholars' views, have pressured governments into adopting policies from a very short list (Schmidt 2002:13–58). The ideas that inform much of public policy certainly opt for uniformity and 'delivery' rather than diversity or democracy (Peters 2003). As mid-level jurisdictions without the powers of states, each administration could be vulnerable to problems ranging from a lack of critical intellectual mass to the threat of flight by disgruntled consumers of public services. Their common legacy of institutional design should likewise have led them to the adoption of policies within a small band. They all shared the model and to a great extent the culture of British institutions such as the National Health Service (NHS), and institutions set on their shared paths by fifty years of common policies. They shared problems, systems, legacies, pressures, parties, labour forces, policy debates, and budget. As one Labour politician in Scotland put it, 'we wanted devolution so we could adapt policies to our local needs, not so we could do something wild' (interview 3–4).

Nor was there any shortage of critics able to point out just how far devolution, the creation of subordinate legislatures by the UK Parliament in

Westminster, is from independence, or even the size of the gap between what the people of Scotland or Wales might want to do and what the devolution settlement allowed them to do. The three new bodies share the formal supremacy of the Westminster Parliament, which created them and could modify or eliminate them at will. They lack important powers. They cannot set any significant part of their taxes, they cannot use the social security that is the main engine of redistribution in a modern economy, and London could always sign away their powers to the European Union (EU). England itself remains the 'gaping hole in the devolution settlement', with an anomalous status: right next to Scotland, which is a highly autonomous by global standards of regional government, England remains directly governed by the UK Parliament in Westminster and therefore by the whole UK electorate (Hazell 2003a:295). A 2003 government reshuffle drove home the extent of interpenetration when Scottish MP John Reid, sitting for Glasgow, became Secretary of State for Health. This meant he ran the English health system but as an MP had no say in the health system in his own constituency.

Perhaps the new bodies would not diverge much, after all. The weight of global politics, society, and economics all look likely to crush different polities into the same shape, while the sharp and powerful legal tools of a supreme Westminster parliament remain available to the centre.

But they have diverged, and diverged a great deal within the first five years. Each of the four political systems of the UK is taking a different path, adopting different goals, ethics, and understandings of policy (Exworthy 2001; Adams and Robinson 2002; Hunter 2003:138–58; Woods and Carter 2003). This book examines their divergence in the case of health, one of the most important, complex, and politically visible policy fields for each government. Facing problems shared by health systems around the world, each administration is placing its own bet on a structure and set of allies that will allow it to run its health system. In a system that allows them considerable latitude to make their own policies, these highly distinct polities have asked and answered different questions of themselves over and over again, and thereby developed new trajectories in health policy. The UK, routinely considered as a single system in international health policy studies, is becoming four different systems.

To foreshadow the empirical arguments, the four systems have bet, respectively, on markets, professionalism, localism, and permissive managerialism, and are thereby creating four different models for health services. Scotland's health policy has bet on *professionalism*, in which it tries to align organisation with the existing structure of medicine. This means reducing layers of management and replacing them with clinical networks, and increasing the role of professionals in rationing and resource allocation. England has bet on *markets*, in which independent trusts, similar to private firms, will contract with each other for care while approximately thirty regulatory organisations will ensure quality. Competition, management, and regulation will be the keys to getting value from health spending while severing the link between frontline health services and the Minister. Wales has bet on *localism*. This means integrating health and local government in order to coordinate care and focus on determinants of health rather than treating the sick. It tries to use localism as the lever to make the NHS into a national health service rather than a national sickness service. Northern Ireland, in and out of devolution, has continued to bet on *permissive managerialism*. This is a system that focuses on keeping services going in tough conditions, and otherwise produces little overall policy and enforces less. It provides stability in difficult conditions – but at the cost of no policy and with the benefit of local experimentation and variation.

This book examines and explains individual policy decisions that created these trajectories. Despite all the reasons for these sibling systems not to diverge, they are diverging on issues as distinct and important as organisation of health services (the role of markets, professionals, and managers); the role of health services and public health in the wider society; the structure of medicine and its relations with the state; the extent of citizenship rights and the welfare state; and the role of public and private funding and provision (or, whether the NHS as a publicly run service should even exist). Why?

The answer, I argue, lies primarily in the natural tendency of political systems to diverge as part of the ordinary course of political problem solving, and partly in the distinctiveness of devolved politics and the relatively high degree of devolved government autonomy in the UK. It is hazardous to assume that any outside constraint will intelligibly shape such policy decisions, even in a small, vulnerable, regional jurisdiction, because it is hazardous to assume that politicians and policy communities will agree a problem exists, agree on its interpretation, and agree on its solution. Politics, writes Hugh Heclo, 'finds its sources not only in power but also in uncertainty – men [*sic*] collectively wondering what to do . . . policymaking is a form of collective puzzlement on society's behalf' (Heclo 1975; Hunter 2003:21). The problem is the uncertainty of politics, where most things seem unaccountably to go away and some things go surprisingly awry but every problem has its Cassandra and every cause has its advocate. In such uncertain conditions, agendas, decisions, urgency, and debates will all vary.

The role of interpretation where there is uncertainty places a premium on understanding how political systems decide their agendas and policies. That means that studying political process, rather than even important outside constraints, may explain how there can be such fertility and experimentation in government as we have seen in England, Northern Ireland, Scotland, and Wales. Small decisions about welfare states might cumulate into big differences but respond poorly to 'top-down' analyses based in great shifts in demographics, trade exposure, capital mobility, ideas, or any of the other major factors that over time shape and constrain advanced industrial political economies. Policy communities suggest ideas and interpret issues, and politics guide what politicians do. Both policy communities and party systems vary, which means that different questions are asked and answered in different places and at different times. Policy communities and party systems will inevitably vary, but the differences between the four parts of the UK create particularly marked divergence, with long-established and distinctive policy communities and very different party systems. Any great, and often rather abstract, external factors such as demographics or globalisation must be processed through such political systems in places with their own histories and structures. As with light when it hits a prism, an external pressure splits, takes on new colouration, and shears off in a new direction when it collides with different political systems.

Explaining territorial political variation matters both theoretically and practically. Theoretically, the autonomy and behaviour of jurisdictions within a state lie at the crux of three important debates. One is the debate about what politics can do in a world where capital, labour, and ideas are all increasingly mobile within and between states. If devolved governments of the UK – or any other country – can diverge, then the constraints of global economy and society are looser and more complex than they might first appear. Second, how much of the autonomy and constraint is a function not of objective pressures but rather of the particular institutional configuration of the state? The UK has developed a particular model of devolution which creates highly autonomous, commanding governments (Chapter 7; Greer forthcoming-a). If politics has an inbuilt tendency to create policy divergence, then the degree of institutional autonomy of mid-level governments will explain their ultimate degree of divergence. Third, territorial policy variation touches the debate about the relationship between size and democracy, an old contest with important entrants such as Machiavelli, Rousseau, Proudhon, and the authors of the *Federalist Papers* (Dahl 1967; Beer 1993:88). What do the new polities of Northern Ireland, Scotland, and Wales do with their autonomy, and why? And what does that tell us of the high hopes some evoke for greater innovation, representativeness, liberalism, and democracy in small communities – or of the pessimistic predictions that they will be beds of conservatism or even anti-democratic politics and reaction? These questions help justify the inclusion of Northern Ireland, which is not just a part of the UK with distinctive politics that deserve respect if not necessarily admiration, but which is also a case, in devolution and in Westminster rule, of policy making and its production of divergence.

Practically, explaining the variation in policy outcomes across territory matters. There is lively debate about health services provision around the world, and the problems and potentials of regional governments are a key topic. What can regional governments do to promote or innovate in health care? Can they, for example, fulfil the hopes that American health policy analysts invested in the states after the repeated failures of federal-level reform in the USA (Leichter 1992; Fox and Iglehart 1994; Grogan 1995; Sparer 1996, 2003; Hackey 1998; White 2003)? What does analysis of politics and policy to date suggest about the future for policy in the UK, for the UK's citizenship rights, its politics, and its public services? If, as this book argues, there are strong forces for divergence in politics that are chiefly constrained by institutions of intergovernmental finance and regulation, then changing the structure of any multi-level system could promote or hinder health policy creativity.

Learning lessons from the experiences of devolution can also feed directly into the UK constitutional debates. Further devolution in the UK is a live political issue. Not only is it likely that Wales will bid for greater power, there is also a gap in the devolution settlement in England. There is a real possibility that there will be new regional governments created in England, and study of the experience of devolution to date can improve the design of such institutions. The experience to date is that the UK has created a permissive environment for devolution, but the institutions that create such autonomous governments are probably fragile and might not survive further divergence.

This chapter explains why the politics of policy should produce interjurisdictional divergence and, often, coherent trajectories for individual jurisdictions, despite various pressures for convergence. Chapter 2 then discusses the UK systems in the context of their shared histories and global debates about health care, identifying the debates analysed in case studies and the legacies that the four systems all share. It highlights that the politics of medicine and health policy are not just the politics of parties, politicians, and interest groups; health politics also includes bitterly fought conflicts between groups that believe in causes such as public health or professionalism, which interact with the clashes in the legislature. Chapters 3–6 then analyse policy outcomes in Scotland, England, Wales and Northern Ireland through case studies of organisation, public health, medical quality, and new public health policies. They also analyse an item that appeared only in Scotland, namely major expansion of welfare entitlements, and examine the politics of acute care allocation in Northern Ireland, a topic that arose in a polity that otherwise made few decisions. They show how policy outcomes and divergence are best explained by analysis of the way policy communities and party systems shape the odds of particular issues being debated and decisions made. Chapter 7 analyses the constraints within which the four devolved systems of the UK must operate. It argues that the UK has achieved a precarious system that maximises diversity. By shielding the devolved countries from normative or financial intervention by the centre or from the consequences of tax-funded services, it permits policy diversity and therefore will permit the natural course of politics to put increasing strains on common UK citizenship rights. The conclusion highlights potential lessons for the UK for its own future and for the study of welfare states, global policy debates, and institutions, while discussing the likely extent of uniformity and diversity in health policy.

Explaining territorial political variation

The reason we should expect divergence is simply that any pressure must be translated through the politics of a place before there is a response. Political systems everywhere have identifiable processes of agenda setting and decision making that vary systematically and that necessarily are foremost in the minds of those with a career to advance, a policy to promote, or a scandal to highlight. That means that the factors that explain individual policy outcomes, above all party systems and policy communities, are inextricably tied to local history and institutions. As such, agenda setting and decision making in different jurisdictions will vary, and the regularities will be primarily those of politics and policy communities. Students of the comparative political economy of the welfare state have long examined divergence in large-scale comparisons between multiple countries. Classic studies found considerable evidence for the ability and propensity of governments to have very different responses to similar problems in response to their politics and inherited institutions (Shonfield 1965; Zysman 1983; Katzenstein 1985; Gourevitch 1986; Hall 1986; Schmidt 2002).

The reason for variation between polities lies in the base elements of politics. Politics is an activity filled with uncertainty and organised efforts to manage, use, or defeat uncertainty. The politician making decisions must balance a large number of incommensurable values and incompatible issues and must usually do so without any sure sense of the likely effects. There are political issues by which a political career lives or dies, such as standing in the party, party strategy, media exposure, or interest group pressures. There are policy issues, the mere selection of which is difficult. A health minister is beset by groups pressing the urgency and claim for attention of issues as diverse as staffing, dental waiting lists, medical regulation, a disease, an ageing population, the resurgence of tuberculosis, and rapidly increasing alcohol abuse. Then, within each issue area, there are many groups pressing the rightness and urgency of their particular solutions. Despite the best, and often effective, efforts of researchers, there remains confusion about ends and means in most areas of policy. The effect of attention to capital spending to the exclusion of staffing or campaigns against sexually transmitted disease is largely unknown, whether in policy or political terms, but it is clear that there is not enough time and political energy to focus on all of the issues.

As a result of the indeterminacy of policy debates, the political process within the jurisdiction is key. Uncertainty in politics, policy, and policy outcomes underpins the 'multiple streams' or 'garbage can' model of policy making. Like many good theories, its explanation of policy decision sounds very simple (its origins are in Cohen, March, and Olsen 1972 and Kingdon 1995; for a formulation that works specifically in the UK, see Zahariadis 1995, especially 27–45; and for a sophisticated study with a focus on decentralisation, see Baumgartner and Jones 1993). It begins with the ingredients of a policy. The most basic formula for a policy outcome is the combination of a problem (something that seems to demand a response), a politician (who can and might actually do something), and a policy (something to do). If one of the three is absent, it is unlikely anything will happen. When the three come together, a 'window of opportunity' opens in which something happens, and a policy is likely to be the result. The window of opportunity generally closes quickly. A pressing new problem will arise, debate will tear down the policy, or the politician will move on (or be moved on). This means that there is fundamental indeterminacy in the policy outcomes from the organised anarchy of politics. What happens is explained by whatever and whoever happens to be in the right place at the right time.

Any individual policy decision is hard to predict but policy trajectories are not as random as the model might suggest. Chance explains their combination but the availability of ingredients is not so chancy. The multiple streams model directs attention to the issues that directly constrain and enable political decision by systematically varying politics, policy, and problem. There are systemic regularities in political systems that reduce, but do not eliminate, the element of chance. Policies have histories and contexts. They will be filtered through policy communities that are entrenched in their jurisdiction, and politicians whose sense of their own and their parties' situation shapes their behaviour. Politicians, too, have histories and roots; their personal and electoral constraints, the organisation and orientation of their party, and the overall party system all narrow the range of policies they can adopt. Analysis of policy communities and party systems – of the origins of policies and the demands of politics – can shape policies and show why, over time, the decisions of a particular political system will cumulate into a particular trajectory, and also when that trajectory will change. These are, of course, 'internal' factors focused on the political process rather than the across-the-board effects of larger problems such as an ageing population, welfare state retrenchment, or factor mobility. Politicians and policy makers might and often do have the greatest will to respond to these larger forces, but choosing which ones get a response, what they actually mean, and what makes an appropriate policy is hard and subject to inevitable randomness. It is also dependent, however, on the nature of the politicians, problems, and policies, and these are creatures of history, resources, and mobilisation. Politicians and policy advocates build their careers on interpreting and proposing solutions, and their dependence on local electors and institutions accounts for the tendency to divergence between jurisdictions. The key implications are that the three 'streams' of problems, politics, and policies are separate; policies can emerge when they surprisingly, contingently, flow together for a time; and while each stream has its systemic regularities their confluence is unpredictable.

Politics

Politics is, in the UK, the ideology and strategy of political parties in government (Zahariadis 1995:34). That incorporates the constellation of interest groups, the number and kind of players in the game, the power of particular groups with vital resources within or over the party, and the politicians' sense of the overall mood in the country, whether impressionistic or based on survey data. All these come together to give politicians a sense of the political costs, benefits, feasibility, and likely outcome of a policy. A policy might win votes but offend crucial groups within the party that could withhold important resources, or it might please activists and the core vote but alienate moderates. These are the decisions politicians must make. Personal failure is generally the consequence of misestimating the importance of different factors in formulating ideology and strategy. Politics is much studied by politics specialists, endlessly documented by journalists, and much discussed by politicians themselves. Politics ranges across wavering public opinion and focus groups, internal party pressure, the make-up of the government and its advisers, and the shifting 'conventional wisdom' that fascinates political classes anywhere. In sum, it is the extent to which a political party sees a reason to address a problem or proffer a solution.

How do politicians in a given party system choose the policies most appealing to them? Parties seek policy, office, and votes in some order. Both office – a seat in government – and votes require that parties have a position in the party system that gives them a stable core of voters and a strategy to win over voters ideologically close to them who vote for another party. If they want success they need voters. Their competition for votes is structured by the party system, i.e. the 'configurations of party competition' (Sartori 1999; Kitschelt 2001:301). This is the relationship between parties and between party competition and social cleavages.

Politicians can choose policies based on the socio-economic preferences of the electors they want to keep and those they seek to win over. One basic way politicians have incentive to differ is the position of their target electorate along a basic left–right continuum, which is defined by a complex of attitudes including attitudes toward the welfare state and cultural liberalism (both less popular on the right). Politicians have conflicting incentives to play to their base and to appeal to new voters who will almost certainly veer towards the centre of the left–right axis. If there are more voters in a particular ideological space to the left or to the right, the party system will shift its centre of gravity, and parties ideologically far away from the voters will suffer electorally.

This is a crude logic helpful in explaining politics (Downs 1957) although its universality is sharply limited to the countries where history has created politics that can be understood as such at all and it is always a simplifying mechanism to understand opportunities rather than a full explanation of party strategy. The left–right landscape already has a geography determined by historical cleavages which constrain the coalitions parties can assemble. The inherited relationship between electorates and parties, and the inherited characteristics of the societies, fix particular parties in particular areas in relation to particular issues (Lipset and Rokkan 1967; Flora, Kuhnle, and Urwin 1999). Such traditional positioning and organisational dependencies thereby dictate the frontiers with other parties that must be crossed to gain voters and the strategies that will win or preserve votes.

Additionally, though, regional party systems can contain a second axis: attitude towards regional versus central government (Caminal Badia 1998; Molas and Bartomeus 1998). Voters and parties in many regions with national identities, including Scotland, Northern Ireland, and Wales, will align themselves in two-dimensional space along not just left–right axes but also according to their view of the appropriate relationship between their people and the central state. This axis ranges from nationalism (desire to secede and turn their region into an independent state), through a commitment to autonomy within the larger state (usually to devolution, in the UK), to unionism (desire for total alignment, or even integration, between regional and state political systems and administration). In policy terms the presence of such an axis shifts party competition. For example, in Scotland and Wales it means that the two major parties are not just on the left. Centre-left and devolutionist Labour combats the left, nationalist Scottish National Party (SNP) and Plaid Cymru, as well as its sometime partners, the centre-left Liberal Democrats (and, in Scotland, the small left-libertarian Greens and Scottish Socialists). It produces incentives for some parties to diverge from each other for the sake of divergence if they seek more nationalist voters. Thus the Labour party in Scotland and Wales, always slightly on the defensive about its Scottishness or Welshness and under attack from nationalists, will often emphasise its difference from England as part of its campaigning.

If the opposition is to the nationalist left of Labour in Scotland and Wales and to the right of Labour in England, the three Labour governments will be pulled in different ways by the need to compete for different voters. Labour fights on opposite flanks in England and in devolved Scotland and Wales. Partisan competition especially sustains a leftward trend in Scotland by creating a threat from the left; Labour could lose votes on the fringes. Labour and the SNP in Scotland might both want to move closer to the centre, but they are dogged by smaller, left-libertarian parties that could rob them of their most left-libertarian voters and which oblige them to pursue policies 'left' enough to keep those voters. There is no such left-libertarian alternative in England, which means that Labour can move quite far right into Conservative territory and only pay the price in lower turn-out (usually lower turn-out in constituencies it wins anyway). Furthermore, the central party with the ability to ally across the board is the Liberal Democratic party, which is a liberal, federalist party on the centre-left in economics, libertarian in social issues, and in favour of both the UK and its thoroughgoing decentralisation. In Scotland and Wales it provides no great rightward tug. The result is that party systems give politicians different incentives relative to their comrades in other places. This simply reflects the differing political preferences, histories, and social organisations of the different regions.

The power of party systems is qualified not only by the poorly defined borders parties exploit to launch raids into each others' electorates. It is also qualified by the organisation and resource dependencies of the parties themselves. Most people support parties because they want or believe in something and think the party agrees. The parties are resource-dependent on supporters of various kinds, and the price of those resources is that the parties can be obliged to pursue certain goals. The organisation of parties and their relationships with other organisations place them under real constraints that limit what they can do. Parties are organisations that mobilise resources such as money, press, activists, infrastructure, connections, and endorsements to achieve an end, and any group that can withhold these resources can play a part in a party's policy. For example, the structure of the Labour party in Wales makes it very difficult for the government to ignore local government and the trades unions because of their strength within Welsh Labour. This means that politicians, for all that they must fight for the party's position in the party system, must do so without crossing the groups on which they depend for their party's existence.

The result is simple: at any given time the structural incentives facing politicians will be different in the different parts of the UK. Scottish and Welsh Labour politicians will be interested in policies that aid them in electoral competition with parties to their left and that will be distinctively Scottish or Welsh, while English Labour politicians will be interested in making a mark in a way that damages a party to their right. Outside the UK-wide Labour party, the differences should be even more marked, since those parties have geographically concentrated votes, even though they should be interested in picking voters from Labour and could therefore move towards its centre-left or devolutionist views. These partisan calculations will shape the response of politicians to policy ideas and problems.

Policies

Policies also have lives of their own. Rather than being devised as solutions to problems already identified, they exist relatively independently, sustained by a support structure of professionals, academics, and adherents in the health services, professions, and civil service, often sharing ideas and world views that cross-cut institutional positions. Policy 'entrepreneurs' sell their ideas, proposing their chosen policies as the responses to any number of problems. The business metaphor of 'entrepreneurs' is intentional. They sell wares by identifying clients, creating or identifying needs, and modifying their pre-existing product appropriately.[2] With luck, they are in the right place with a plausible policy just when a politician needs a solution to a problem. All their years of preparation, analysis, and argumentation serve to make their solution seem feasible and acceptable (rather than outlandish) and give it a better chance of being the outcome of this fundamentally indeterminate process.

Who shapes the cost–benefit analysis and sense of plausibility and feasibility of policy ideas? Who helps or hampers policies and nudges policy ideas and advocates in or out? The environment for policy advocates and spring from which policy ideas flow is the policy community, a 'shared-knowledge group having to do with some aspect . . . of public policy (Heclo 1978:103; there is voluminous debate about the logic and terminology of policy networks, communities, and so forth, but the core idea is quite simple: see Heclo 1978; Richardson and Jordan 1979; Rhodes 1981; Walker 1989). What the communities provide is 'a way of processing dissension' (Heclo 1978:120). Therefore, by definition, there is one policy community per government, even if some are very small, and they seem to grow and orient to governments (Keating and Loughlin 2002). They are the ones who shape perceptions of costs, benefits, and feasibility; they are the groups and institutions that host the policy entrepreneurs and ideas over time and influence how easy or hard it is to sell an idea. Policy communities are built on local institutions and organisations, are relatively stable, and will tend to have systematic biases towards one set of policy advocates or another. This is because it takes resources to participate in politics. The distribution of resources (which ones are present, and in whose hands they lie) dictates the lines of battle and the likely victors in policy communities. These resources vary territorially as they lie in different social institutions and the particular histories of institutions. This also means that they are based in concrete, territorial, organisations such as the Scottish Royal Colleges of medicine or the Welsh Local Government Association, and will fight for their own autonomy and environmental stability.

What does it take to enter a policy community? Samuel Beer (1982:331) analysed the currencies of influence, dividing them into the three attributes of an organisation that mean its leaders can have influence in politics. There have been other efforts to develop this core insight of resource dependency for specific situations (above all Rhodes 1981), but Beer's retains its simplicity and applies particularly well to policy. The first resource is *advice*. This reflects the strong likelihood that political decision makers lack information or policy ideas that they need to make decisions. Policy advocates who can supply timely and desirable advice to politicians win a hearing and influence, if nothing else because they supply ideas and help condition politicians' and other advocates' sense of feasibility. The second attribute is *acquiescence*. This is the ability to shape, support, or stop implementation of a policy. For example, in the politics of health care the support of the professionals is usually necessary if a policy is to have its desired impact, since they will be responsible for implementing it and can easily, authoritatively, ruin it. As a result, their representatives have influence over the evaluation of ideas in the policy community since they can both directly exercise their influence to make the policy fail (such as through industrial action) and indirectly since they are expected to predict whether their constituents will accept and implement the policy. The third attribute is *approval* – the help a policy gains from the group's acceptance. Beer suggests that it begins with a general public acceptance of the right to participate, such as the general sense in public opinion that doctors should have a say in health policy (which multiplies the effects of their political activities), but it includes collective action, such as memberships, organisational resources, media contacts, and money.

Policy communities around the world are clearly and often tightly linked together across borders. Even if governments learn very little from each other, the policy advocates pressing ideas upon them are often in close touch (this is the key insight of the 'policy advocacy coalitions' framework in public policy studies, which fits well with this argument: Jenkins-Smith and Sabatier 1994; Sabatier 1998). Civil servants, academics, the press, and other politicians can all affect the outcome by shaping the politicians' impression of the costs and benefits of a policy and thereby influence whether the politicians will adopt the proposal in response to political opportunities and problems. Policy advocates learn and intellectually link different jurisdictions as they suggest policies and problems. Participants in a political arena are more likely to learn from advocates within and adopt their policies because of their domestic politics rather than out of a process of learning that leads politics to converge on a 'good' or 'evidence-based' policy – they are more likely to get what one Northern Irish civil servant called 'policy-based evidence'. Policy advocates, wherever they live, ensure that the same ideas can be found within each arena; their relative strengths or weaknesses, rather than any abstractly good properties of their arguments, explain their success or failure in shaping the policy ideas available. Each policy community will ensure that different questions get asked and different answers offered.

Problems

The third element that should arise and sometimes unpredictably collides with the other elements to produce policy is the problem. What leads to particular issues gaining visibility and importance? Kingdon usefully distinguishes between 'problems' and 'conditions' (1995:109). A problem is something that seems to demand attention, and that is amenable to attention. A condition is something disagreeable that we can or must live with. Poverty is a condition (the poor are always with us), but child poverty or homelessness are problems that get treatments. Issues travel back and forth between the two categories. Problems typically gain their status through media attention and can often compel politicians to respond. Sometimes politicians or policy entrepreneurs can engineer a condition's transformation into a problem in order to have something to treat (as happened with quality improvement in Scotland). Major policies often come about when there is a 'focusing event' – an event in the public eye that focuses attention on an issue. The scandal of deaths in a bad paediatric heart surgery unit in Bristol, for example, focused attention on medical quality and thereby gave politicians a need for a response and policy advocates an opportunity. The policy implications of this problem's emergence and the response reshaped English and influenced all UK health care (Bridgeman 2002).

Problems are the least predictable aspect of the political system, from the point of view of both politicians and those who seek to explain a given policy decision. The processes that define problems – that turn conditions into problems – can vary dramatically. They can be driven by politicians, by relatively routine operation of a policy area, or by a crisis (Heinz *et al.* 1993:397). The common denominator for crises and politicians is usually the media, which is easily capable of deciding on a problem and forcing politicians to respond. The reasons a problem might attract media attention are varied and if important enough can drastically reshape the agenda. Such 'focusing events' can include criminal investigations (as when Manchester serial killer and GP Harold Shipman directed public attention to quality control in the NHS), commissions of investigation (such as one that detailed the failure of London social and health services to look after an abused child named Victoria Climbié), statistics on regular release (such as waiting list statistics), individual campaigns, and campaigns by policy advocates or politicians that bear fruit for reasons as small as a well-timed press release on a slow news day. There are three reasons why the core structural sources of problems facing the UK are relatively consistent, and certainly not different enough to explain the degree of policy divergence we have seen. The UK health services share institutional basics, they face similarly brutal media environments, and they deal with similar population problems. Routine issues and crises should not vary enough to explain much of policy: politicians' ability to raise issues is better explained by their tactics and strategies (the politics) rather than the nature of health services.

STRUCTURAL PROBLEMS OF PUBLIC HEALTH SERVICES

The incidence of problems is broadly constant; they will erupt regularly. If there is an error in every million medical encounters, then the UK could have several scandals a week. Even if there is not, newspapers and news programmes have pages and time to fill and often their own agendas, and health services are an inexhaustible source of interesting stories that can be serious problems for a government. Problems of structure and accountability are shared across the UK, if not most of the advanced industrial societies (Klein, Day, and Redmayne 1996). The health services daily face the gap between citizenship rights to necessary medical care and the effectively infinite expansion of medical needs and costs in societies. Like health systems elsewhere in the world, that means that UK health services are rationing systems that must define their baseline services, control their costs, and yet provide the level of health care that comes with citizens' rights to free and universal health care. They are beset by patient needs, patients' perceptions of needs, escalating technology and drug costs as science improves, increasingly long-lived populations, and the problem of health care's labour-intensiveness, which means that payers (governments, health insurers) must expand health care spending just to stay in place (Pierson 2001:83–7). This means that all who finance and deliver health care face this rationing problem in some way, regardless of whether they are operating in a public, private, universal, or other kind of system.

UK systems have their own particular sub-group of problems. The defining characteristic of the NHS model is that the state directly employs or contracts with the medical professionals and owns the infrastructure. Other countries have more arms-length relations with providers, and therefore tend to have politics centred around the regulation of professions and corporatist arrangements. The NHS model gives the Minister or Secretary of State responsible for health the problems that come with being the employer of a huge, assertive, and articulate workforce. In England, Northern Ireland, Scotland and Wales, the health system is the largest single employer, public or private. Health workers are far more independent, professionalised, organised, expert, popular, and legitimate than their political masters or managers. It is almost certainly true that the Minister responsible for health has a harder job than the chair or chief executive of any large corporation. The private firm will be smaller, engage in less complicated operations, have lower political salience, have fewer conflicting goals, have far simpler accountability, be less transparent, and have a more tractable workforce.

These background conditions create the following series of conditions associated with health systems, including the NHS. First, they are always rationing, millions of times a week. They must routinely deny care that somebody might deem 'necessary' or that would turn out to have saved a life. This produces, at a minimum, waiting lists for elective surgery. Second, and consequently, a system never spends 'enough', as Enoch Powell pointed out shortly after his time as Minister of Health (Powell 1966). Whole new categories of expenditure are ignored even by gloomy analysts and could erupt as problems. For example, every UK health system faces a worrisome pensions bill that expands with each new recruit. The whole UK, like many other rich countries, faces a serious professional shortage that may not be solved by current quiet attempts to recruit doctors and nurses from poor countries. Third, a health service is a huge and immensely complicated organisation (or federation of organisations) that almost certainly cannot be understood. No two hospitals work in the same way, which is why hospitals have apparently until now not even been able to share scheduling database software (Berg 1997:109). Fourth, because of their size, complexity, and integration with the lives of everybody in the UK, the health services are always under wide and complicated pressures that make their fortunes difficult to predict.

These features of UK health services mean that rationing and organisational failure routinely erupt as problems. Rationing erupts in the form of waiting list polemics, or press stories about 'crises' in individual hospitals, such as 2001–02 polemics about Glasgow's Beatson cancer centre or Northern Ireland's Royal Victoria hospitals – both triggered by an irate doctor speaking to a journalist about the consequences of a gap between desired and available resources. In the UK the legacy of low levels of capital investment since the 1970s also shows. Organisational failure problems erupt when one of the hundreds, if not thousands, of organisations that make up a health service goes wrong. The organisational features of the health service produce the conditions of rationing and difficulty of controlling organisations, which erupt into various problems when figures, a scandal, or a tip to a journalist bring it into the public eye. Sometimes this is just the life of a complex health system, but often there is a real issue involved that politics will interpret and to which the political system might respond by adopting a policy.

IDENTIFYING PROBLEMS

In the struggles among journalists and policy advocates to define the nature of any given catastrophe, the media is vitally important. Editors' search for stories means that press attention is to a great extent available to anybody who can offer a problem as a good story. The UK boasts harsh and intensely competitive media markets. In each polity there are a large number of newspapers competing for readers and maintaining a strong focus on their regional politics. In Northern Ireland the Protestant *Newsletter*, Catholic *Irish News* and middle-of-the-road, Unionist *Belfast Telegraph* maintain great pressure on politicians. In Scotland the fiercely competitive quality press (the *Herald* and its smaller rival the *Scotsman* as well as their Sunday kin, the *Sunday Herald* and *Scotland on Sunday*, as well as regional papers in Aberdeen and Dundee), the tabloids (above all the *Daily Record*), and Scottish editions of London papers all compete on the basis of their attention to Scotland. With the many smaller and evening newspapers they keep Scottish politics under a harsh spotlight (Scottish media outlets resemble mountain goats, it is said, in their ability to survive for long periods of time on almost nothing). In England, the largely London-focused 'UK' newspapers (the *Guardian, Daily Telegraph, Independent, The Times, Sun, Daily Mirror, Daily Express, Daily Mail*, and some other tabloids) as well as the local press also keep up the scrutiny. As media climates go, all three governments face a large press willing and able to identify a problem. The Welsh media market is highly fragmented and dominated by non-Welsh media. The *Western Mail*, ostensibly Wales' national newspaper, is not the dominant newspaper or even the dominant quality newspaper and faces stiff competition in the north from the Liverpool press. There are other routes to problem status, but the dominant one is the mass or technical media.

ILLNESS AND PUBLIC HEALTH

Finally, the societies in which the four health systems operate have substantially similar problems. There is marked tendency in the UK to identify the South East of England with England, and to attribute too much health and wealth to England. In reality, the picture is mixed. Every country has areas of prosperity and good health or of poverty and sickness. Standardised mortality rates measure likelihood of death relative to a national norm of 100, so a lower number is good and a higher number is bad. They show wide variation within regions, and certainly show that England faces severe problems among much of its population. Glasgow has a standardised mortality rate of 144 while Westminster in central London scores 71, meaning mortality rates are more than twice as high in the Scottish city than in central London – but the standardised mortality rate in Swansea is 98 and in Manchester it is 127. The South East of England might be well-off and healthy, but the North West (with a larger population than Wales or Northern Ireland) is neither. Tables 1.1, 1.2 and 1.3 make the demographic point: the devolved countries have severe challenges, but so does much of England. Even London might be rich and young overall but is also an extremely unequal and diverse city with a great deal of poverty and unemployment and a frighteningly high incidence of problems such as drug abuse and homelessness. The essential demographics and population risk factors of the different societies are not identical but are similar enough to shape the problems that the health systems face. Drug addiction, cancer, and coronary heart disease preoccupy doctors across the UK, while obesity, alcohol, environmental carcinogens, and tobacco worry public health specialists across the UK.

So this analysis holds the problems constant, ignoring their systematic biases because they are not regional and therefore not candidates to explain policy. The key problems that the four systems of the UK face are the same, since they stem from the basic characteristics of any health system (the gap between the beneficial and the possible, made worse by demographics, costs, and technologies) and from their basic nature as large organisations (very) theoretically run by a minister. Throughout the case studies of England, Northern Ireland, Scotland, and Wales, the problems that emerge will be of either rationing that proved unpopular or organisational failure. The problems do not vary enough to be interesting explanations of divergence or devolution. They are a regular series of stimuli to which the four systems react

Table 1.1 Standardised mortality ratio by local authority, 1999

Local authority	SMR (UK = 100)
Sedgefield	117
Newcastle-upon-Tyne	110
Manchester	127
Liverpool	126
Harrogate	93
Sheffield	99
Leeds	98
York (unitary authority)	85
Northampton	101
Stratford-on-Avon	92
Birmingham	105
Cambridge	78
Watford	115
Great Yarmouth	99
Westminster	71
Richmond-upon-Thames	79
Sevenoaks	81
Guildford	77
Exeter	97
City of Bristol (unitary authority)	95
Cardiff	100
Caerphilly	117
Swansea	98
Glasgow	144
Edinburgh	109
Aberdeen City	111
Belfast	104
Derry	111

Source: National Statistics (2001) Regional Trends 36: 180–7.

differently according to their politics and policy ideas. The problems of the four UK systems are as similar as we can expect them to be for any group of jurisdictions. The fact that the systems still diverge both poses the question that this work addresses and explains how problems can be put aside as a category of analysis.

Conclusions

The garbage can, multiple streams model of policy making was developed to capture the contingency and unpredictability of decision making and the difficulty of defining influence, but by identifying the ingredients of a policy it can identify the crucial regularities in policy making. Looking at the origins of policies, politics and problems identifies their rootedness in local history and circumstance while stressing the chance and interaction in their outcomes. Even if there are systemic regularities in policies and parties, these will not explain every decision, and sometimes policy, problem, and politician will come together and for some reason nothing will happen. This gives us a tool to see how political systems differ and to explain their divergent policy outcomes. It can also capture systematic regularities; the composition of party systems and policy communities, above all, shape these seemingly random policy outcomes. They reflect social and political institutions that can be studied and that vary territorially. Wherever there is meaningful variation in territory, which is most places, policy communities and party systems will shape politics by changing the odds of a particular policy emerging.

It is worth noting that the model has very little automatic policy learning or interchange. Policy advocates learn from each other and meet in international meetings, and many members of the world's health policy communities meet up at international conferences dedicated to policy learning, but the structure of policy communities and party systems pose nearly insuperable obstacles to real 'learning' of the sort that would produce convergence on a 'good' or 'efficient' policy outcome. Policy communities and party systems are deeply rooted in their societies and policy ideas must take their chances in the confusion of politics. This means we should, based on this model, neither expect learning and convergence nor mere adaptation of supposedly 'good' ideas to local topography and demography. Only if policy advocates are close in spirit and argument between two jurisdictions, and party politics encourage governments to select the same ideas from those advocates, would we see similarity, and that is hardly learning from experiments in other laboratories of democracy. Ideas will travel as they always have tended to travel – via determined advocates who participate in global debates and local politics. This does not mean that ideas do not travel; the history of both health and social policy is necessarily global. They mean, though, that there is little pressure to converge on a 'correct' solution because there is little pressure for two jurisdictions to see the same problem or same solution. No wonder that, as Sparer and Brown found in an analysis of US health policy, 'laboratory adoptions and adaptations are probably more the exception than the rule' (Sparer and Brown 1996:196). If the public health advocates are weak in England, England will not learn much about public health. If the market reformers are weak in Wales, the Welsh policy community will not learn much about new developments in market-based managed care. There is a global menu, but each country will order different items at different times and want them prepared differently.

Table 1.2. Demographic trends by region

	Standardised mortality ratios (1999) (UK = 100)			Good state of general health (1998–99) (% 16 and over)		Smokers 1998–99) (% 16 and over)		Non-smokers (1998–99) (% 16 and over)	
	All	*Males*	*Females*	*Males*	*Females*	*Males*	*Females*	*Males*	*Females*
UK	100	100	100	62	57	29	26	72	74
North East	110	110	110	57	50	26	29	74	70
North West	108	109	107	59	57	29	31	72	68
Yorkshire and the Humber	100	101	99	61	54	29	27	71	72
East Midlands	99	99	99	59	59	25	26	74	75
West Midlands	102	102	101	57	56	31	25	69	75
East	93	91	95	63	59	25	23	75	77
London	95	96	93	65	59	33	27	67	73
South East	92	90	93	66	61	16	21	74	79
South West	90	88	91	63	60	15	24	76	76
England	98	97	98	62	58	28	26	72	74
Scotland	104	104	103	61	49	29	27	62	74
Wales	118	119	117	65	58	33	28	72	72
Northern Ireland	–	107	106	58	53	28	29	72	71

Note: Figures are based on International Labor Organization definitions of un/employment.
Source: National Statistics (2001) Regional Trends 36: 47, 67, 93, 95, 99, 155.

Research design

The first rule of analysing devolved policy making is that England must not be taken as a baseline. There is a strong tendency, found even in Northern Ireland, Scotland, and Wales, to retain the pre-devolution habit of seeing England as a template with marginal variations on the periphery. While England is undoubtedly important, and Northern Ireland, Scotland, and Wales hear more about it than vice versa, it nevertheless has a different health system. The UK has four political systems (one, Northern Ireland, with its democratic self-rule periodically suspended) and four health policies, and there is no *a priori* reason to give any one of them primacy.

The key question is why there has been policy divergence in the UK despite the short period of time since devolution, the similar institutional baselines, the strong interconnections between the four systems, and the shared or similar pressures facing them and all health systems in a global intel-

Food energy derived from fat (1998–99) (%)	ILO unemployed (spring 2000) (%)	Economically active (spring 2000) (%)	Economically inactive (spring 2000) (%)	GDP per head: indices (1999) (UK less extra-regio = 100)	Still births (1999) (%)	Perinatal mortality (1999) (%)	Infant mortality (1999) (%)
39	5.6	78.7	21.3	100.0	5.3	8.2	5.8
39	9.2	74.3	25.7	77.3	5.1	8.3	5.5
39	5.4	76.8	23.2	86.9	5.4	8.7	6.6
38	6.1	78.2	21.8	87.9	5.2	8.3	6.2
39	5.2	81.1	18.9	93.6	4.6	7.9	6.1
38	6.3	78.0	22.0	91.7	6.2	9.9	6.9
37	3.6	81.2	18.8	116.4	4.9	7.1	4.6
39	7.1	76.5	23.5	130.0	5.9	8.9	6.0
39	3.4	83.4	16.6	116.4	4.5	6.9	4.8
39	4.2	82.0	18.0	90.8	5.3	7.8	4.6
39	5.3	79.3	20.7	102.4	5.3	8.2	5.7
39	6.2	74.0	26.0	80.5	4.8	7.8	6.4
40	7.7	77.9	22.1	96.5	5.2	7.6	5.0
39	7.2	69.9	30.1	77.5	5.7	10.0	6.4

lectual arena. The answer lies in the particular ways that political systems, working under conditions of great and structural uncertainty, respond to pressures. They do this in a way that is very loosely connected to outside pressures but systematically influenced by their 'domestic' legacies of party systems and policy communities. Outside forces do not impose their own coherence on politics, but domestic political systems do; therefore, the divergence in domestic political systems mean that even systems which might be expected to run in parallel will diverge.

There are three ways the empirical data can confirm or disconfirm this argument. The first is simply to seek out a correlation between the presence and strength of particular groups and particular outcomes. Does the make-up of the policy community vary with the outcomes? The second is to examine the processes leading to the policy outcomes. Does the political and intellectual process that defined alternatives and the costs and benefits of a particular policy idea show the impact of different groups with advice, acquiescence,

Table 1.3. NHS trends by region

	NHS hospital waiting lists (as at 31 March 2001)							In-patients (all specialities) (1999–2000)			
	Percentage waiting				Total waiting (=100%) (thousands)	Mean waiting time (months)	Median waiting time (months)	Average daily available beds per 1,000 population	Cases treated per available bed	Cases treated per 1,000 population	Average list size per GP (30 September 2000)
	Less than 6 months	6 months but less than 12 months	Less than 12 months	12 months or longer							
North Yorkshire	78.8	20.5	99.4	0.6	118.7	3.8	2.8	4.2	44.5	187	1,774
North West	78	18.3	96.3	3.7	156.2	4	2.7	4.1	49.3	203	1,880
Trent	80.2	18.4	98.6	1.4	99.1	3.7	2.7	3.8	48.4	184	1,871
West Midlands	80.2	17.4	97.5	2.5	84.1	3.7	2.7	3.6	48.1	174	1,899
East	73.9	20.9	94.7	5.3	116.9	4.4	3	3.3	46	153	1,853
London	71.6	22.4	94	6	135.1	4.6	3.2	4	41.9	168	2,030
South East	70.7	22.6	93.3	6.7	189.5	4.7	3.4	3.1	46.1	144	1,845
South West	76.3	19	95.3	4.7	95.6	4.2	2.9	3.9	46.7	182	1,637
England	75.6	20.2	95.8	4.2	995.1	4.2	2.9	3.7	46.2	173	1,853
Scotland	66	20.2	86.2	13.8	65.6	–	–	5	35	176	1,695
Wales	83.7	15	98.7	1.3	82	3.2	2.1	6.8	27.9	190	1,426
Northern Ireland	58.6	19.6	78.2	21.8	52	–	–	5.1	38.4	196	1,673

Source: National Statistics (2001) Regional Trends 36: 101, 103.

and approval in the territorial policy community? The third is a particular opportunity afforded by the pre-devolutionary structure of the UK, namely the opportunity to examine insider politics before devolution and the cast they put on to the formulation and implementation of policies determined in London. Before devolution, three territorial offices (the Northern Ireland Office, the Scottish Office, and the Welsh Office) were responsible for the administration of government in the three areas (Rose 1987; Kellas 1989; Deacon 2002). Thus, the Scottish Office in 1997, just before devolution, combined the main activities carried out in England by the Home Office, the Department of Health, the Department for Education and Skills, the Ministry of Agriculture, Fisheries, and Food, the Department of the Environment, Transport, and the Regions, and the Department of Culture, Media and Sport, as well as marginal parts of other departments. In each case the policy agreed by the Cabinet and usually led by the English ('UK') Minister or Secretary of State would then have to be fit into the activity of the territorial office, and conversely the territorial offices could develop their own activities, quietly, and on the margins (Williamson and Room 1983; Hunter and Wistow 1987; Hazell and Jervis 1998). As a result we can see in retrospect the policy communities at work, and thereby establish the extent of their presence and local roots, as well as identify the legacies that shaped the devolved policy communities when they met their new elected politicians.

The data in this book is based on semi-structured interviews conducted in the health services of the four countries from autumn 2001 to spring 2003. Informants were anonymous in almost all cases, due to the political pressure surrounding health systems, but an appendix giving basic indentifying information is included. Informants were selected by two methods. One was centripetal, starting with two regions in each country involving a major city and a rural area (Glasgow and Argyll/Clyde in Scotland, London and the East Midlands in England, East Glamorgan and North Wales in Wales, and North and West Belfast and the West of Northern Ireland). Starting with doctors and management at that level, a snowball strategy was pursued by asking them to suggest further interviewees, particularly among their superiors. A few interviews outside the chosen regions checked for ways in which the choice of sites might have distorted data. The second selection method was complementary, starting with academic informants in each country and asking for recommendations in the policy process. The geographically and organisationally dispersed sources of interviewees reduced the likelihood of bias. The interview data was transcribed and subjected to deviant case analysis. In many cases the reconstruction of particular events could also be cross-checked with other published sources. Analysis of the press and government documents supplemented the data. Short visits later for targeted re-interviews as well as participant observation of invitation-only ('Chatham House rules') meetings in the four countries afforded opportunities to check facts and interpretation, while talks to practitioners were a valuable source of responses to ideas worked out here. A survey conducted independently by the project, of health elites, was also valuable information.

The two comparator countries discussed in Chapter 7, Canada and Spain, are chosen as parallel demonstrations of theory, i.e. cases in which theories of intra-state divergence (rather than policy making in general) may be tested (Skocpol and Somers 1994). The logic was that each system forms a paired comparison with the intergovernmental relations, broadly defined, of the UK, which between them show variance in most relevant aspects (see Ragin 1987; Ragin, Berg-Schlosser, and de Meur 1996 for a more sophisticated use and extension of the method of difference used to select the two countries). The prominent variables, therefore, are institutional and related to the broad context of constitutional development and operation. Spain shares with the UK a recent history of decentralisation (rather than federation) and asymmetry (social and institutional), as well as an intergovernmental financing formula and EU membership. It differs because it was a centralised state (on the French Jacobin model) before regionalisation, it has a strong regulatory role for the central state in setting frameworks, and it has a different political culture and non-Westminster institutions. Canada shares with the UK a weak regulatory role for the central state, a political culture, and Westminster institutions, while it differs in being a long-established federation with discretionary central funding for health. Both Spain and Canada are multinational countries with universal access to public health services, which might limit generalisability

Each empirical chapter then works to a template. The first section discusses the pre-devolution inheritance, explaining the historic legacies that gave each part of the UK its distinctive party system and policy community as well as health service organisation. Beneath the theoretically centralised UK policy-making system there have always been distinct policy-making arenas, and these sections on inheritance discuss their institutions and the organisational distinctiveness they created. The second section of each chapter discusses the policy community and politics (institutions and party system) inherited at devolution, analysing its make-up and consequent incentives, and finishes with a short recounting of the political history of each. The third section contains the policy case studies. It discusses the policy outcomes in organisation, new public health, public–private relations, and quality, as well as (in Scotland) long-term personal care for the elderly and (in Northern Ireland) acute care reorganisation. The other chapters introduce the politics and debates (Chapter 2) and the institutional autonomy of the UK governments that allows them to diverge so (Chapter 7). A concluding Chapter 8 draws broader lessons.

Notes

1 See Bogdanor (1999) for devolution, and Keating (1998) and Sharpe (1993) for regional government.
2 Martin Laffin refers to this as a 'horseshoe' model, in which advocates pitch ideas in the hopes that they will catch on a politician (personal communication).

2
Medical politics and the politics of medicine

Dealing with the doctors is even worse than negotiating with the French.
(Department of Health and Social Services official, cited in Hennessy 1989:421)

Health care is one of the largest policy areas in the UK and probably the most complex. Health care absorbs 6.8 per cent of UK gross domestic product (GDP) and the UK government is committed to unprecedented (more than 7 per cent per year) real increases in health spending until 2008 (Department of Health 2003a:31)(Tables 2.1 and 2.2). The UK governments, unlike most advanced industrial states, can decide their health spending in their general budgets; it is therefore as a result of Labour's political decisions that health spending has taken the particular growth trend that it has. Other health systems do not have this tight political control, and see remarkable costs; the USA's rapidly accelerating costs, underpinned by public health residual financing but driven by private provision, are almost 13 per cent of GDP.

Because of its size and importance in the political economy, health is a compelling topic. It matters in itself and it matters because it demands the attention of any group interested in taxes, spending, workforces, or policy areas it affects such as higher education, biotechnology industries, and local service sectors. Health is also one of, or the, most clearly devolved policy sectors in the UK. It benefits from the Barnett formula of block grants and it is lightly regulated by the central state (Table 2.3). As a consequence, in all three devolved polities the institutional limitations on them are small and we can see more of the extent of variation.

Within health, however, there are multiple policy areas, and multiple ways of viewing the same issues or institutions. Marmor (2004) and Healy and McKee (2002:69) point out that there is almost no such thing as a simple concept in health policy. Consider the hospital. A hospital fulfils many functions, and it looks different and calls for different policies and politics depending on whether it is viewed primarily as a device for rapid treatment of patients, a site for medical education, an apparatus for reinforcing inequalities

Table 2.1. Identifiable expenditure on health and personal social services compared to total comparable services[a] spending by country, 1997–2002 (£ million)

	England			Scotland			Wales			Northern Ireland		
	Health and personal services	Total comparable services	%	Health and personal services	Total comparable services	%	Health and personal services	Total comparable services	%	Health and personal services	Total comparable services	%
1997–98	43,642	193,971	22	5,751	24,901	23	3,077	13,801	22	1,760	9,279	19
1998–99	46,351	199,912	23	6,017	25,699	23	3,245	14,335	23	1,856	9,648	19
1999–2000	50,462	210,555	24	6,473	26,724	24	3,477	14,741	24	2,018	10,067	20
2000–1	54,171	222,978	24	6,877	29,065	24	3,710	15,561	24	2,170	10,462	21
2001–2	60,196	246,138	24	7,658	32,026	24	3,934	17,052	23	2,320	11,175	21

Note: [a]Comparable services: services provided by developed governments, and equivalent services provided by the UK government in England, e.g. education, health, local government and culture.

Source: HM Treasury Public Spending Statistical Analysis 2002–3: 91–5.

Table 2.2. Per capita identifiable expenditure on health and personal social services compared to total per capita spending on comparable services[a] by country, 1997–2002 (£ million)

	England		Scotland		Wales		Northern Ireland	
	Health and personal services	*Total comparable services*	*Health and personal services*	*Total comparable services*	*Health and personal services*	*Total comparable services*	*Health and personal services*	*Total comparable services*
1997–98	886	3,936	1,123	4,861	1,051	4,715	1,054	5553
1998–99	936	4,039	1,175	5,019	1,106	4,888	1,106	5750
1999–2000	1,014	4,232	1,265	5,221	1,184	5,019	1,202	5996
2000–1	1,083	4,460	1,360	5,746	1,259	5,282	1,290	6217
2001–2	1,224	5005	1,512	6,324	1,355	5,874	1,374	6616

Note: [a]Comparable services: services provided by developed governments, and equivalent services provided by the UK government in England, e.g. education, health, local government and culture.

Source: HM Treasury Public Spending Statistical Analysis 2002–3: 91–5.

of power in society, a site for research, a refuge for the incapable, or a form of economic and community development. Trying hard to shut small hospitals in favour of rapid outpatient treatment at big centres, a common policy, might improve quality, teaching, and efficiency, but it transfers responsibility for transport and home care on to families and local government, damages a community's sense of self and can have devastating consequences for local labour markets and economic development. It is no wonder that those who are concerned with community pride or a refuge for their relatives will disagree with technocratic decisions to improve quality and throughput through centralisation.

The core debates in the NHS are shared across the UK, and by and large are shared around the world. This is because the social institution of modern medicine, and the channels of communication that link policy advocates and administrators, are thoroughly global. Medicine and science have since their inception tended to cosmopolitan social organisation, with doctors, journals, scientists, and ideas crossing borders freely. Each step in communications technology and organisational infrastructure ties different national health systems together more closely. The result is that advocates can find allies in almost any country who share a vocabulary and set of understandings. This precocious 'globalisation' means that health policy probably anticipates the development of other policy sectors in the future. We can expect that to the extent other fields develop international networks, shared understandings, and coalitions, they will come to share with health care its combination of international debates and parochial conclusions.

Life, death, and scarce resources

For its first fifty years, despite the important variations in Northern Ireland, Scotland, and Wales, the nation in the NHS was Britain (Northern Ireland had its own health service, but in the minds of many, it was also the NHS). The politics were as often as not English and the policies metropolitan; the politics of the territorial offices failed to seize the imagination or even make much of an impression on the peoples of the UK. The history of the NHS, written as the story of the keystone of the UK welfare state and in the context of UK politics, is the subject of a sizeable library with some excellent studies from different perspectives (Hennessy 1992; Timmins 1995; Rivett 1998; Webster 1998; Ham 1999; Klein 2000) and comparative studies (Anderson 1972; Fox 1986; Hollingsworth 1986; Moran 1999; Tuohy 1999).

The four NHS systems share exposure to international debates, shared histories, and many common problems born of their common structure. They have the problems of health services in general and the problems of their particular model of health system in particular, and their histories are of efforts to grapple with those problems.

Problems of health services

Just what is the problem you're trying to solve with all this? (Australian policy maker to an English group, September 2003)

Any health system is built around the need to provide services in a context of deep uncertainty and essentially unlimited demand. Whether it is a fee-for-service insurer in the USA or the Swedish health service, the payer bears the obligation to provide health, despite the fact that the procedures and services that provide health could easily outpace the resources available. A sustainable system, therefore, must also be built around the need to ration services. There never seems to be an easy way to bridge the gap between the potential amount of extra treatment and tests that could be desirable and the actual funds that the NHS can extract from the taxpayer or the US Health Maintenance Organisation (HMO) can squeeze out of a big employer's health insurance fund. As a result, anybody charged with running a health system faces the problem of how both to provide services and not provide services.

The necessary uncertainty of medical treatment exacerbates these problems. Every patient is unique. Even if illnesses and risk factors are similar, they are numerous, and in each person they are reshuffled into a new combination. As a result, it is impossible to construct easy algorithms that allow mechanisation of most treatment. Neither extracting information, nor diagnosis, nor treatment, nor follow-up is easy enough to be routinised. When it is impossible to routinise a high-stakes activity, Western society habitually hands over the problem to professionals (doctors, nurses, lawyers, clergy, academics). These professionals have undergone training and socialisation that will allow them to make difficult judgements using what is often trained intuition when the ethical issues are serious and there is very little information.

This solves one set of problems but creates new, management, problems. There is a great deal of literature on practice variations that documents extreme variations in the way patients are treated between different parts of even the same city (Dartmouth Center for Evaluative Clinical Sciences 1998). This reflects the differences in patients and the professional, often tacit, conservative, experience-based judgements of doctors. It also reflects the sheer difficulty of identifying an effective treatment, which has been the subject of many clarifying attempts by advocates of improved medical quality – and which is dwarfed in difficulty by the difficulty of getting a correct diagnosis. The consequence of this uncertainty, combined with the high personal and professional status of doctors, nurses, and most other health workers, is that the politician and the manager are always on the defensive when trying to ration health resources that can easily vanish into treatment.

The professionals can look more like a curse than a help to a hard pressed minister or official (or health insurance executive). They are articulate, difficult to control, numerous, and enjoy far more public sympathy than any minister. They are socialised into powerful institutions and organised into powerful lobby groups. The professional organisations might be powerful in politics but still find it hard accurately to represent and control their members. If the British Medical Association (BMA) or Royal College of Nursing (RCN) signs up to an agreement, that might not mean that the majority of its members will sign up to it and it certainly might not mean that any changes in the actual professional work will ensue. Efforts to change medical practice from the top down invariably end in struggles for control and authority on individual wards across the country, which as often as not are won by professionals jealous of their autonomy and backed up by an authority managers cannot match.

In short, every modern Western health service faces a series of linked challenges. They lack the resources to perform all the medicine that might produce health gains. They must construct a system, therefore, that rations. It is easier to construct a system that provides, such as a supermarket, rather than one that can equitably, legitimately, and sustainably decide *not* to provide. In the systems committed to some degree of equity and citizenship rights (systems outside the USA), there is an extra tension. If the NHS or Canadian Medicare or the French health funds take seriously their responsibility to provide equitable outcomes to the whole population, and not just equal access, then they also face a tension between the need to increase access and use among disfavoured populations and the need to limit overall access and use. Worse still from the point of view of planners, the basic unit of medical interaction – the decision made in an encounter between a professional and a patient – is difficult to control. Outcomes like waiting lists and problematic practice variations, and the budgetary strains or bad headlines that make them problems for decision makers, are nothing but the cumulation of millions of small medical decisions about whether to prescribe a medicine, ask for a scan, or send the patient home. In these decisions, health systems necessarily rely on professionals. Only professionals have the skills (or willingness and status) to ration, and only they have the legitimacy to ration where it matters most, namely at the level of the individual patient with a complaint. The result is what Rudolf Klein called 'the politics of the double bed' (Klein 1990). Professionals and payers (in the UK, the state) are stuck with each other, no matter how they might quarrel, since the state pays but the professionals are the only group that can provide the health care that the state wants and the only group that can provide the rationing that the state needs.

NHS issues

The NHS is the prototype for a subcategory of universal, public health services (Freeman 2000). The NHS model is a health service in which almost all care is funded out of general taxation and directly provided by public bodies that employ or are prime contractors with professionals. The salient characteristics of an NHS-model system are the low organisational costs and low political costs of change compared to other health systems (Greer 2004a). It is not easy to change health policy, but it is easier to do so than elsewhere. In NHS systems, therefore, the Minister is much more engaged than his or her counterparts in other countries.

The *political costs of change* are the costs to a politician associated with getting a policy into law. They are roughly equal to the number of opportunities opponents have to stop a policy, and they are low in the UK's Westminster systems (including Scotland and Wales). Federalism, with shared competencies, separation of powers, judicial review, weak parties, and corporatism, raises the political costs of change since it introduces groups (judges, subnational governments, other legislatures) that proponents of a policy must pacify in order to make the change. The great strength and greatest weakness of the centralised Westminster system is the ease of policy change. The government can put its business through the legislature, there is limited judicial oversight, and there are few genuinely shared health powers between the UK and devolved bodies. Once a government makes a decision, it is usually able to push it through without much trouble.

Within the three systems in Great Britain the political costs of change can still vary, but only in extreme situations where party discipline breaks. 'Shifting the balance', the 2001–02 English reorganisation, was very questionable but went through (Department of Health 2001b). It had low political costs since it was done with very little parliamentary oversight and the main losers were a group (managers) who were weak due to their unpopularity in the political arena. Foundation hospitals policy, by contrast, has high political costs with major rebellions on key legislative votes. These have been held amidst a storm of backbench–frontbench conflict over universities, justice, Iraq, and health, and are a symbolic focus of opposition to a whole range of market-based government policies. It took that much symbolic value and that much political turbulence to make legislating hard for the government. Such narrowly won or lost conflicts are far more common in other systems, whether they are seen in the one-vote margins characteristic of the current US Senate, the tiny Bundesrat (federal upper house) margins by which German policy advances, or the hard-fought intergovernmental conferences by which Canada is changing its federal health policies.

The *organisational costs of change* are the costs in terms of performance that come from a policy change. They amount to the degree of implementation failure that the policy faces, as measured by the amount of actual visible policy failure and as driven by the number of different groups whose non-cooperation can scupper a policy. In systems with shared health powers, such as Canada and Australia, governments willingly sign agreements that they do not deliver. The Canadian federal government's organisational costs of change are driven up by its reliance on provinces to deliver any health services. The provinces' costs of change are driven up by their reliance on a substantial amount of federal funding and the constraint it brings. Both accuse each other of bad faith. Australian governments' costs of policy change are driven up by blame and cost-shifting between Commonwealth (federal) and state parts of the health system (Wilkins and Greer 2003). Sweden uses its powerful local governments to separate the central government from delivery decisions but thereby incurs the higher organisational costs of inducing elected local governments to change policy because the central government wants them to. In the few areas where UK local government is allowed to matter, its ability to frustrate or reinterpret central government policy in line with its independent electoral mandate is impressive.

In systems with genuine corporatism (not the voluntaristic partnerships of British history), the government might be only a member of labour-management boards or reduced (as in Germany) to setting the legal framework rather than actually making decisions. The German federal state regulates rather than runs its health insurance, and therefore has few real levers with which to influence health service organisation or delivery. Finally, contracts also raise the organisational costs of change relative to direct employment relations. If the German government can induce funds to make the decisions that it seeks, the funds then still need to extract the outcome from the doctors they pay. As a result, the organisational costs of change in Germany or similar social insurance systems are relatively high.

Again, the NHS-model systems face lower organisational costs of change than systems in other parts of the world. In each part of the UK one government owns and pays for most of the health system. There are no fixed countervailing powers within the system. No UK government relies on any other government to deliver or fund health services on its territory. There are no unions or employers' organisations necessarily involved in health decision making. They are pressure groups that can be strong but still can be brushed aside. Local government might have representation or rights with regards to health services but is not vital to policy change. Subordinate units of the NHS are weak. It need not be so, and semi-forgotten organisations such as the English regional boards were more able to resist central pressure, but today there are few managers or board members who think they exist other than at the Minister's pleasure.

The NHS model, therefore, has low political and organisational costs of change. Ministers can, as anybody in the NHS will testify, reorganise almost on a whim (and the reasons given for some recent reorganisations have been startlingly trivial). The concentration of power and political authority in the Minister of Health also entails highly concentrated accountability. As long as there is general agreement that there should be public, democratic accountability through a minister for tax-financed services, there will be a remarkable degree of public, press, and political concentration on the person of that minister. This means that, in the old phrase of Aneurin Bevan, the dropped bedpan anywhere in the system does resonate through the Minister's office. It reflects not just the simplifying assumptions of politicians and the public and the politicians' desire for attention; it also reflects a learned and much reinforced public view that the Minister of Health so far outranks other people in the health service that it is not worthwhile to pay attention to anybody else's doings. The result is pressure on the Minister to intervene, to set targets, to do something, and the result is yet more centralisation and instability.

Legacies

So how, then, have the governments of the UK to 1998 used their imposing power in their efforts to balance equity, value, and restraint? Why have they done what they did? And what legacies did they leave to shape services, politics, and debates today?

Removing financial barriers: 1948

Most writers agree that the creation of the NHS was through rationalisation rather than revolution. These authors focus on pre-existing consensus in favour of equality and rationalisation (Eckstein 1959; Powell 1997; Klein 2000) even if it is striking that other countries with similar histories of health service provision up to 1945 did not create anything like the NHS, and historians sometimes stress the political effort that it took to establish the NHS rather than something less radical (Morgan 1984:154). That the UK could convert its patchwork of local, voluntary, and private medicine into a unified state-run system is a dramatic difference from countries with comparable pre-1945 histories, such as the USA (Hacker 1998; Moran 1999; Tuohy 1999). But whether the NHS is an incremental evolution or a revolution, it still built on a pre-existing infrastructure of health services.

What happened in 1948 was, essentially, the removal of barriers to access to the health service, made possible by government control of finance (Powell 1997). In other words, the health sector was nationalised but left intact (rather like some other nationalised industries). The logic of the settlement was that the state removed the entrepreneurial autonomy of the hospitals and health services but left the clinical and professional autonomy of the professionals – above all the doctors – intact (Tuohy 1999). This meant that some sources of opposition to professionals on the local level – local governments, insurance funds, and charity boards – ceased to matter. Instead the state and the medical profession climbed squabbling into Klein's 'double bed' (Klein 1990).

The removal of barriers to access did not entail the development of equal provision or equality of access. Health services were provided in the same way as before, and by the same people, but without money changing hands. There was no inbuilt effort to reform the system. Rather, the tripartite structure of the first NHS outside Scotland (see Chapter 3) reflected inherited divisions. Health services in the NHS, excluding public health, were built on three more or less separate pillars: general practice; teaching hospitals with their own boards and autonomy (reflecting their status in medicine and society, particularly in London); and ordinary (mostly ex-Poor Law or local government)

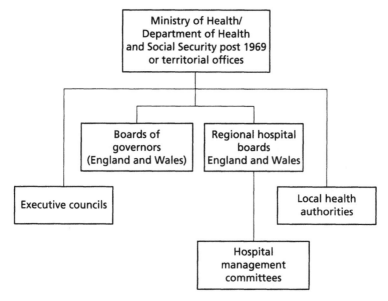

Figure 2.1: Structure of the NHS, 1948–74

hospitals without their own boards, governed by districts that as often as not mirrored the local authority administrative units that had previously managed the hospitals (Figure 2.1). It was essentially a system of financing that put the state and the professionals together as principal and agent in making existing health services available. This did not entail changing the social institutions of the health services. The professionals provided the service, the government funded the service, the inheritance determined the structure and without significant new capital spending or determined government policies the NHS coasted and the Department of Health became increasingly dozy (it did not even have Cabinet status from 1968 to 1988).

Providing services according to existing patterns but with increased equality created unexpected problems. Ham writes that 'One of the assumptions that lay behind the NHS . . . was that there was a fixed quantity of illness in the community which the introduction of a health service, free at the point of consumption, would gradually reduce. It was therefore expected that expenditure would soon level off and even decline . . . In fact, the reverse happened' (Ham 1999:13). The first response was the appointment and report of the Guillebaud Committee, with a remit to discuss the cost of the NHS. It concluded that spending on the NHS was decreasing as a percentage of GNP and that if anything it deserved more money (Committee of Enquiry into the Cost of the National Health Service 1956). The next response was to supply that money, in the 1962 Hospital Plan – the first plan for the NHS and until the Blair government the only one. The Hospital Plan attempted to restructure the NHS to improve equity by ensuring the equal provision of hospital facilities; in this it represented the most significant effort by the government to direct the growth and development of the whole health service rather than fund and widen access to that which was already established. Its designer, Enoch Powell, proudly explained that the government was planning hospitals on a scale unseen elsewhere, 'certainly not this side of the Iron Curtain' (Mohan 2002:2). It did this primarily by developing a model of hospital provision centred around district general hospitals and formulas calling for all parts of the UK to have equal provision measured in terms such as hospital beds per capita (the formulas ignored differences in need). The plan was expensive and changed the face of medical provision, even if various problems meant that large parts were not enacted, underfunded, prey to stop-start economic policies, or otherwise unattained (Webster 1998; Mohan 2002).

Professionalism: 1974

The NHS in 1974 was already remarkable for the reasons it is remarkable today. It was one of the few health systems owned and operated by a state that funded it out of general taxation. Its reorganisation in 1974 made it doubly remarkable in international terms by formally converting it into a contract between professions and the state, structured after an analysis of how health services work.

The logic of the 1974 reorganisation was that the old governance of the NHS was not adequate or good value. The political need to enshrine major status and social differences in order to establish the NHS in 1948 was long gone, and the structures, mirroring the organisation of medicine before the NHS, were increasingly seen as inappropriate in a well-established NHS. The result was that the very committed Conservative Keith Joseph (known as the 'mad monk' and later to become an ardent Thatcherite) was able to decide upon and create a new shape for the NHS.

The organisation's intellectual genesis was partly with McKinsey consultants but crucially with the team at Brunel University led by Elliott Jaques (also known as the originator of the concepts of organisational culture and the midlife crisis). Jaques and his team, students of organisations who had conducted studies of work and organisation, based their analysis of health services on an analysis of where decisions were made in practice (Jaques 1976, 1978; Hands 2000). Efforts to build a wholly multifunctional NHS added multiple layers and organisations (Figure 2.2), but the essence was focused on the frontline professionals.

Jaques' argument was in essence simple. In health care, the frontline

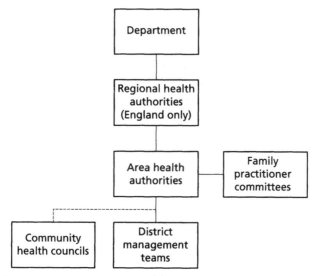

Figure 2.2: Structure of the NHS outside Northern Ireland, 1974–82

professionals make the key decisions. The NHS (or almost any health service) does two things. It provides care and it rations care. Both of these core activities are done by professionals. The basic unit of the health services is the interaction between a professional and a person with a problem. The diagnosis and treatment decisions of that professional are more legitimate in the eyes of the patient and the public than any decisions made by others. These decisions cumulate into the whole allocation of resources. If the professionals are not responsible for overall use of resources, their decisions will cumulate into serious misallocations (or excessive use) of resources. If doctors feel constrained by people or rules they do not respect, their greater legitimacy and commitment to seek the best for the patient will lead them to subvert the rules and, in all likelihood, undermine the overall budget. If they take no responsibility for rationing decisions, including resource allocation, their spending could rapidly cumulate to crisis levels. The problem for the NHS, in the eyes of the Brunel team, was to harness this unchangeable aspect of medical decision making in order to produce a health service that made intelligent decisions overall.

The conclusion was that the professions, as social institutions, should be responsible for decisions. This took the form of a technique called 'consensus management', in which putatively representative boards of professionals and others made managerial decisions at levels from the hospital upward. It came with an overall lack of management; the NHS employed 'administrators' who occupied a subordinate position in the service and who were not responsible for overall decisions and direction. Instead, consensus management was geared to making decisions when (and only when) the professionals who would have to implement it were agreed; it would thereby make them responsible for decisions about the resources upon which they drew and would harness their knowledge. It was therefore highly decentralised. The hierarchical formal structure of administration had relatively little to do with the key decisions.

The evidence is that consensus management worked (Schulz and Harrison 1984; Greer 1987). It improved doctor–patient trust and professional responsibility. It also, crucially, made rationing decisions compatible with professional and patient preferences (Harrison and Schulz 1989:192–3). Without a legitimate, responsive way to make individual-level rationing decisions but with the necessary responsibility to ration limited resources, the NHS could be in serious trouble (Harrison 1995). Focusing the rationing decisions on professionals both created a high degree of compatibility between management decisions and professional (i.e. the real activity of the service) and fed professionals' extensive knowledge of patients and populations upward into decision making. While there is surprisingly little clear evaluative literature on consensus management, the verdict should be that Jaques did design a structure suited to providing health care on limited resources. Nevertheless, it was abandoned. The government's decision to switch to a corporate model based on supermarkets is a remarkable case of the autonomy of politics vis-à-vis experience.

Corporate rationalisation: 1983

> If Florence Nightingale were carrying her lamp through the corridors of the NHS today she would almost certainly be searching for the people in charge (NHS Management Inquiry 1983: 12).

There were a number of different criticisms of consensus management. Critics argued that its design was too complicated and rigid (the blueprint for organisation came in the form of a large, very detailed book sent out from the centre), that it had too many levels of organisation, and that decisions were not made because either the consensus committees could not agree or because the representatives of some group were unable to secure their group's compliance. What these criticisms amounted to is the assertion that the NHS could not be a self-governing collective of professionals contracted by the state anymore and that it should be an organisation that could have a strategy defined for it and then be led in that strategy. It is noticeable that the evidence for any of these problems is generally anecdotal.

In 1980s Britain the burden of proof was against professions as a form of governance. This reflected overall strong impulses in the UK policy stream of the day to improve the management of the public services (and to introduce management where there was none). This managerialism, based on often rather stylised images of the private sector, was increasingly dominant as criticisms of the 'corporatist' aspects of the post-war British settlement became a theme of the Thatcher government that entered into office in 1979 (Pollitt 1993). In the Thatcherite vision, one accepted by many of the Conservatives' business or business-friendly followers, the public services could be made more efficient and responsive if managed with private-sector techniques. At the same time, the Conservatives' efforts to reduce public spending in their first governments increased the constant volume of complaint about supposed NHS underfunding. This upsurge of problems, in a febrile political environment, coincided with a government interested in business and its techniques and a policy stream with many managerialists. The Prime Minister commissioned a businessman from the Sainsbury supermarket chain, J. Griffiths, to report on the administration of the NHS. The output – a twenty-four-page letter which many writers assume must have been a report – was a short analysis suggesting that the problems of the NHS included dispersed authority (nobody in charge) and consequent inability to determine goals and strategy and implement them. It suggested the introduction of a management board and a supervisory board and outlined a management structure divided by classical functions (personnel, property) and existing geographical tiers. It explained the problem as Griffiths and his team saw it:

> One of our most immediate observations from a business background is the lack of a clearly-defined general management function throughout the NHS. By general management we mean the responsibility drawn together in one person, at different levels of the organisation, for planning, implementation, and control of performance [which means that] there is no driving force seeking and accepting direct and personal responsibility for developing management plans, securing their implementation, and monitoring actual achievement . . . it appears that . . . the NHS is so structured as to resemble a 'mobile': designed to move with any breath of air, but which in fact never changes its position and gives no clear indication of direction (NHS Management Inquiry 1983:11–12).

The government proceeded to act on most of the specific recommendations. The impact was dramatic: the NHS would now be expected to be managed like, and work like, a company. The government was effectively to restructure its pact with professions into a standard employee–manager–owner relationship, with the government as the sole owner, the board as its agents in oversight, and management as responsible to the board for delivering the goals.

It was never entirely clear why such efforts needed to be expended on giving direction from the top or what was wrong with consensus management.

The shift to general management was a triumph of a managerial sensibility and ideology over a design based on experience of health services. There was nobody like Jaques involved in the production of the Griffiths letter. It is difficult to imagine the Conservatives of 1983 asking university sociologists to design a health service. Nor was a team of academics required to produce a policy that amounted to introducing into the NHS a form of industrial organisation seen in almost every other complex organisation. Such isomorphism – organisational form that resembles forms generally seen as 'legitimate' – is a powerful force that can overpower considerations of efficiency or desirability, and it certainly happens in health care (DiMaggio and Powell 1991). There is a broad social understanding of what bureaucratic management is about and what managers do (and an extensive industry competing to add or subtract definitions) and by contrast very few organisations in 1983 or now that are run on the professional-corporatist model of the 1974 NHS.

The new managers were supposed to be a new breed, and the old 'administrators' were hardly guaranteed success in the new, hard-charging role of actually setting goals (or, equally likely, implementing top-down objectives on the wards) (Day and Klein 1983). The whole NHS began to undergo a dramatic culture shift. From now on the 'non-negotiated order' of the NHS, in which powerful professional groups held trump cards, would also include managers who were answerable to the Department and Minister but who found it difficult to get the tools to make anybody else answerable to them (Cox 1991; Wall 2001). The managers' fundamental difficulty was that they could not understand the context of decisions by individual professionals. Even if the manager was a doctor, each patient is unique. This pits managers with relatively weak tools against professionals' legitimacy, their influence over patients, and much closer sense of the patients. Such importance matters in health, a setting of high stakes, great uncertainty, and with a prominent role for intuition and context (Harrison and Pollitt 1994; Harrison 1995). The managers were seen as the servants of the government department – which effectively could fire them – and as such were much less likely to win the trust of patients or professionals.

The NHS did indeed establish its managerial structures and hierarchies in a form fairly close to the design laid out by Griffiths in the 1983 letter, and the three territorial offices followed in rolling out health service management. It seems hospitals and other health service organisations did run better for the inclusion of some general management. The new regime also changed the politics on the ward floor and in Westminster and Whitehall by introducing managers responsible to the state into an environment previously wholly dominated by professionals and creating a new form of health policy community member, the student or advocate of management (Harrison 1995). It did not, however, change core aspects of health care politics. Almost every group continued to have incentives to complain, threaten crisis, and demand better funding. Health services became no less complex, and errors remained possible – and errors could at any time could be presented to an interested media as evidence of underfunding or bad policy by one of an increasing number of professional and interest groups. In short, while the NHS now looked formally like a private company, its managers remained caught between professionals and politics. Rather than being accountable just to shareholders, the NHS was accountable to everybody to whom the Secretary of State was accountable – interest groups, the press, the Treasury, and voters. That meant it was unable to develop the core goals akin to shareholder returns on capital or cease to be a drag on the government of the day. Had it developed such goals, it was still unclear whether the equipment it had developed to reshape the system – its management corps – was sturdy enough to do it. The government was investing great energy in the creation of a managerial cadre seen as good in itself and as a tool to steer the system, but in essential ways it was unclear what the tool and the new central control was for.

Market reform: 1989

The 'problem' of rationing flared up with particular intensity in the winter of 1987 when fifteen heads of Royal Colleges and others created a media storm around the government's supposed reluctance to fund or operate the NHS properly. After weeks of especially intense talk about crisis, and with the government under attack, Margaret Thatcher made the dramatic announcement on the television show 'Panorama' one evening in January that she planned to convene a group to review the structure and functioning of the NHS. Thus began the most visible, dramatic, and contested change in its history. A political problem – a winter crisis combined with some particularly public complaints by the medical profession – combined with a conviction politician and a radical set of policies to change both the NHS and health politics.

The first remarkable attribute of the review convened by Thatcher was its size and membership – it was small and it was defiantly non-corporatist. None of the insider groups whose participation had so shaped the NHS was invited. Not even the BMA and Royal Colleges, hitherto epitomes in the literature on corporatism (Eckstein 1960), were included. It was a small group of confidants that reviewed proposals as radical as a switch to an entirely different financing mechanism. The review gradually closed in on the concept of the 'internal market', one of a set of proposals associated with Stanford University health economist Alain Enthoven. It would be implemented by the aggressive Kenneth Clarke, in the new Cabinet post of Secretary of State for Health. The form it took was a set of concrete proposals which created something like a market (Klein 2000:158–62). The goal of the proposals was to introduce the benefits of competition and organisation into health services, an area notoriously resistant to the analyses and solutions of economics (McDonald 2002). Enthoven, more or less accurately seen as the most influential advocate, is a classic policy entrepreneur, equipped with an answer and perpetually seeking its questions. The internal market is a classic example of a Christmas tree, namely an answer bedecked with the questions that it is supposed to have answered.[1] Enthoven, for example, sold health care markets as the way to escape measurement and data collection (because markets are automatic) and as the way to require measurement and data collection (because markets build in incentives to do so) (Enthoven 1979, 1989). Enthoven's internal market was of a piece with other solutions then popular around the world which fell under the name 'new public management' (Barzelay 2000; Lane 2000). Key to them was the development of new methods of introducing competition and contracting, using quasi-market relations in order to unlock efficiency and create incentives to provide better services at cheaper prices, or to at least get prices and level of provision right (this in turn was part of a larger global neoliberal movement towards markets in many forms). Advocates of the internal market might not have dominated the policy community around the NHS, but the adoption of policy ideas is always somewhat contingent and market-based ideas were certainly present in every field and country by the late 1980s (Saltman and van Otter 1995).

A radical solution therefore emerged from the near-random confluence of a politician, policy idea, and the problem of a winter beds crisis in the Midlands. The confluence of a determinedly pro-market government, serious political problems with the NHS, and a suitable policy idea, would change the NHS. The internal market would replace the older top-down, planning-based models. In its place, purchasers and providers would be separated. Providers (largely acute service trusts – effectively hospitals or groups of hospitals organised into firm-like trusts) would compete for the custom of purchasers. When purchasers bought services from their chosen providers, the money would follow those patients. The acute trusts would be released from the supposedly stifling central planners and given autonomy but would be newly, and more effectively, disciplined by purchasers. Purchasers would come in two forms. Health authorities would be reconstituted as contractors for services, thereby creating a purchaser–provider split everywhere. The other kind of purchaser

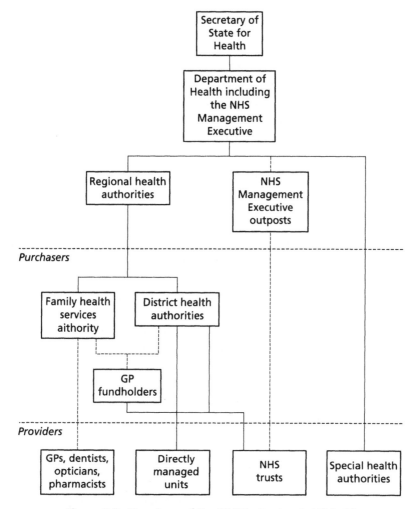

Figure 2.3: Structure of the NHS in England, 1991–96

would be 'fundholding' general practitioners (GPs), who could select desirable providers for their patients rather than be constrained by higher authorities (Figure 2.3).

There was serious resistance from the interested interest groups, coupled with sceptical reactions from much of the press and public. The BMA resisted particularly strongly and memorably. A BMA poster showed a picture of a steamroller, captioned as Margaret Thatcher's plans for the NHS. 'What do you call a man who refuses to listen to doctor's advice?' asked another BMA poster over his photograph. 'Healthy' replied that man, Kenneth Clarke (Elston 1991:70). Clarke's insouciance highlighted the problem of these interest groups. They might have considerable reservoirs of advice, acquiescence, and public approval, but a Westminster government is formally unconstrained and increasingly willing to take on the medical profession (Klein 2000:230–2). Indeed, the process of creating an ostensibly automatic, structured market created enormous new central capacity to intervene in the health services as part of forcing through change (Giaimo and Manow 1999). The last twenty years of the NHS have conclusively shown that pro-market, decentralising reforms tend to centralise (Greer forthcoming-c). They leave behind a residue of yet greater power for the central government as a result of the power Whitehall must seize in order to push through its own disengagement. The power tends to be used to a greater extent than the disengagement is successful.

The government went ahead but appeared to be frightened by the responses and tried to introduce the internal market with a minimum of disruption – the Department of Health, with a calming new ministerial influence, began to suggest that health authorities should try to avoid radical changes in patient and funding flows (Ham 2000). In a situation with very limited capacity and tight central control, 'anything resembling a functioning market was the exception rather than the rule' (Paton 2000:15). That said, the change was dramatic and had mixed consequences for patients and people working in the NHS (Robinson and Le Grand 1993; Le Grand, Mays, and Mulligan 1998). GP fundholding proved more popular than most observers expected. The concept of the trust began to establish itself as the core building block of the NHS. Whereas previously the NHS had been based on geographical units that more or less reflected the organisation of the professions, now it came to be based on firm-like trusts. Whereas previously the government had been funding, and later trying to manage, the whole social institution of UK medicine, now it was owner of a large number of firm-like organisations, each one with management, internal hierarchies, autonomy, and overall surface resemblance to private companies. The autonomy and internal hierarchy of the trusts, their power over employees (outside the porters), and the ability of the new chief executives to act like their private sector equivalents remained sharply compromised. But there was at least something that looked like an ecology of firms rather than a profession.

New Labour: 1998

When New Labour entered office, it came with a basic, oft-repeated ethos that appeared in both its manifesto and in its English White Paper: what counts is what works (Department of Health 1998b:§2.5). New Labour overall wanted to establish its reputation for competency in economics and management (the

Conservatives having lost their previous popular image as superior economic managers with the currency devaluation of 1992). This meant, across the UK, working with the well-established building blocks of trusts. In England it also meant collapsing the whole purchaser side into what became, within years, primary care trusts. What is remarkable, though, is the story that begins with these 1997 White Papers. England would continue to build on the trusts and the logic of markets. Wales would shift its focus from the purchaser–provider split to the purchasers – who they are and what they are to buy. Scotland would begin to roll back first the market and then the managers. And Northern Ireland would demonstrate a fundamental inability to develop new policy solutions, but demonstrate equally an aversion to any efforts to make markets more of a reality. In other words, when the Labour government first wrote separate White Papers and then devolved the health systems of the UK, the legacies would remain but the common story of development would end. Differences in the origin of ideas and the distribution of winners and losers would vary across the UK and change the policies the four systems would pursue (Table 2.3).

Table 2.3. Devolution comparison of legislative competences in health

Westminster	Stormont	Holyrood	Cardiff
Regulation of the health profession	D	R	R
Abortion	=	R	R
Human fertilisation and embryology	=	R	R
Surrogacy	=	R	R
Human genetics	=	R	R
Xenotransplantation	=	R	R
Medicines Act 1968: Licensing	D	R	R
Regulation	D	R	R
Enforcement	D	D	D
Medical devices regulation	=	R	R
Pharmaceutical price regulation scheme	D	R	R
Welfare foods: Policy	D	R	R
Administration	D	D	D
EU relations	Excepted	R	R
International relations	Excepted	R	R
Policy and management of the NHS and health services	D	D	D
Policy and management of the social services	D	D	D

Notes:
D: devolved, executively devolved or transferred; R: reserved to Westminster (Scotland); no Assembly competence (Wales); = : reserved but Assembly can legislate with Secretary of State approval and Westminster veto.

The next section introduces the policy advocates that the particular history of the NHS in its fifty years as a British national service would bequeath to each country. The rest of the book discusses how the policy communities and party systems that had been previously submerged emerged to shape what were now four national health services in the UK.

Issues and advocates

Health politics in the UK reflects the common issues in all global health systems – issues driven by shared technology, institutions (such as the basic institutional form of Western medicine), policy advocates, and communications between professionals. These include, above all, the tension between medicine's effectively unlimited ability to consume resources, its increasing ability to perform expensive new procedures of value, and the reluctance of payers to fund all of it. They also include efforts to shift medicine away from that basic tension between purchaser and provider, by trying to reduce illness and keep people out of hospital, or, alternatively, by trying to unlock the potential in the scientific aspects of Western medicine to produce better quality and implicitly more efficient health care. They are also, then, shaped by the basic organisational form of the NHS. The NHS model is of direct state provision funded from tax finance, which effectively means the government running the health service as a department. That means that the government responsible for an NHS service bears a tremendous weight of responsibility for running the system in the eyes of the public and enjoys a remarkable degree of freedom to redesign and manage the system. The government charged with an NHS-model system is accountable for it and must in some sense 'run' it or find an agent to do so, whether management or professionals, and it will have to wait for the effects on the service of long-term efforts to improve population health. Or, if the government gives up and seeks some more automatic mechanism, the NHS must be deconstructed in some way if it is to use other mechanisms (such as market discipline) to produce high-quality, efficient health care.

Policy case selection

There are multiple reasons why the arguments in health policy across the UK are so similar, even if the course of the debates and the policy outcomes are very different. There is the shared historic legacy from the common health politics before devolution, when the dominance of Westminster and Whitehall guaranteed common health policies. There is the fact that the UK is embedded in international networks and policy advocates. And there are the common issues facing health services – constants of scarcity and constraint that affect anybody supplying health services.

Most health policy problems, for all their variation and dependence on other issues, also reflect key issues of choice amidst scarcity (Mechanic 1989:20). There is never enough money, staffing, or time to do everything desirable in any walk of life. Health care, however, adds severely complicating factors. The issues matter more to the people involved; few people want to think about choice under constraint when it comes to their life and health. Rationing care on financial grounds is also a subject of serious debate; even the USA operates a sizeable government-funded residual health network (the existence of which allows its politically powerful private sector to concentrate on desirable insurance prospects).

Shared legacies of UK policies and politics shape the health politics of England, Northern Ireland, Scotland, and Wales. The basic design of the UK health services was always similar, with territorial offices' variations on the margins in almost all cases. Scotland had separate NHS legislation largely due to the requirements of Scots law, and Northern Ireland merged health and social services (to improve services and strip powers from its bigoted local governments). Only in the year before devolution were there three separate White Papers on health (Scottish Office 1997; Department of Health 1998b; Welsh Office 1998b).

This book chooses cases according to two sets of criteria that should capture a range of outcomes important in themselves and valuable as indicators of differences and similarities in health politics and policy. First, each chapter focuses on four major issues in health policy that attract attention and activity globally and which matter in NHS systems: the organisation of health services; the degree of attention to 'new public health' (a focus on promoting health and reducing inequalities in health outcomes); efforts to improve medical quality and the evidence base of activity in the system from the top down; and the relationship between the public and private sectors in service provision. The empirical case studies discuss each agenda in each country. If there is no activity, that is also interesting – why do some items not make it on to the agenda, or fail to arrive at a decision? Failure to discuss an issue, a non-decision (failure of an item to appear on the agenda due to the weakness of proponents and/or strength of opponents) (Bachrach and Baratz 1962), is an interesting negative indicator. Choosing consistent policy case studies in each country reveals non-decisions as well as decisions. Such a case selection strategy, however, does not always reflect the major agenda items in a country. Scotland's decision to expand the bounds of the welfare state by providing for the personal care of the elderly is an agenda item not shared with any other part of the UK. Northern Ireland, meanwhile focused on acute services allocation rather than policy.

These topics also matter for practical reasons. They occupy textbooks, ministers, politicians, newspapers, and employees. They feed through to patients: poor medical quality can lead to rationing decisions that patients find unfair, or major disasters up to and including mass murder. Organisations run by managers, professionals, or local government will invest differently and over time produce differences in the way patients are treated. Even in the short term, responses to issues such as waiting lists and times vary depending on who runs hospitals and who can apply pressure. New public health is radical and marginal in a system that runs hospitals, not buses or schools, but even marginal policy changes (such as free fruit in schools) could have serious effects in the future. Finally, the NHS across the UK is an ethical imperative as much as a system of organisations. At the heart of the ethical stances commonly associated with the system is provision by the public sector. Introducing private provision, whether as a subcontracted laundry, a privately owned hospital, or a whole private clinic, makes many people uneasy and can provoke opposition. These policy areas are issues of life, quality of life, and death.

This section introduces the advocates involved in these struggles to define the way health policy works. The terms used and also a caveat are borrowed from Alford (1975:192):

> If my concern were to explain the actions of various individuals and groups with respect to a particular piece of legislation or administrative decision, lumping diverse groups and individuals together into a single structural interest would be too crude. But for the purposes of explaining the main contours of the present system, its resistance to certain kinds of change, and its readiness to adopt others, finer distinctions would entail a short-term time perspective.

Representation: the three faces of a profession

It is important to distinguish carefully between different aspects of the complex social formations that influence health politics. A profession or defined occupational group (such as managers in the NHS systems) is not a unitary actor; it is a group of people with common socialisation, ideological, and ethical stances, perspectives on the world and understandings of events, and a set of organisations and social networks. In discussing health politics, it is all too easy to confuse the different aspects of a group. Political studies, for example, has a long tradition of confusing medical associations with medical professions.

The first face of a profession is the profession as a social institution. The characteristic of a formal profession such as the doctors and nurses of a health service is that it is a social institution that to a very considerable extent social-ises its members and structures their behaviour. Studies in the sociology of the professions, and to a lesser extent in the study of any clearly defined occupa-tional group, catalogue the devices used to socialise individuals and demar-cate professional borders. Professional apprenticeships are not just immersion in professional institutions and world views; they often include what appear to be needlessly unpleasant experiences (such as throwing trainees into envi-ronments where they work thirty-six hours under intense pressure with little help) (Becker *et al.* 2002). The impact of these apprenticeships is to make a deep impression on the young professional's sense of self and problem-solving skills, while marking them off from those who are not members of the pro-fession. Beyond initial socialisation, professions have profound and marked regularities of behaviour that often confound outsiders. Doctors' rationing decisions, or decisions not to ration in some cases, have largely defeated efforts to manage them from without. Doctors are essentially conservative in both practice and channels of information gathering because they are reluc-tant to experiment on patients. Technology and practice adoption, therefore, is far from guaranteed and practice divergences are endemic.

The second face is that of the profession as ideology. This is the highly contested understanding of what the profession's role is and should be. The debate can be cast in many terms but often focuses in on the place of the pro-fession in society and the ethical concerns that come with professions. Thus, for example, professionalism as an ideology includes as core concepts clinical autonomy and science. There is a significant divergence between ideology and practice in most professions, since ideology is the business above all of the most articulate members of the profession, often university-based, and also because other groups try to impose their definitions on professions. Thus, for example, it is a running debate whether nursing is or should be subordinate to medicine. Another example is that science is not the practice of most doctors, whose commitment to patients makes them extremely conservative in changing practice with every report of scientific advance that might later turn out to be useless or misleading (Greer 1988). The result is that the ideol-ogy of the profession stresses the scientific basis of medicine but the scientific studies done in medical schools and research laboratories often go unadopted by doctors sceptical of journal articles.

The third face, then, is the profession as its leaders. This refers to the medical and policy elites – most visibly the associations (the BMA, RCN, and unions) and professional organisations (the Royal Colleges), and the high-status professionals who individually advise ministers and departments. These groups claim to speak for the profession and often play a dominant role in the development of particular professional ideologies. These elites and groups make up the members of their health policy communities and the advocates. They shape the policy streams since they engage in the policy communities and actively propose to align goals, means, and ends while trying to veto proposals they find disagreeable. The problem is that their representativeness is always in question. The real connection between professional leaders and their profession is invariably questionable. Neither medical organisation politics nor high-level research activity are typical of the profession, and there are strong reasons to question whether the recruitment process and demands facing the leaders of either university laboratories or professional lobbies throw up typical professionals.

The result is that the politics of professions and occupational groups are just as hazard-filled as other arenas in politics. The problem is of representation – the extent to which words and people represent the reality of professionals at work. It should be stressed throughout this work that its focus on the policy communities should not be taken to suggest that English health services are filled with marketeers or that ordinary Scottish health professionals long for the 1974 NHS. They might or might not. The political science literature on the topic is overwhelmingly the study of professional elites and ideologies. Professions as social institutions, the real core of professions in society, appear in politics primarily when policy analysts do autopsies on policy failure or unintended consequences and find professional resistance on the wards caused the undesired result. The literature is filled with changes impelled from top down within professions or from outside by others, which failed when they simply could not change entrenched professional values and activities that had evolved over many years. The people and ideas that offer advice and acquiescence to politicians and guide the policy stream are often weakly representative of the professionals on whose preferences they consult and for whose supposed interests they fight. The advantages of these professional elites, from the point of view policy makers, is simply that a flawed representative is superior to no representative.

Advocates

There are four major groups of advocates in health services with broadly shared understandings of means and ends. Professionalists essentially promote an agenda of interest to professionals and policy solutions based on them, sometimes harkening back to the pre-Griffiths NHS. Corporate rationalisers dominated the health services from 1983 until the internal market with a call for management. Market reformers want to go further, using self-correcting markets to provide health services. New public health advocates do not want to join the other three groups in fighting to control hospitals; they want to shift the agenda to population health rather than services. They are the only group that has never set the tone of the NHS. All four face the sheer complexity of health services and the resilience of the social institutions that are professions, so there are always problems to solve. While the politicians and top civil servants might see sequential domination by one organisation after another, it is fairer to argue that the NHS was never a pure type of anything (Exworthy, Powell, and Mohan 1999).

Professionalists

Q: What effect would you say devolution has had on your work here, in this hospital?

A: That's not the thing. What matters is what is changing in practice. In thirty years we will barely need hospitals . . . telemedicine and new procedures mean that we have to rethink practice in all of medicine . . . within ten years acute hospitals will just exist to house the servers with patient records and a place for outpatient surgery . . . and the surgeon won't even have to be there . . .

Q: Do you mean devolution doesn't matter?

A: That doesn't matter much. The science is what's changing medicine.

Q: And devolution . . . genuinely doesn't make a difference?

A: That'll change financing, some of the policies, but not what we do. . . . (Author's interview with an acute trust medical director, autumn 2001)

> My officials would come to me and say that we needed to put more incentives into the policies to make the doctors work better. I would tell them that they're doctors! What they want to do is treat patients. That's the incentive, treating patients! (Sam Galbraith, doctor, professor, former MP and MSP, and former minister with the Scottish Office health portfolio, 2001)

> I told the civil servants that if you really want to drive a surgeon mad, go put a padlock on the operating theatre. Don't let them at the patients, they'll really hate that. (Retired Department of Health professional civil servant, 2002)

The legitimacy of professions – the ideology of professionalism and the goals of professional elites – combined with the resources available to professions can sustain policy advocates who focus on the importance of stable or increasing professional roles in resource allocation and on issues salient to them. The salient issues tend to be medical innovation and quality, and the argument is that better development of new techniques and application of scientific advances would produce a more effective medicine. Professionalists are usually located among the professional elites (doctors resident in teaching hospitals), organised through Royal Colleges, and linked by medical journals.

Viewed from the high point of 1974–83 the influence of professions in the organisation of the NHS anywhere in the UK is small, and viewed from any point before the mid-1980s the formal influence of professional elites and organisations is much diminished. No system in the UK makes the social institution of the profession its organising principle, although that is the direction of Scottish health policy (see Chapter 3). An issue that is a good indicator of professional influence is medical quality. Quality is a difficult term for a large category of activity that was defined in a prominent 1972 Nuffield Trust lecture by founding figure A. L. Cochrane (Cochrane 1972). It has grown markedly in importance since the early 1980s (Walshe 2003). Quality subsumes a variety of campaigns in medicine, such as the campaign for evidence-based medicine (in which doctors are urged to use the techniques judged best in clinical trials), technology assessment (which tries to establish the costs and benefits of new technologies and their diffusion), clinical governance (efforts to manage medical quality), and reduction of practice variations (which tries to eliminate the wide variation in what treatments doctors choose). It is an international movement, with centres as disparate as Dartmouth College in the USA, Oxford University in the UK, and McMaster University in Canada, and multiple journals and societies such as the International Society for Technology Assessment in Health Care (which reorganised in 2002–3 into HTAi, or Health Technology Assessement International). Quality offers a promise to policy makers quite different from that of management. Whereas management offers the use of businesslike methods of organisational change in order to improve efficiency, quality offers to close the gap between professional ideology and professional practice and thereby improve the functioning and value for money of the health service.

Professionalists' chief organisations are the Royal Colleges, which muster considerable status and ability to advise. They directly play a role in accrediting hospitals for training. As hospitals depend on trainee doctors for staffing, this gives Royal Colleges considerable authority over investments and staffing decisions of health services. Royal College decertification can close a department in a hospital, and since hospital departments are interdependent a few decertifications can close the hospital. The Royal Colleges, unlike the BMA or UNISON (the public service workers' union), are mostly weakly organised outside London. They pay the price of a reputation in Cardiff and Belfast as being distant and out of touch (Tables 2.4 and 2.5). The profile of quality is now an indicator of professionalist elites, since they typically seek to put it on the agenda (even if it can be integrated with market-based ideas), and its control is then an indicator of ability to influence the policy stream as it may be used as a government technique to control and regulate doctors or as a professional technique to improve its performance without state intervention (thereby possibly warding off state intervention).

Corporate rationalisers

A: And we are also working on a patient choice model that will allow us to keep them away from the big [nearby city] teaching hospitals.

Q: Isn't that hard? Don't doctors try to exercise some influence over whether or not the patients go to people they respect, hospitals they respect?

A: Well yes . . . the solution will eventually be plans that mean we employ them and tell them where to jolly well send the patients! [laugh] (Author's conversation with a primary care trust manager, England, August 2003)

The essential tenet of corporate rationalism is that the health services can best be run – planned, developed, operated, and improved – if there is an identifiable management cadre in executive positions throughout firm-like units that employ and organise the professionals (Pollitt 1993; Harrison and Pollitt 1994; Hunter 1994). This basic agreement on the importance of management permits enormous variation in objectives and arguments; health service management theory and studies, like other branches of management, include many perspectives and practitioners with differing views. It would also not be remarkable; most of the economy and public sector in the world, and certainly in the UK, is managed. A student must return to the 1930s to find serious debates about the phenomenon of management as something new. However, the particular organisation of professionals – with their powerful social institutions, control over key areas of discretion such as the irreducible patient interaction, and constant flow of unique challenges – has defied management in fields from law to medicine and academia. Equally, the 1974 NHS was a remarkable case of a complex organisation built, formally, on professional activity – on the state effectively employing the whole social institution of British medicine. As a result, within living memory the UK has had a non-managed health service with nobody, as Griffiths put it, 'in charge'. The result of the problems with managing professionals and the recency of an alternative model mean that the managerial function in the NHS, unlike in supermarkets or laundries, has rivals.

Corporate rationalisers include the vibrant group of those who recommend more use of management and management techniques and those who study the use and dissemination of particular management techniques. This encompasses organisations for managers, above all the NHS Confederation (a UK-wide peak organisation for managers that in 2003 became an employers' organisation for contract negotiations), as well as organisations for particular types of manager (such as the NHS Alliance, which is for primary care managers in England); journals to match (above all the *Health Services Journal*, the leading publication for managers); specific organisations dedicated to the extension and improvement of management, above all the

Table 2.4. Territorial structure of major health organisations

Institution	Staff changes in offices in the devolved territories	Office structure changes since devolution	Other comments
Royal College of Physicians RCP	The Wales office has one part-time member of staff. The Belfast office has one full-time member of staff. Their main duties are to support the local regional adviser and to provide local services to members and fellows.	Regional offices exist in Wales and Northern Ireland. The opening of the Wales office was partly influenced by devolution. There is no specific infrastructure to link the RCP with the devolved bodies. Instead the RCP engages with them through other means: on specific projects, where they may seek funding from the devolved bodies, and responding to consultation exercises.	
BMA Scotland	In Scotland there are three offices; one in Edinburgh with twenty-three members of staff, one in Glasgow with five members of staff, and one in Aberdeen, which has three members of staff. Devolution did lead to an increase in staffing numbers in Scotland.	In the Edinburgh office new posts were created to deal with the Scottish Parliament and Executive. These included a public affairs officer and a research and information officer, so as to maximise parliamentary and political influence in Scotland. In addition, additional support was given to the general practice secretariat. The Edinburgh office also moved into new and more prestigious premises. The Aberdeen and Glasgow offices have seen less change, although assistant secretaries in both offices have taken on a significant role in assisting with national policy and negotiations attached to it, providing specialist advise and expertise on policy and negotiations.	The new posts have since been reviewed to see how effectively they are working. Some changes have been made to the roles and responsibilities of the posts.

BMA Wales	The Wales office has not undergone any structural changes since devolution. However, most of the work of the office is now taken up with dealings with the National Assembly for Wales. For instance when it came to negotiations on the consultant's contract, the office dealt almost exclusively with the Welsh Assembly Government.	The Wales officer has fourteen members of staff. Devolution led to the office employing one additional member of staff – a press officer.	
NHS Confederation	No special structures have been introduced to deal specifically with devolution. However, each office is resourced to deal with public affairs, policy, and the media. Each office is resourced from its own income and manages expenditure accordingly. Advice from the central, London office is also available for the offices in the devolved territories.	Since devolution, staff numbers in Scotland and Wales have increased from one to four. The Northern Ireland office has one staff member. There are plans for expanding staff numbers to cope with the devolved bodies.	
UNISON	Unison Scotland has developed internal mechanisms to cope with devolution (without increasing its budget.) A policy and information team has been established, providing policy advice and specialise support for the organisation. Specialist support services cover bargaining, equalities, legal, and communication and policy research. Unison Wales has not developed an internal policy capacity like Scotland. Instead it signed contracts with University of Wales, Swansea, to conduct its research and policy work.	Devolution has not led to changes in staffing numbers. Overall staffing budgets have not changed since devolution; however budgets have been spent differently, where devolution has changed the nature of their work.	Unison is currently reviewing its organisational structures and operations.

Note: The RCP does not have an office in Scotland, given the presence of the Royal Colleges in Edinburgh and Glasgow.

Table 2.5. Membership numbers for the Royal Colleges broken down by
nation

Royal College	England	Wales	Northern Ireland	Scotland	UK total	Total
RCN	292,000	20,000	12,000	34,000	358,000	–
RCP	13,300	700	300	700	15,000	–
RCS	6,310	345	79	–	6,734	–
RCP and RCS (G)	–	–	–	–	8,000	13,500
RCP (E)	2,361	134	253	1,738	4,486	7,909
RCS (E)	6,313	418	259	1,205	8,195	14,228

Notes:
Royal College of Nurses (RCN): primarily England/Wales/Northern
Ireland/Scotland
Royal College of Physicians (RCP): primarily England/Wales/Northern Ireland
Royal College of Surgeons (RCS): primarily England/Wales/Northern Ireland: the
figures are low because the RCS has excluded retired members, so the figures
presented here cover 'active members and fellows' of the RCS; the figures also
exclude members of the Faculty of Dental Surgery
RCP and RCS Glasgow (G): total membership figures are given, which do not
distinguish between the RCP and RCS
RCP Edinburgh(E): membership is broken down by nation; the figures cover
follow, members and associate members
RCS Edinburgh: membership is not broken down by nation; the figures cover
fellows and members
Total: includes overseas members.
All figures are as of August 2003, except Edinburgh, which are as of March 2004.

Institute for Healthcare Management (born of the merger of the important
Institute for Health Services Management and a primary care management
organisation); and, less directly, the university centres for health policy
research and associated think-tanks that regularly sponsor work on what management should do. Managerialism is an almost existential aspect of the life
of the management cadre; born of the government's initial determination that
administration was inadequate and management was needed, the NHS management cadre exists because of the assumption that organisations require
leadership, hierarchy, strategy, and relations with the environment, and that
managers should provide it. The core agreement on these understandings of
health service organisation – that the NHS needs management – defines this
group.

Corporate rationalisers' role in policy is based on their good fit with advocates in many policy fields, their impressive advice capacities (probably no
other group in the health service has so many advocates with the ability to
produce new strategies and policy ideas, on any level of generality), and on

their role in acquiescence. The management cadre was introduced into the health service following the Griffiths letter precisely to create a group that could implement policies and act as a tool of the centre, and to the extent that it does this means that this is the group the centre will consult about implementation and to whom policy makers will attribute that power.

Market reformers

The managerialism of corporate rationalisers and the professionalism of medical leaders are both sets of goals connected with the operation of organisations rather than the structure of their environment. There is a second organisational strategy, however, that tries to focus on creating a structure of external incentives that will produce desirable outcomes. Market reformers are strong in many areas of public policy worldwide, and focus on the introduction of market mechanisms and logics as a way to give health services organisations and consumers incentive to improve. Rather than the state effectively owning and trying to lead a large organisation through whatever mix of professional and managerial power, this strategy would have the state employ market mechanisms that discipline health services organisations into improving quality and efficiency. In the context of the UK, market ideas build on the structure inherited from the internal market, namely the logic of contracting between acute trusts and those who represent or are patient consumers, i.e. GP fundholders, primary care trusts, or, in some proposals, patients themselves. If purchasers are given funds to contract for care, and there is competition among providers for the funds, and the funds and patients move together, then the providing organisations should be obliged to improve. Some of the most extreme, who at times appear to have the ear of the Conservative party, recommend undermining the effective state monopsony for health care in the UK (the equivalent of monopoly for purchasers, in which the state is the only major purchaser). This is despite the international evidence that competition in financing, as against delivery, raises costs while monopsony lowers costs (Marmor 1999).

After introducing competition between trusts, the most successful (arguably, most successful overall) market reform technique has been public–private partnerships. These range from outsourcing work such as laundry and catering through to the construction and operation of all but professional services in new hospitals. Most go under the name of PFI, the private finance initiative, although they are also called PPP, for public–private partnerships, and involve the construction and maintenance of a particular type of facility in return for a regular payment and possible transfer at the end of the contract. Their advantages are debatable and debated, and while they have the immense attraction of getting a new facility without immediate capital costs they also put severe pressure on running costs for decades afterwards and incur the opposition of unions (for the critics, see Pollock 2004). The front-line for their extension varies; England's government repeatedly considers full-scale PFI facilities, including the professional staff, while the National Assembly for Wales restricts them to building and maintenance and, almost uniquely in the UK, trumpets its decision to build a wholly public, non-PFI hospital in North Wales. PFI and the extent of market mechanisms in organisation are the two best indicators of market reformers since they show UK-wide divergence; more exotic private-sector involvement is pursued only in England.

Market reforming policy advocates have their bases in the larger infrastructure of health policy and new public management organisations, and can benefit from the overall strength of market logics in UK public administration and debates. Explicitly right-wing think-tanks such as the Institute of Economic Affairs, Adam Smith Institute, Centre for Policy Studies, Civitas and Policy Exchange are interested, as well as various thinkers writing in more rightist publications (Kandiah and Seldon 1996). The civil service in the centre has long experience with contracting, as does much of local government, with the result that they can rate the feasibility of market mechanisms highly. Much of the management cadre, likewise, is experienced in operating in environments structured as quasi-markets. There is no overall organisation but in an environment such as that of the UK public sector, permeated with new public management ideas, there is sufficient support to keep market reformers in policy communities.

Population health advocates and localists

Finally, there are the advocates of new public health and an overall focus on local population health and its determinants (Hunter 2003). Public health is any collective action to improve population health outcomes (Porter 1999:4), and within that category new public health refers to a concrete movement calling for health policy to focus on the full range of health-promoting factors rather than medical services and for public health to go beyond 'classic' environmental health policies. The new public health movement arose out of the failings of health services around the world to produce the equity and overall well-being that they were expected to produce once financial barriers to access were good. Inequalities of health and poor health indicators in the UK, for example, survived the NHS (Powell 1997). Studies of the determinants of health over time carried out by students of history, poverty, and social policy, as well as examination of impressive data from countries such as Sweden that produced much greater health improvements, began to suggest that a variety of factors outside the control of the health service explained much of health (Wilkinson 1996), while much-debated work (most famously by McKeown) argued that medicine contributed relatively little to health (McKeown 1979:xv). Poverty alone does much to explain health inequalities: there are some very good hospitals in London, but the poverty and social exclusion in parts of London overwhelm their influence on local population health. The watershed for this line of argument was the Black Report, which was commissioned by Labour in 1979 and reported in 1980 to a frosty Conservative government (which tried to bury it and thereby accidentally guaranteed its fame, and publication not by the Stationery Office but by Penguin) (Black Report 1992). The report amassed impressive evidence that the NHS had not eliminated dramatic inequalities in health and that poverty explained much of the inequality and ill health.

Throughout the 1980s a large amount of research on health demonstrated that interlocking sources of deprivation explained much of ill health. Identified causal chains multiplied. Poor public transport leads to unemployment and failure to take up educational opportunities by those trapped in remote areas; unemployment leads to domestic violence and drug or alcohol abuse, while producing children who can suffer from all of their parents' problems as well as new ones such as foetal alcohol syndrome or the consequences of abuse or neglect. The result was the new public health movement (Ashton and Seymour 1988; Baggott 2000). This research met with the discipline of public health, then highly marginal in the NHS and in many ways restricted to infectious disease control. Seeking to get away from hectoring about lifestyle or passive waiting for meningitis outbreaks, many public health scholars and practitioners began to campaign for attention to 'the wider determinants of health'. Their first policy victories came from a Conservative administration, which both commissioned an influential report and enacted the 1988 *Health of the Nation* White Paper, the first explicit public health White Paper in England (Independent Inquiry into Inequalities 1988).

This is an uphill battle. Fox (1986) argued that the guiding theme of health policy in the very different health systems of the USA and UK has been 'hierarchical regionalism', which is the assumption that diseases are best treated by the medical model in facilities arranged in a hierarchy of complexity and territorial scale, from GP surgeries to smaller, less sophisticated hospitals, up to the big academic medical centres. Sociologist Samuel Bloom (2002:201) in endorsed Funkenstein's 1971 observation that

> Most faculty members [demand] that [medical] schools remain institutions whose chief goals are basic biomedical research and the care of hospitalized patients whose illness is biological in nature. Some charge that they are not

conscious of their social responsibilities. This is not true. They see them differently. In interviews with faculty members at a number of medical schools, they state that the problems of the delivery of medical care and the education of new types of family physicians should be the concern of 'other schools' . . . They seriously question whether medical schools can or should take on social factors that breed disease.

Or, as one university-based interviewee in Scotland put it, 'jobs make the difference to people's morbidity, and that's for of the Chancellor of the Exchequer, not the Minister of Health' (3–4) .

In the face of such conviction advocates of new public health face serious problems of marginality. Their key institutional bases are in marginal areas of health policy, above all public health and academic public health and sociology. Local government is often sympathetic to a greater role in health services and policy, but, according to public health advocates, there are a variety of stumbling blocks – 'when you say public health to local government, they think "drains – that's our job"' (5–3), so in the eyes of public health specialists working on wider determinants of health 'they need educating' (5–1) such as the time that 'a [director of public health] from the NHS came to an event, and sat on a stage and answered questions for hours. That built credibility' (5–7).

The public health professionals therefore are marginal within the health services, have only uncertain relationships with local government, which likes localism but tends to want to invest local authority in itself, and control a very small part of the budget. They face major organisational constraints, since from this marginal base they are asking large, well-entrenched, and sometimes professional organisations to change their activities and goals. They are also organisationally fragmented. Unlike clinical elites, they lack powerful organisations with a hand in running or regulating health systems, such as the Royal Colleges. What they do have is a substantial number of ideas that can be placed in the policy stream from multiple academic and policy sources, and enough capacity as advisers to establish a credible position in the policy communities of the UK. Nevertheless, this organisational marginality and the nature of the new public health agenda means that adoption and implementation of new public health is the exception rather than the rule (which is why Wales is so interesting for its adoption of new public health tenets).

Issues

These four groups tend to focus their attention on four issue areas that serve as the principal outcomes studied in this book. The first issue is organisational form. This is the organisational structure of health services – the location of decision-making power and resources, including the balance between markets, management, and professions. The second is the public–private relationship, i.e. the extent to which policy tries to incorporate private provision into the health service via routes such as private finance initiatives (PFI), which use private providers for plant and services, franchising management to the private sector, or contracting with private sector medical firms. This public–private relationship is an indicator of the presence of market reformers' ideas. The third is the quality agenda, which refers to efforts to use policy to improve quality, whether as a regulatory technique to prevent slipshod but cheap performance in a market, or as a professionally dominated device to improve professional autonomy by reforming top-down from within the professions. It is an indicator of professionalists' ideas, with or without the addition of market reformers' interest in regulation. The fourth is the new public health agenda, which focuses on the reduction of inequalities, organisation and resources of the public health function, and organisational structures designed to promote population health through service integration. It is often tied to localism since local government, along with public health specialists, is its best champion. In addition to these four issues, present on global health agendas, two countries have developed additional focuses. Scotland, uniquely, added a new universal right to personal long-term care, and Northern Ireland, while ignoring other issues, focused its attention on the allocation of acute hospitals. Those two countries accordingly have those case studies included as reflections of what their devolved systems did do.

Conclusions

The four health systems of the devolved UK each inherit a set of problems shared by health systems around the world and shaped by the inheritance of a common health policy arena and NHS model. Ministers charged with health in each country face problems of cost escalation, increasing demand, and questions about quality and value for money, and they face them from a common position – as the chief executive officers of giant organisations. Different advocates have influenced the design of the systems over time, and the memories of each structure are still embedded in organisation, culture, and ideas, while the NHS is also subjected to policy ideas such as planning and privatisation that inhabit the political environment around it.

As with other policy areas and as in other countries, the geographical distribution of the institutions that sustain policy advocates differs and produces different policy communities. The policy communities from which devolved and UK politicians fish their ideas have rapidly grown apart and should continue to do so as new policy developments shape their policy communities. Combined with separate party systems, we should expect that the four systems will differ quickly and permanently. The next chapters show how the different balances of these groups, based on different social institutions, produced differing policy communities that shaped different policy streams – and as a result lent coherence to policy streams. Over time as politicians solved political problems, they picked up policies favoured by the policy advocates most prominent in their local policy communities. The result was that the advocates who had won little in Northern Ireland, Scotland, and Wales, now won a great deal, while those in England found their policies largely confined to its borders.

Note

1 I owe the term 'Christmas tree' to Nigel Edwards of the NHS Confederation.

3
Scotland: professionalism

> I don't use the word 'consumer' myself. I prefer to use the word 'patient'
> (Scottish Health Minister Malcolm Chisholm MSP, cited in Templeton 2003)

Scotland is the star case of devolution. In 1997 Scottish devolution was an extremely important issue on the political agenda, with powerful political coalitions behind it. Its profile was high enough to bring Wales and discussions of English regionalism along in its wake; its promises were of a new Scotland with new politics, and the passage of the referendum supporting a Parliament was an electoral landslide accompanied by jubilation. Scotland could finally have a representative political system that at least partly reflected the complexity and distinctiveness of its national institutions and culture. The impact of devolution in Scotland on health politics and policy, then, should show what devolution can do under the best of circumstances – when it is long-prepared, popular, supported by an overwhelming coalition, and freed from the legal restraints and institutional complexities that hamper Northern Ireland and Wales.

The trajectory of Scottish health policy since devolution is one of professionalism. The politics of Scottish health policy are strongly influenced by the country's impressive medical elites, while market reformers and corporate rationalisers look more English and have had their strongest bases south of the border. Scotland has continued to forge ahead with quality improvement, leaving it in the hands of professional leaders, and has invested in public health. There is little talk of more markets or private-sector participation, and the only important effort to include the private sector is PFI. The result is that Scottish health policy bets on professionals as the state's allies in providing effective, efficient, legitimate health care and health care rationing. The logic, if not the forms, are close to the 1974 NHS – and the criticisms are the same as well.

Inheritance

The case of Scotland highlights how the UK, for all its ostensible centralism, is a union state rather than a unitary state. Made up of several different polities conjoined at different times, London never tried to establish uniform rule across the UK. Rather, when England united with Scotland, it united with a well-established kingdom and distinctive society. The ensuing Union left Scotland's organisations great autonomy to develop distinctively (Hutchison 1986, 2001; Devine 1999). The combination of critical masses of wealth, population, and social institutions such as law, universities, charitable associations, and local government all meant that Scotland would have a distinctive institutional trajectory that its leaders could defend against centralisation. As a result, Scotland, of the three devolved countries, is the one with the most complicated, competitive, and well-worked out policies.

Once the geopolitical threats Scotland posed to England had been neutralised by the 1707 Treaty of Union, Scotland's elites were broadly left alone to continue governing in Scotland by a central state that easily incorporated and over time buttressed them. As a result, Scottish institutions developed relatively autonomously, with their own elite leadership intact and few directly coercive measures causing centralisation (McCrone 1992; Paterson 1994, 1998). The basic geopolitical fact that made a separate, successful Scottish state possible before 1707 also allowed Scotland to assemble an imposing civil society: the central belt between Glasgow and Edinburgh, the site of dense economic and social interactions and surrounded by inaccessible hills, was a defensible and desirable place in which to build social institutions.

The welfare state occasioned the greatest changes, in a nineteenth and a twentieth-century wave. However, in most cases Scottish elites were willing and able to adapt the increasing degree of state intervention to maintain their, and Scotland's, autonomy. This autonomy meant that regular campaigns for Scottish autonomy (Mitchell 1996) failed for want of elite support and the political elites mostly looked askance at the secessionist Scottish National Party (SNP), a party movement with a large protest vote. Only Margaret Thatcher's violation of a Scottish consensus in favour of conviction politics rooted in English electoral support led Scottish organisations to conclude that the informal, administrative autonomy of the Scottish Office was not enough (Greer 2003). The result was the overwhelming coalition of Scottish organisations in favour of guaranteeing their autonomy that ushered in the Scottish Parliament.

The legacy of institutional distinctiveness over time is that Scotland, much more than Northern Ireland or Wales, is endowed with an important complex of institutions and interest groups that shape health politics. The great cities – Edinburgh and Glasgow above all, but also Aberdeen, Inverness, and Dundee – house important concentrations of political and policy resources. Medical politics alone shows the density of Scottish regional organisations and case studies of policy show their influence. The four medical schools of Scotland are among the world's elite and sustain a concentration of high-status academics who can make authoritative claims to command advice and acquiescence.

Interest groups and the press in Scotland are also strong, relatively devolved, and operate on a scale that allows them to create a different policy agenda. The BMA and specialised Royal Colleges tend to have specific Scottish organisations, while UNISON and the Scotland-only Scottish Trades Union Confederation have important resources and strong connections with the Scottish Labour party. Their doings are all reported by a Scottish press that dominates its market – only the *Guardian, Independent*, and *Financial Times*, with their comparatively small circulations, publish single UK editions. Every other paper in Scotland is Scottish (such as Glasgow's *Herald* and tabloid *Daily Record* and Edinburgh's *Scotsman*) or a special Scottish edition of a UK paper. Even so, the Scottish press outsells Scottish editions of UK papers. From this complex of institutions Scotland can select a different agenda, and there is almost no room for members of the policy community who do not have roots in the capacious Scottish institutions.

Territorial office politics

The Scottish Office was the oldest and the most imposing of the three territorial departments and has been on the scene for every chapter of the development of Britain's modern welfare state. It was born in 1885 as part of the ongoing institutional adaptation of Scotland's autonomous organisations to the British welfare state (Hanham 1965; Mitchell 2003). As Victorian and Edwardian social reforms went on, continuing to take the form of appointed special-purpose boards, the key question was what part of the central government would supervise (and increasingly subsidise) them (Harris 1983). After 1885 the demarcation was clear: in Scotland, it would be the Scottish Office. The supervisory duties over the increasingly numerous boards that in England and Wales accrued to the Whitehall departments gathered into the Scottish Office.

In the mid-twentieth century, and above all with the Attlee government, the policy mix in the British welfare state changed from an emphasis on appointed local boards providing residual public services to larger organisations directly providing services and run by the state (the total mobilisation of two world wars marked the arrival of direct provision and planning).

Government departments grew enormously as they took on nationalised industries and the demands of directly providing services such as health care and social security and working closely with the providers of education and transport. In Scotland, one department – the Scottish Office – took over most of the direct administration of social policy, if not of industrial policy and planning (i.e. the nationalised industries) (Hutchison 2000). The Scottish Office, rather than the Department of Health, was to administer the NHS in Scotland (Nottingham 2000).

Formally, the Scottish Office was a large Whitehall spending department with a UK Cabinet minister bound by collective decisions (Milne 1957; Parry 1987; Kellas 1989; Midwinter, Keating, and Mitchell 1991). The ability of the Scottish Office and its policy networks to resist a determined government was minimal, and the desire to do so of Secretaries of State for Scotland, in office as UK politicians, was often equally minimal (Holliday 1992). The Scottish Office was one more part of the UK-wide civil service and profoundly influenced by Whitehall's culture. It also lacked policy capacity relative to its Whitehall peer departments such as the Department of Health. The combination of Cabinet unity and a unified civil service meant that when the Scottish Office was working on a policy, the Department of Health in London was usually in the lead. The Scottish Office was, like the other territorial departments, working on its own version of the same policy with information flowing through bilateral contacts among officials. Governments preferred to launch all policy papers together, with simultaneous release of the policy and its Scottish variant. This practice led to the Scottish Office civil servants staying up all night working with documents faxed from London to have the documents prepared by the 9 am deadline. It gave rise to unkind comments from interviewees about civil servants using word processors automatically to replace 'UK' with 'Scotland' in government drafts. Symbolically enough, it was not until 1935 that the Scottish Office even established a permanent base in Edinburgh rather than in its quarters in Whitehall; its imposing Edinburgh headquarters, St Andrew's House, only opened during the Second World War.

Informally, however, the Scottish Office institutionalised a different style of politics to complement the formal refraction of every decision from a UK Cabinet through a territorial office. The ability of the Scottish Office and its Secretary of State to adapt policies – and their incentive to do so – was impressive in light of the constraints. Divergence in Scottish politics came from the simple ability to experiment that came from being a large department with relatively stable staffing, and one that was comparatively insulated from direct policy oversight by London and that had to write its own version of most major policy papers. There was too much to oversee for the centre (Cabinet,

Treasury) to oversee it all in detail or to want to oversee. Before the 1960s and the strengthening of 'central' coordinating departments around the world (Tuohy 1992:31), the centre did not really try to control this 'dual state' in which two formally hierarchical administrations, for the UK and Scotland, respected each other's spheres (Bulpitt 1983). The resulting informal autonomy meant that implementation of many initiatives could diverge, either formally in the Scottish versions of policies or informally in the circulars and informal advice civil servants passed on to the system. This is to some extent the autonomy of any large department. The Scottish Office had more.

The basis for this autonomy was the interaction of the structure of Scottish politics (the presence of both nationalist–unionist and left–right axes) with the political institutions to create a distinctive party system. Scottish politics were made more competitive by the presence of the SNP, which at once was a nonpartisan Scottish vote, an all-around protest vote, and a party to the left of Labour. Scottish politicians and elites were able to take advantage of this threat to the Union in order to lobby London, because to a degree unknown in the rest of the UK their institutions (local government, health service, parties, universities, professional organisations, unions, and Scottish Office *inter alia*) were bound together in networks of resource dependency that were different from organisations more completely dependent on London (Greer 2003). The result was autonomy defended and complemented by a strong territorial lobby and policy community.

Meanwhile, the Scottish Office resembled other territorial offices (for which it was the prototype) in the politics it created. Partly due to the structure of Scottish society and partly due to the need to apply policies formed in a UK agenda to Scotland, the Scottish Office developed close links with a policy community built around professional elites in the medical schools and Royal Colleges. Much like the other two territorial departments, the Scottish Office had to write the policy papers and develop implementation strategies on the ground in its region (and unlike the other territorial offices, it was unlikely to find itself wholly without qualified, interested, advisers, no matter how obscure the field). The inherited characteristics of Scotland's distinct health system would thus shape policy communities and policies.

Five points stand out. First, the Scottish health system has a stronger tradition of deference and what now look like authoritarian practices. As late as the 1930s Scotland's social welfare institutions were quite progressive in their willingness to address need, had a markedly authoritarian streak, and enjoyed a high degree of autonomy from state and society. For example, the Royal Scottish Society for the Prevention of Cruelty to Children (known as 'the Cruelty') held a Royal Charter and worked as a sort of nonstate police. Its uniformed workers would among many other activities greet Govan shipyard workers suspected of alcoholic dissipation, take away wages the workers would otherwise spend on alcohol, and deliver the money to their families – an extraordinary level of social intervention by a charity in a tough neighbourhood (Blane 2002). Scottish public health and police were until the start of the twentieth century formally bound together in a way foreign to the rest of the UK (Carson and Idzikowska 1989; White 1994; Hamlin 1998:192). The eighteenth-century concept of police having broad powers to organise society long held sway, with the result that Scotland developed a nearly unique system of police boards that ran both conventional criminal justice operations as well as public health. Academia mirrored the link, with public health and forensic medicine bound together until the late 1890s and high-status academics moving between these and other medical chairs and posts as medical officers with local government and police boards. This tradition was badly eroded by the Second World War, but Scotland remains a place where the collective status of public health and its willingness and ability to intervene remain high.

Second, Scottish medicine had a long tradition: it had some of the oldest medical schools in the world, a deserved reputation for innovation and excellence, tight links to universities, and high social status. The presence of the large teaching hospitals at the famous old universities of Glasgow, Aberdeen, Edinburgh, and Dundee (St Andrews), the status of professions and higher education, and the universities' tight connections with elite society meant that medical elites' status in society was high, their influence over their institutions' environments impressive, and their power within medicine great. They were well organised into three Royal Colleges. In a small society with fewer status rivals, Scottish medical elites were world class and known for it. As a result, medical elites at the major institutions in Scotland retained, residually, a higher status and more power within medicine than many of their colleagues in the rest of the UK.

Third, Scotland also developed a strong tradition of public health medicine and intervention, from physicians through to health visitors, district nurses, and other primary care professionals. The tradition in part reflected the disastrous health of the Scottish population in the nineteenth and twentieth centuries – particularly the populations of the west, but really the rural poor and the industrial working class throughout the country. Scotland's industrialisation was always at least in part based on having lower wages than comparable regions in the rest of the UK, and this combined with Scotland's early industrialisation and unusual landholding structure to produce immense problems of overcrowding, poor housing, and poor diet (Smout 1987; Knox 1999). Pioneer social reformer Owen Chadwick was not alone when he judged Glasgow to be the unhealthiest city he had seen (White 1994:153).

In response, some members of Scotland's medical professions, municipal governments, and social reformers developed one of the UK's strongest traditions of public health interventions, at the same time as surgeons in Glasgow were developing the Caesarian section to overcome the problems of childbirth by women with rickets, a bone-warping disease caused by poor nourishment. This strong tradition of public health leadership and advocacy still survives, just as the problems that originally caused the interventions – problems of poverty, unemployment, unhealthy lifestyles, and social exclusion – also live on. The public health tradition at its least creditable could dovetail with the authoritarian streak in Scottish public policy, but equally formed a basis for many of the most meaningful interventions in Scottish health by creating the leadership, organisations, and climate to act. The Scottish Office was probably ahead of England in hearing, and to some extent adopting, the new public health agenda, and to this day Scottish public health is better organised, with the Public Health Institute of Scotland and then Health Scotland acting as an umbrella (and antedating similar English efforts).

Fourth, the high degree of local autonomy Scotland enjoyed doubly insulated local elites and their institutions from central control. Policies until the postwar era had to go from London through the Scottish Office and through boards before arriving at the Scottish front line. At both the levels of the Scottish Office and local elites on boards, Scots elites and politicians could, for better or for worse, protect their own ideas and innovations from central control. The Scottish Office, itself, was slow to undertake a process of centralisation; for much of its history officials spent their whole careers in single areas (Parry 1987). The result was a different environment for experimentation. Scottish elites could gain support for their ideas and carry them out according to local politics rather than central policy ideas. Scottish politics might have been more or less politicised or restrictive, but it was different. The inherited connection between policing, academia, and public health made innovative service integration possible, if not guaranteed (Hunter and Wistow 1987).

Fifth, Scotland's Highlands and Islands have for a long time been seen as different and deserving of different policies and organisation. This area was organised independently in Parliament with the nineteenth-century Crofter's party, and even now the party is gone separate legislation and policies mirror the area's special place in Scottish culture. In health, it split from the rest of the UK with the arrival of National Insurance. The structure of crofting (sheep farming in the area) made the logic of National Insurance inapplicable, while finding doctors to set up as small businesses in the area was very difficult. The result was the creation of a special health service for the Highlands and Islands, with staff doctors and funding from general taxation (McCrae

2003). The extent to which the UK learns from the Highlands and Islands is questionable (there is a tendency to view it, and its policies, as exceptional rather than instructive). Nevertheless, it meant that part of Scotland had something similar to the NHS, and the Scottish Office was administering something like the NHS, long before 1948.

Outcomes in Scottish health policy in the NHS before devolution are the sum of marginal changes to UK policies. As with the other territorial offices, pre-devolution outcomes are more interesting as indicators of the policy advocates at work than as policies, for they were far less important than the outcomes in London (and, consequently, much less studied). The need to develop separate policies – even if they were conceptually the same as the policies the Cabinet agreed for the rest of the UK – meant that the Scottish Office could often vary policies. This could happen formally, in details, only very occasionally on a large scale (as with the integration of teaching hospitals in 1948) and very often in implementation and areas of administrative discretion. Small Scottish Office policy capacity relative to Whitehall limited its possible variance on paper, but increased it in practice by making administration more dependent on collaborators in the health service.

Organisational distinctiveness before devolution

The formal organisation of the NHS in Scotland before devolution was not particularly distinctive. First, and most importantly, it was a responsibility of the Scottish Office rather than the Department of Health. The organisation was flatter because it lacked regions. Scotland was about equal in population to a small English region and so there was little point to having the extra tier. The one significant structural difference in Scottish NHS organisation reflected broader differences in the internal and external relations of Scottish health elites. In England and Wales teaching hospitals were outside the normal NHS acute care structure and had their own boards. This reflected largely the social and professional power of the big London teaching hospitals, which dominated medicine in England and Wales and sought to preserve their autonomy against control by lower-status large hospitals (often old Poor Law hospitals with the stigma of low-status clients) (Hollingsworth 1986:38–41, 53–8). By contrast, in Scotland there was a long tradition of much tighter integration between universities, hospitals, and local government, which meant that the teaching hospitals could be integrated, mainly because the Scottish universities attained ascendance over their hospitals while the reverse happened in London (Rivett 1986:60). As a consequence, integrating the teaching hospitals merely reflected power relations within a different and less internally differentiated medical and social services world – what appeared to be the subordination of teaching hospitals actually reflected their peak position in a more integrated health system.

This distinctive treatment vanished when the 1974 reforms merged the various pillars of the English system so that it converged on Scotland's model. Throughout the UK the 1974 reforms were actually designed to use professional structures to provide efficient health services, unlike the 1948 structure, which was designed to make the NHS politically acceptable. In Scotland the system resembled the rest of the UK. The Griffiths reforms led to the creation of a corps of managers with a chief executive to run the NHS in Scotland, much like the head of the Management Executive in London. When the government imposed the internal market, Scottish structures were easily adapted to the same basic strategies as used to marketise the English system. The health boards were the main purchasers, especially as fundholding made very little progress. Trusts did form relatively rapidly, as managers of important hospitals sought more independence. Nevertheless, the internal market cut across the traditions and the traditional hierarchies of Scottish medicine and met profound cultural resistance on all levels.

Summary

For all the distinctiveness of Scottish culture and identity, most of the distinctiveness of Scotland's health politics could be explained by the dependence of the Scottish Office, in its marginal policy formulation and implementation, on the clinical elites of Royal Colleges and academic medicine, who offered the advice, acquiescence, and approval that the lightly staffed Scottish Office needed. The Scottish Office, responsible for administering the health service in Scotland, did not formally pursue separate policies, because the Secretary of State was subject to Cabinet discipline and the civil servants relied on their colleagues in the 'UK' departments. The lack of administrative capacity, however, combined with the distinctive structure of Scottish politics (the presence of a nationalist opposition) to create distinctive Scottish patterns of spending and implementation. These reflected the preferences and arguments of the groups that loomed large in Scotland and could provide advice, acquiescence, and approval. Very important, compared to their colleagues elsewhere, were the medical elites of the Royal Colleges and the great hospitals; they were perfect insiders and had fewer competitors for the policy ideas, such as medical quality control, that they supported. Scotland differed also in the structure of its informal social institutions, such as in the culture of public health, but above all Scottish distinctiveness was the product of the interaction of the Scottish Office, Scotland's party system, and the different weights of UK-wide advocates.

Policies and politics

The new government of Scotland is the Scottish Office with a legislature on top. Much of the argument for a Parliament was founded on perceptions of the indignity (the unresponsiveness and unrepresentativeness) of UK rule for Scotland. The main targets of devolutionists were therefore the effective powers of the Secretary of State and the quangos – as in Wales, the indignity of Westminster rule was magnified when it was by boards appointed by Westminster politicians. Whether out of practicality or due to their satisfaction with Scottish governance, activists made few other calls for restructuring Scottish administration. The result is that devolved Scotland is an old administration run by a new representative body. The Scottish Parliament alone bears the weight of expectations of a new politics. It is indeed new; it is the legislative body enjoying all the competencies in Scotland except those enumerated in the Scotland Act 1998 as belonging to the central state.

The policy community

To run the health system Scottish Office policy makers developed strong links with those who could supply them with information and advice, implement their decisions, and give them legitimacy. Thus, like the other territorial offices, policy influence in the Scottish Office came primarily from advice (reflecting its information-poor nature), acquiescence (cooperation – the influence that comes from being a crucial group for implementation), and approval (the ability to endow a policy with legitimacy, or deprive it of legitimacy). The groups that could provide this were, above all, the professional and medical elites who were so strong in Scotland's hospitals, universities, and Royal Colleges. Their influence, organisation, power within medicine, and capacity to formulate policy ideas are Scotland's most distinct property. Their resources (information and capacity to carry opinion formers) fit well with the needs of and opportunities provided by the Scottish Office. In Scotland, therefore, the 'reign of professional ideas' that marked all three territorial offices was particularly glorious (Hazell and Jervis 1998:44). This is not to suggest that Scottish medical elites had a particularly distinctive Scottish agenda; that is only true at the margins (many are not Scots by birth). Nor does it suggest Scotland diverged in big policy issues; Scottish Office changes had to be only at the margins. What it does mean is that policy advocates that depended on medical elites – such as those opposed to market and corporate rationalisers and in favour of professionally led quality improvement – were stronger in Scotland than in areas less endowed with elite physicians.

The influence on policy debates of medical elites and their institutions are particularly visible in a number of areas (even despite the marginal nature of Scottish Office changes to UK policies). First, Scotland's big teaching hospitals and universities took large parts of the budget and were broadly autonomous; the medical school in Dundee built itself up with very little oversight and considerable public investment. Second, very few acute services, no matter how costly or little-used, existed in England that did not exist in Scotland. The Scottish institutions were capable of doing any procedure, and politically they could win the rights and resources to do it even if planners would prefer to have fewer sites performing a procedure. The Scottish medical elites could win the support of the Scottish territorial lobby. Third, Scotland made strides ahead not only of England but ahead of most Western countries in developing a real focus on medical services quality, through networks of elite physicians that tried to identify consensus on medical techniques and diffuse them to raise quality, as well as improve data and medical education. The losers in post-devolution policy were mostly those who relied on the UK agenda but found that they had few allies on the ground in the Scottish health system. For example, partisans of the internal market or use of the private sector (even in the form of PFIs) were in hostile terrain.

Politics: institutions

Before devolution there was some debate about the extent of the gap between Scotland's strong and distinctive 'civil society', its imposing but only marginally autonomous administration, and its weak, or often nonexistent, political arena. Devolution created an autonomous political arena, the Scottish Parliament, to resolve this anomaly, but it inserted the Scottish Parliament into a well-entrenched administrative system. The politics of Scotland's institutions are shaped both by its old administration and by its new political system.

First, formally, Scottish institutions changed little. The Scotland Act effectively transferred the powers of the old Scottish Office to a pair of bodies called, respectively, the Scottish Parliament and the Scottish Executive (Burrows 2000; Mitchell and Scottish Monitoring Team 2001). The ministers and top civil servants remained in St Andrew's House and the Scottish Office premises in Leith; now they reported to the Parliament.

The Executive is powerful in that there is no formal restriction on what it can do with the health service and its block-grant funding gives it effectively unlimited power to move funds between programmes. Scotland could, theoretically, abolish the NHS. What the Executive does not have, however, is significant control over its level of financing as the pre-devolutionary funding formula was carried over almost unmodified. Like the other devolved administrations, the Scottish Executive depends on the UK budget. The Scotland Office continues its existence as a somewhat vestigial UK Cabinet department (merged into a new Department for Constitutional Affairs in 2003). It occupies a budget line that includes the Scottish Executive budget and then forwards the funds due to the Scottish Executive under the Barnett formula. This means that legally the Scottish Executive depends on the UK budget – in which it does not even have its own budget line. Scotland does have the right (confirmed in a referendum) to make a 3 per cent change in the income tax paid by Scots – its only new right to tax – but this could not be an important part of the Scottish revenue base and would be politically extremely difficult to levy for such a small reward (and if relatively well-funded Scotland were to lower its taxes it would provoke outrage in the rest of the UK).

The decision to build the Scottish Executive out of the Scottish Office means that the Scottish civil service remains part of the unified UK civil service (the terminology is confusing – the Scottish Executive refers to both the civil servants serving the executive of the Scottish Parliament, i.e. the old Scottish Office in Scotland, and the 'government' of Scotland itself). The formal institution of the unified civil service has dramatic consequences for Scotland by bringing along a large number of informal institutional structures that restrain governments (Kirkpatrick and Pyper 2001; Parry 2001). Intergovernmental relations and administrative style have not changed much, with old civil service traditions adapted in the course of events to resolve disputes and develop policies – an oddly informal way of conducting relations that resembles classic Whitehall networking as much as intergovernmental relations (Hazell 2000a; Masterman and Mitchell 2001; Trench 2001a). When informal civil service mechanisms do not head off conflicts, as in the case of long-term care, there is nothing else. Unlike in other recent cases of regionalisation in Europe, the Scottish Parliament did not have the opportunity to construct its own public service corps or even develop its methods from a clean slate, and that has both eased its arrival and constricted its options.

The major innovation, then, is not so much the Scottish administration as it is the Scottish Parliament itself. One of the regular tropes of Scottish politics, especially salient in the Scottish Constitutional Convention's *Claim of Right for Scotland* and subsequent debates, was that Scotland's new Parliament could usher in an era of 'new politics' (Harvie and Jones 2000; for an example, see Wright 1997). This concern appeared in everything from the design of the new debating chamber (a horseshoe, seen as less confrontational than a Westminster-style chamber in which the government and opposition literally face off) to important aspects such as efforts to increase female representation and the choice of a proportional representation system. The result was that the Scottish Parliament has a more open institutional structure (Mitchell and Scottish

Monitoring Team 2001; Winetrobe 2001). Committees and a petitions process open up the agenda and many operating procedures are designed to create a more transparent, participatory politics (Midwinter and McGarvey 2001).

The electoral system matters more. Electoral devices can dramatically change the character of any policy, and in Scotland they do produce a different politics. The Scottish electoral system combines single-member constituency seats for Members of the Scottish Parliament (MSPs) with additional Members elected from regional lists to provide greater proportionality. This produces dramatically different results than the first-past-the-post system still used for Westminster elections, by representing parties that do not have pluralities in many or any constituencies. The list seats open the way for new parties to enter politics – both the Green Party and the Scottish Socialist Party have representatives in the Parliament. It also allowed the Scottish Conservatives to make a comeback from their 1997 elimination by rewarding their low-double-digit support, and gave the SNP a major boost relative to Westminster elections. Labour MPs, increasingly annoyed by the proliferation of left-libertarian parties built on protest votes, began to discuss the advantages of alternative electoral systems that would staunch the flow of votes from their party into smaller alternatives (3–30) (Table 3.1).

Without the manufactured majorities of a plurality system, it was virtually certain that Scotland would not have an overall single-party majority and would have a coalition government. This indeed happened in the 1999 and 2003 Scottish Parliament elections. Labour won a plurality but had to go into coalition with the Scottish Liberal Democrats. Labour took the two largest spending portfolios (health and education), while the Liberal Democrats usually refused to be a back door for lobbies. As a result, the Liberal Democrats' most obvious influence was on high politics issues with major implications for party strategy – such as the debate over whether to fund long-term personal care.

Table 3.1. Scottish elections under devolution, 1999 and 2003

Party	Seats	
	1999	*2003*
Conservative	19	18
Labour	55	50
Scottish Liberal Democrats	17	17
Scottish National Party	34	27
Green	1	7
Scottish Socialist Party	1	6
Others	2	4

Just as the civil service is an important formal institution that exercises informal restraints, the Labour party is an informal institution that exercises great influence. The close connections between the Labour parties in Scotland and the rest of the UK, aided in Scotland by the numerous Scots in the first two UK Labour governments of 1997 and 2001, provide both a strong socialising influence and back channels to bargain and resolve problems. The influence of the Labour party is such that, for all their differences, Scottish and other UK Labour politicians have been through a common socialising institution and have a common, informal, institutional framework in which to develop common preferences and quietly resolve problems, as well as an incentive to party discipline in front of the electors.

Politics: the party system

Finally, there is the party system. The Scottish party system has never been quite like the English one; from the nineteenth century there was a Scottish predilection to vote Liberal, then home rule debates created a Unionist party that was for decades culturally distinct from the Conservatives (Kellas 1989; Mitchell 1990, 1998; Field 1997; Hutchison 2001). Most dramatically, after 1964 the rise of the SNP changed the dynamics of party competition (Bennie, Brand, and Mitchell 1997). By the morning after the 1997 general elections, the Scottish party system looked comprehensively different. The two major parties were the SNP and Labour. Parties that failed to present themselves as adequately Scottish, regardless of their policies or publicity, failed – wiping out the Conservatives (properly, the Scottish Conservative and Unionist Party and Association) (Seawright 2002). The SNP's activist base and many voters are to the left of Labour, leading to a party clash between a centre-left Labour party (broadly to the left of English Labour) and a left nationalist party. As a result of this structure of party competition, the centre of gravity has shifted to the left (even if Scottish median voters are not far from their English counterparts). In addition Scottish voters appear to have developed a tendency to dual voting – electing Labour effectively to defend their interests in Westminster but often expressing themselves by supporting other parties in Scottish elections (Bennie, Brand, and Mitchell 1997; Brown *et al.* 1999; Hough and Jeffery 2003).

The result is a markedly different set of policy debates. Given the capacity of parties to drive the media's agenda, this in turn forces political debate left – the opposition party in the Scottish Parliament is broadly to the left of Labour on key issues such as private finance and long-term care, and is capable of making news. Meanwhile, in England, the opposition party is not just supporting the private sector; it is questioning the premise of publicly provided care. The Labour parties in Scotland and England have to fight on completely different flanks. For the Scottish Executive a shift to the left is safer than a shift to the right, and the reverse holds true for the government in England. In addition to this marked difference, Scotland also sustains the Conservatives, the Liberal Democrats, independent MSPs (exiles from the SNP and Labour) and individual representatives of the Green Party and the Scottish Socialist Party. When this situation is combined with the limited restrictions on Scotland, and its growing block grant, Scottish Labour's incentives are almost all to move leftward and, ideally, in a distinctly Scottish direction.

The first Parliament

The Scottish government elected in 1999 represented the new politics in its diversity and more proportional representation, and took office amidst both high hopes and a predictable storm of media criticism. Bad luck and political mis-steps, combined with the intense media scrutiny politicians face in Scotland, meant that the headlines of the Parliament's first four years were variable. Stories about politics came against a backdrop of highly public arguments about the large cost overruns and construction problems of its building, which did not improve the public image of a body that Scots supported but about whose power they remained very sceptical (Curtice 2003).

Scotland's most prominent political events, which often overshadowed real changes in politics and policy, do not all make a happy story (Mitchell and Scottish Monitoring Team 2001; Taylor 2002). The first major incident was the sudden death of Donald Dewar, a senior Scottish politician and long-time advocate of devolution who had been the Secretary of State for Scotland responsible for devolution, leader of the Scottish Labour party, and the first First Minister of Scotland. In the ensuing elections Henry McLeish, the junior minister for devolution in Westminster, became First Minister, with the goal of establishing a separate identity and agenda in the UK, Europe, and the world. His most dramatic act, though, was the decision to fund long-term personal care for the elderly, which was the most important divergence in policy in the UK in the first four years of devolution. McLeish had to resign, however, in a murky, minor scandal over constituency party expenses which was handled poorly, and he was replaced by Jack McConnell; one expert discussion of Scottish politics had to explain Scotland's 'Third year, third First Minister' (Mitchell and Scottish Monitoring Team 2003). McConnell led Scottish Labour back into office in 2003, still, in coalition with the Liberal Democrats. The result was that by 2003 Scotland was almost entirely governed by politicians without Westminster experience, and most of the Labour MSPs had spent time in the Scottish Executive in some post under Dewar, McLeish, or McConnell.

The first years of the Scottish Parliament, then, were rocky for two reasons. On the one hand, the highest-profile issues were mostly unflattering: apart from an outpouring of sympathy at Dewar's death and some positive reactions to the long-term care decision, the most visible issues were the expensive building, McLeish's resignation, and scuffles for the Labour leadership. The SNP, despite being the chief opposition, failed to advance in public opinion or votes, while the protest parties (the Scottish Socialist Party, linked to the old Labour left entryists of the 1980s, and the Greens) were high profile but small, with one charismatic MSP each. Instead of new politics, Scotland had Scottish politics – but politics nonetheless. On the other hand, the shock of introducing plural, democratic party politics into an established policy system and administration irritated many participants; managerial and medical interviewees in Scotland expressed frustration with the demands on their time from the new Parliament and Executive and the reduction in the autonomy and informality of the health system. Senior management turnover was high. From the 'reign of technocracy' the Scottish policy arenas suddenly became subject to a partisan, nonspecialist, democratic parliament with all the noise, misunderstanding, and politics that parliaments bring. Even if this inconvenience is a requirement of a healthy democratic system, those who suddenly faced it were often volubly unhappy.

Policy outcomes

The Scottish health policy landscape is therefore densely populated with groups based in very high-status, important medical institutions who are willing and able to participate in policy, who can claim to speak for medicine and prognosticate its future, and who are more than able to suggest policies and force issues on to the agenda. Furthermore, the channels between officials and professionals that the old Scottish Office opened up in its efforts to govern Scotland remain intact. Before devolution, Scottish Office officials and ministers had to make and implement complex decisions within very tight staffing and research limits. While much of the solution lay in reliance on London, the Scottish office also maintained tight links with the medical elites of Scotland's Royal Colleges and its mighty university teaching hospitals. These channels remained open after devolution. The introduction of an elected parliament for Scotland did not change the availability of Scottish policy information or its sources; if anything, it made Scotland's insiders more important because Scotland's politicians developed an aversion to using English policies. We see the effects of their influence on the agenda and policy debates in Scotland's relatively coherent professionalism.

Organisational form

Like England and Wales, Scotland reorganised its health system just after devolution. The chief partisans in the Scottish debate were classically those of corporate rationalisation versus professionalism. In 1998 Scotland had inherited the Conservatives' internal market, even more poorly implemented than in England. Its main consequence had been the development of hospital trusts as the core of the system – autonomous and powerful, and beholden to the obligation above all to balance their books. Nevertheless, this was at least formally a market system; health boards still had to purchase from trusts (fundholders were rare compared to England). Neither professionals nor the Labour party liked the structure and there was pressure to get rid of it, mainly because of the ideological offensiveness of trusts to many (perceived as a marketising Thatcherite imposition) and the discomfort of many professionals with the trusts, which had so clearly improved the status of managers.

The importance of professionalists in the Scottish policy community, reflecting their role in important Scottish health institutions, and the weakness of corporate rationalisers and market reformers based in England, showed in policy from 1998 onwards. The changes the Scottish Office could make to formal policy were becoming greater as devolution loomed and a major Scottish party finally governed Scotland. While the first Labour government's policies reflected broad New Labour pragmatism, policy design became increasingly devolved as the Northern Irish, Scottish, and Welsh civil servants and ministers prepared for devolution. This meant that Scottish Office officials and ministers were able to pursue a policy more grounded in the policies suggested by the Scottish policy community rather than the plans from London. As a result, Scotland's 1998 NHS reforms were a transition between a London policy framework with Scottish distinctiveness to a Scottish policy framework. Scotland's White Paper, *Designed to Care*, split the difference between market and hierarchy quite differently from the other systems (Scottish Office 1997; Bruce and Forbes 2001).

The distinctive feature of the Scottish 1998 system is the dashed line between the boards – with policy responsibilities – and the trusts – with administrative responsibilities (Figure 4). The structure sought to preserve the administrative autonomy of trusts (i.e. hospitals) to self-organise while leaving broader strategy issues to boards. It was a question of graphic presentation as much as true intent how the structure was drawn; the fact that boards are above trusts seems to suggest hierarchy, but what *Designed to Care* actually intended (its civil servant author insisted in an interview) was a division of labour: 'you could turn the diagram on its side'. The system is a halfway

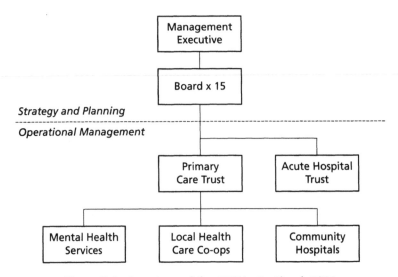

Figure 3.1: Structure of the NHS in Scotland, 1998

point between the inherited, English-inflected market reformers and the resurgent Scottish professionalism.

The Scottish Parliament thus arrived to find a system with trusts formally confined to self-administration and with boards in charge of policy. The Executive's initial intent was not to change the organisation, but the perpetual political incentive for ministers to alter the system and the additional political issue of developing a Scottish alternative led to the Scottish health plan *Our National Health* (Scottish Executive Health Department 2000). The purpose of this plan was in part to sort out what Scottish health policy actually should be by synthesising many previous plans; more cynical observers suggested that it was to be a distinctive Scottish homologue to the English *NHS Plan* so the Minister did not seem to have fallen behind (3–1, 3–3) (Department of Health 2000b). Much of the plan was long lists of what the health services should be doing on a number of fronts, but it also included proposals to tighten further the hierarchical aspects of the Scottish health service by further merging trusts into boards (most noticeably by having the trusts directly represented in the boards); any larger changes would have required complicated legislation. The result was further erosion of trusts and further concentration of formal power at the board level. Edinburgh then keeps a close eye on the boards.

The trend continued with what one Scottish journalist called 'the mystery of the pointless White Paper'. This was the 2003 White Paper *Partnership for Care*, released on the same day as some bad waiting list figures and never subject to much attention (Scottish Executive Health Department 2003). It

seemed anodyne and puzzled some observers, but its intent was clear: to eliminate the market reform elements in the Scottish health system, roll back the
corporate rationalisation, and instead turn the system into a 1974–style
compact between the professions and the state. It was a professionalist goal
fit to Labour party preferences and electoral strategy.

The White Paper promised to abolish the trusts, which Labour had
wanted to do for some time but had resisted doing because of the legal,
administrative, and accounting complexity of dismantling trusts. As in the rest
of the UK, the trusts had in 1991 been made the core building blocks of
service provision outside primary care, and undoing them meant coping with
complicated questions of finance and organisation. *Partnership for Care*
finally did it and was therefore, in purely managerial terms, centralising. It
announced that the chief administrative units of NHS Scotland would be the
fifteen health boards, which would provide care in unitary bodies that abolished the purchaser–provider split. At the same time, it formally introduced
the managed clinical network as a key part of the health services. Managed
clinical networks were partly justified by the need to use resources better, but
they were fundamentally new attempts to harness the professions as institutions to the goals of the government (namely, quality and value for money).
Managed clinical networks would be based on problems such as cancer care
and would use resources and formulate needs by cooperative medical discussions. In early 2004 an intense debate took place within Scottish health services as to whether the managed clinical networks should have their own
management or not and whether funds should be routed through them rather
than through (potentially uncooperative) board management.

Partnership for Care, then, marked at least a theoretical shift in Scottish
health policy – a shift both forwards and backwards. It was a shift backwards
in time as it expunged the new public management from the NHS, eliminating key attributes such as the purchaser–provider split and the heavy reliance
on contracts as well as the trusts that form the basis of any such systems.
Instead, it returns to the concept of a pact between state and medicine in
which doctors play a major role in the allocation of resources – thereby giving
up on many claims made that management, disciplined by competition,
would allocate resources better. It was a shift forwards the future in that it dis-
pensed with the particular, stylised, logic of new public management and
managerialism, which was based on a relatively unrealistic image of the private
sector (which is not always composed of internally hierarchical, independent
organisations that deal only by contract – many firms with 'knowledge
workers' are more flexible and network-based than the model of trusts as
monads suggests) and a relatively unrealistic image of medicine (which is fundamentally based on small networks of like-minded doctors who use their

mutual trust to overcome the uncertainties of referral and treatment – and which rarely match trust administrative borders). After *Partnership for Care*, the manager–professional frontier shifted yet again. Managed clinical networks are a far cry from the professional-dominated system that was the UK under consensus management, but they have been part of an overall rollback first of markets, then of the autonomous trusts that made up a market, and now of management itself.

This shift could have two signal advantages if it works. The first is that it will use the professionals rather than try to work against them. There is considerable evidence from the days of consensus management that professionals, given fixed budgets and autonomy to spend them, will be responsible – and happier, too (Schulz and Harrison 1984; Harrison and Schulz 1989). The UK has spent two decades trying to manage professionals in increasing detail. Scotland's efforts to work with rather than against professions, if successfully implemented, might work as well or better, and might increase the public legitimacy of rationing while creating a role for management that is better aligned with medicine and therefore more effective. Second, it might align organisation with the development of medicine. When hospitals were primarily about palliative and remedial care rather than high-technology interventions (i.e. until recent decades), it made sense for them to be organised as independent, territorial units similar to hotels or schools. Much of what they did was catering, laundry, and basic personal and medical care. By contrast, now, medical treatment is increasingly specialised and hospitals have steadily less in common with hotels. Managed clinical networks respond to this logic – they try to allocate resource flows and activities according to the technical demands of the process rather than by territorial 'patches'. The shift from a bricks and mortar understanding of industrial organisation to one more focused on flexible networks has been visible in less complicated and professionalised private sector organisations for decades now. If hospitals are no longer building blocks but rather network nodes, then it is Scotland that is responding appropriately and it is England that is entrenching an outdated, industrial-era model. Scotland's effort to focus less on territorial areas and buildings and more on the nature of the work might look not so much like Old Labour corporatism as like internet-era innovation.

New public health

Devolution began when the new public health advocacy coalition was on an upswing. New public health had been gathering strength for years in academia and increasingly among active specialists (above all public health physicians and some managers), and the arrival of the Labour government in 1997 helped with the publication of a new public health strategy and the creation of funds for social inclusion and health promotion (Scottish Office 1998). The issue at stake was the extent to which the health service engages with work on the wider determinants of health. However, it is relatively difficult to develop firm indicators for the amount of attention a system is paying to new public health, since much of the work takes place on the level of individual institutions where policy advocates can assemble the resources and protection from interference that allow them to build health improvement structures (Greer 2001a).

Scotland's public health policy entrepreneurs are marginal in organisations, but they do have strong bases in the boards and in the impressive medical faculties of public health, which have allowed them to slip ideas into the stream of policy ideas. From their point of view, Scotland improved, with top-sliced funding and ministerial support increasing. It is now a much better environment for new public health advocates. However, public health and health promotion are relatively low-status in medicine. This means that it takes very little to improve public health's status – a small amount of 'top-sliced' funding, going directly to public health with a ring fence around it, can have a tremendous impact in terms of giving advocates seed money and improving their morale. Likewise, if the omnipresent (after devolution) Health Minister includes visits to health promotion projects or asks after a health promotion initiative, the support from above is far greater than when public health received a vanishingly small amount of attention from absentee Scottish Office ministers. This is despite the broad lack of interest of politicians who are still, in Scotland, more concerned with the health service than with public health – the first devolved Minister, Susan Deacon, showed little interest but that was still far more than before devolution. It is important to stress that these changes are relative and from a low base: an interviewee who had worked closely with Deacon had not noticed any great interest in public health during her career or in her office (3–19); another, working in public health, was very pleased with the increase in attention to the issues (3–10). More to the point, Scotland also tackled inequalities in health services finance. The Parliament commissioned a review of resource allocation led by Professor John Arbuthnott and changed its funding formula to reduce inequalities in provision (National Review of Resource Allocation 1999). It also pursued regulatory public health strategies with vigour, restricting machines vending unhealthy products in schools and attacking tobacco advertising. It did not try to reorganise to improve service integration; Scotland's health policy community lacks interest in being mixed with Scotland's local governments.

The attention is a relatively good outcome for the new public health advocacy coalition when viewed comparatively. Scotland's formal documents have been similar to England's, with the same broad priorities. They reflect the policy consensus (and epidemiological case) that cancer, coronary heart disease and stroke, accidents, and mental health need attention ('we selected our own priorities, and of course they were the same as England's' reported a minister). To some extent their efforts caught the eye of the press and politicians; after enough repetition the line that Scotland is 'the sick man of Europe' began to make public health seem like a problem. At the same time, the Scottish electoral rules, by effectively turning a four-party system into a six-party system with a pair of left-libertarian challengers, has pushed public health issues further to the front. The Scottish Socialist Party, for example, is eager to attack Labour over its lack of support for the initiative to distribute free fruit in schools.

Public health's higher status relative to England, as measured in public health directors' role in the boards, the role of public health academics in policy, and their prominent position in many medical networks means that they have been able to win funding through essentially professional arguments that have yet to create real opponents and which fare well in left-wing and profession-dominated Scotland. Their organisations are as dense as anywhere in England, and are better linked. At first the Public Health Institute of Scotland (PHIS) has served as an umbrella organisation (there is no English equivalent) until it was merged in April 2003 with the Health Education Board for Scotland, a more traditional health promotion quango, to produce Health Scotland, a larger organisation with much inheritance from the professional public health chamber PHIS. Public health leaders profited from a higher organisational density than in England, culminating in the PHIS and then Health Scotland, which was to bring together the whole range of public health practitioners in Scotland. While in the long term the new public health coalition contains a deeply destabilising call for resources to shift from cardiac surgery to smoking cessation, from neonatology to pre-natal care, from automobiles to bicycles, and from cheap school food to free fruit, in the short run it can benefit from the integration of some of its leaders into powerful professional circles and enjoy victories for some of its ideas, such as came from the SSP's interest in its fresh fruit idea, which obliged Labour to be more interested, or the SNP and Labour interest in reducing tobacco advertising.

Public and private

It is thanks to Labour in England that the public versus private provision debate achieved such a high profile in the UK. The main questions are how much of the health service will be directly provided by the state, as in the classic NHS model, how much of it contracted from non-state organisations, and from whom will it be contracted. The discussion is tied closely to the market versus hierarchy debate in health service organisation – if there should be market-like decisions by primary care commissioners about what hospital to use, and hospital trusts should be autonomous, then perhaps the roles of hospital trusts and primary care providers could be opened up to more organisational forms. The practical policy relevance of the debate is that countries' outcomes are arranged along an axis from near-total NHS provision (the classic NHS model seen until Thatcher), through contracts with the private sector to provide physical plant and maintenance (traditional PFI, or private finance initiative), through 'public–private partnerships' to extend the PFI model into clinical services, through a hypothetical system considered by English Labour in which all sorts of organisations compete to provide the best outcomes for the government, to the option of undoing the NHS entirely and shifting to a private system based on insurance funds (as some Conservatives support). In this continuum, Scotland is firmly on the PFI outcome, with the government committed to using PFI for facilities but uninterested in expanding non-NHS provision. Thus, new capital projects of any size are PFI.

The result was that Scotland had a legacy of PFI projects and expertise in its policy community and its politicians saw PFI as a way to solve their perceived capacity and quality problems. Expansion was not a likely prospect, however. The institutional bases of these groups were weaker in Scotland. The private sector in health and the consultants and City firms working on PPP were less visible. There was little in the electoral logic of Scottish politics to make Labour want to call such groups forth. Market reformers advocating private-sector-led 'modernisation' were weaker in Scotland and the government's incentives to change the health service were mostly to demonstrate its competence by increasing capacity and supplying new facilities. The civil service had long grown accustomed to PFI mechanisms.

The result, on the one hand, was that PFI remained core Scottish policy despite the strong influence of professionalists in the Scottish policy community and the weak influence of market reformers. Problems of capacity and reconstruction, such as the reconstruction of Greater Glasgow's hospitals during the first Scottish Parliament, could be met by constructive policy suggestions that offered to solve the problem and that a legacy of PFI work had rendered plausible. This is the logic of the multiple-streams model of decision making. Even if the opponents of PFI are stronger in Scottish politics than the proponents, there has not been a combination of problem, politician, and policy that would lead to a policy reversal, while problems of capacity routinely call forth politicians and PFI advocates. On the other hand, greater commitment to the private sector is unlikely. Problems of medical (as against capital and support) capacity attract solutions that are well articulated by many in the Scottish policy community and which do not rely on the private sector but rather on medical organisational innovations such as managed clinical networks. The persistence of PFI testifies to the chancy nature of any political decision, but Scotland's professionalist-dominated policy community explains why there are few widely circulated ideas for further private sector involvement.

Quality

As elsewhere, the question with quality is the extent to which it is a major policy and the extent to which it is controlled by the professions themselves (i.e. professional elites) as against politicians and their top officials. Scotland was a leader in promoting quality work even before devolution and has since retained a powerful infrastructure for quality promotion. This head start in developing quality policies as well as Scotland's lack of a quality crisis (as seen several times in England) meant that the Scottish professions broadly control the direction and specific elements of the quality agenda. By contrast, in England the quality agenda is far less of a buttress for professional autonomy, since the work programme of the National Institute for Clinical Excellence (NICE) the Commission for Health Improvement (CHI) and the successor Commission for Healthcare Audit and Inspection (Healthcare Commission) is highly politicised and far more regulatory.

Scotland's quality campaigns began in the early 1990s. As one participant observed, 'it was not politically driven . . . The ministers allowed an alliance of senior officials and clinical leaders to get on with it' (3–15). This took the form of a series of organisations, above all the Clinical Resource and Audit Group, and the Scottish Intercollegiate Guidelines Network (SIGN). These were organisations operating with assistance from the Scottish Office (above all those working with the influential Chief Medical Officers of the decade) and the Royal Colleges to reduce practice variations and distribute consensus recommendations of optimal treatments. This voluntary, encompassing organisation of medical elites was without parallel in the rest of the UK, where the Cochrane Collaboration at Oxford and similar endeavours were not sustained by such a strong movement across their whole countries (3–13, 3–15). There was no equivalent political take-up for the idea in England until years later – roughly 1996 with the publication of *A Service with Ambitions*, which was more hortatory than effective on quality organisation issues (Department of Health 1996).

It was in 1998 that quality moved on to the UK agenda; the reassertion of faith in the professions and professionalism that came with Labour, and the focus on standard-setting in the public service, meant that Labour was open to the policy proposals that produced CHI in England. Scotland developed parallel organisations in a classic example of institutional adaptation that kept Scotland in line with the rest of the UK, but meaningfully distinctive. *Designed to Care* established two core organisations to improve medical quality. One, the Health Technology Board for Scotland, had the same remit as NICE, the English technology assessment agency. It was not expected to differ significantly from NICE (both due to resourcing and due to the weight of public expectations). It still entailed the possibility of a distinct Scottish agenda as well as direct attention to the differing characteristics of much of Scotland's services (such as its remote and rural care issues). The Clinical Standards Board for Scotland (CSBS) built on the pre-existing organisations in Scotland and focused on developing service quality recommendations and standards rather than an enforcement role (which, unlike CHI, it did not have). These organisations only really became active in mid to late 2001, when there were already discussions of merging the various regulators into one organisation. CSBS 'has not yet had time to make enemies' (3–15) and has become the core of NHS Quality Improvement Scotland, which includes formerly independent nursing, midwifery, and technology boards.

Overall, therefore, the quality agenda before and after devolution reflects the power of Scottish professional leaders to move an item on to the agenda ahead of most of their peers by taking advantage of the Scottish Office's administrative autonomy and their strength on the ground in Scotland. They won a highly profession-oriented model of quality regulation that focused on the concerns of professional elites and their work to improve medicine. The extent of quality improvement work (great), its timing relative to the rest of the UK and the world (early) and the extent of professional autonomy built in (great) all point to the well-organised leaders of Scottish medicine using the administrative autonomy of the Scottish Office to make advances and then retaining their distinctive model after devolution.

Range of services: long-term care

By far the most dramatic case of policy divergence in any field since devolution was the decision by Scotland to fund universal long-term personal care for the elderly (personal care is non-professional assistance with daily tasks), discussed by Rachel Simeon (2003) (Health care, i.e. care requiring professional help, was already funded, and 'hotel' costs, or the cost of room and board, were still only funded on a means-tested basis). The decision was a dramatic one (Woods 2002:43–5). This was a classic decommodification decision that decreased the need of individuals to rely on their fortunes in the market. It broke with UK policy and New Labour sensibilities and incurred a large bill for Scotland that other governments opted not to pay. It was, in fact, one of the only large extensions of the otherwise retrenching UK welfare state since the 1970s. It also marked a major intervention in a larger set of debates about how to operate a welfare state in the changing demographic conditions of the West, i.e. with an increasingly large elderly population with fewer carers.

The origins of the decision were in a focusing event that was actually a hangover from pre-devolution politics – the report of a Royal Commission. The Great Britain Royal Commission on Long-Term Care, under Professor Sir Stewart Sutherland, was set up in 1997 by the new Labour government to consider the problems of caring for the elderly. Its recommendations, released in March 1999, were expansive. It argued that there should be universal provision of personal care for the elderly. Suddenly there was a problem (the effect of the Royal Commission was to make poor care of the elderly a problem rather than a condition), a policy, and a politician – McLeish – who wanted to make a mark and do it as distinctively Scottish and social democratic.

McLeish surprised his civil servants and advisers by announcing on the television programme 'Newsnight' that he would consider adopting the conclusions of the Sutherland report (MacMahon 2002). The salience of the Scottish cleavage between nationalism and unionism gave McLeish the incentive to demonstrate his Scottishness by adopting a position not taken by the other UK governments. McLeish had been meeting with groups interested in the aged for some time, and they suggested that the Sutherland proposals might be a valuable policy attractive to many Scots and responsive to Scotland's demographics (3–30). The commitment triggered a conflict between two broad groups. On one side was the UK government, which had opted for means testing (Department of Health 2000c) and did not appreciate Scotland appearing to show it up (one Scottish Labour politician speaks of English colleagues angrily telling him Scotland's budget was 'because of the deprivation you have in Scotland, not so you can do things we can't do'). This view was popular within the Scottish Labour parliamentary parties. On the other side were the pro-aged coalition and, initially, the media. Crucially, however, the other parties were all in favour. The Liberal Democrats saw a way to identify themselves as distinctive and pro-welfare state (repeating an operation from earlier in the session when they obliged Labour to revoke tuition fees for university students). The Conservatives saw a way to cause problems for Labour and identify themselves as a Scottish party (i.e. become less of an extreme on the Unionist–nationalist axis). The SNP had three reasons to support the Sutherland recommendations: its own left bias, its desire to develop distinctive Scottish policies, and its interest, as the main opposition party, in promoting Labour divisions and making the party look subservient to London. The result was that Labour faced a potentially over-whelming parliamentary coalition in favour of Sutherland – a coalition includ-ing its own coalition partners. 'So thanks to proportional representation we have a policy now that was not supported by the majority party' concluded the irritated Scottish Labour politician.

The intergovernmental institutions of the UK, meanwhile, proved unable to constrain Scotland. They did try. Within the UK Labour party, there was great anger at Scotland for having made their colleagues in the rest of the UK look stingy. Within Whitehall, as a consequence, there was no effort to help Scotland when it tried to defray part of the costs. The Scottish Executive pointed out that the universal long-term care decision replaced the UK-funded support for personal care, routed through the UK Department of Work and Pensions; as a consequence, Scotland had saved the UK the cost of all previous funds for existing, means-tested, long-term care in Scotland (called 'attendance allowances') by replacing it with a Scottish programme. It thus requested that the Department of Work and Pensions transfer to Scotland the money it would have spent on long-term care in Scotland. The Department, driven by the irritated UK Cabinet, denied the request. McLeish did not raise the issue at one of the regular intergovernmental ministerial meetings intended to resolve disputes (joint ministerial committees) since he did not expect to win. Meanwhile, the opposition of other Labour figures was impressive. The only problem was that McLeish, were he to give in, would be seen to be controlled from London and thus on the wrong side of the Unionist–nationalist cleavage in Scotland. The fury of Westminster was easier to bear than the fury of the Scottish political system.

So Scotland received no help. However, the decision was a dramatic dem-onstration of just how much formal power to diverge Scotland does have. First, the rigidity of the Barnett formula and Labour's UK-wide spending increases gave Scotland a large budget increase, much of which was spent on long-term care. Second, there was no normative framework set from above. No part of the UK government had a formal right to interfere in Scottish social policy decisions.

The Sutherland decision is a classic policy emerging from the temporary merging of politician, problem, and policy. In coalition politics, McLeish's agenda and partisan logics all pushed for the decision. McLeish as a politician who had recently entered office in the shadow of an imposing predecessor, and who was interested in making a mark and making Scotland distinctive, faced a party system in which Labour had to compete for votes to its left and was regularly attacked for being subservient to London. This meant that the personal and party strategies of McLeish and Labour could both benefit from the Sutherland decision (even if many within Labour disagreed) and the other parties saw the opportunity to demand it. The policy advocates produced the Sutherland report, which was not a new idea but which came at the right time, while the problems of the elderly were regularly in the news. As a result, the window of opportunity opened, and the Sutherland decision emerged. Scotland, unlike the rest of the UK, combined politics with problem and policy in a way no other part did – and it did so mainly for reasons connected with sheer chance and one man's strategy.

Conclusion

Scotland's inheritance at devolution was not so much a distinctive set of Scottish health policies as a distinctive policy community and party system. The party system and the Labour party reward policies that are to the left of England and distinctively Scottish. Politicians have sought both rewards, most publicly in McLeish's decision to break ranks with UK Labour and enact long-term personal care for the elderly. The policy community fits with the incentives to adopt distinctive, leftward-trending policy. It reflects the density of professionalists in Scotland, where professional elites have for centuries enjoyed high status and considerable autonomy in their institutions and where they had been entrenched in Scottish Office policy communities. The politicians and professionalists enjoy an elective affinity in the affirmation of the value of professionalism, the great universities and hospitals, and public sector workers. Relatively well endowed with policy and administrative capacity relative to the other devolved countries, Scotland has been able to enact the policies that emerge from the interaction of politician and politics.

Specific policies broadly reflect the nature of the policy community, which is explained by the histories and density of social institutions such as Royal Colleges and teaching hospitals. Not just the good organisation, accomplishments, status, and density of professionalists but also the place they held in Scottish Office policy debates led them to be able to espouse a serious set of proposals based on professional values rather than markets, management, or locality. The second test of the argument, whether the role of the policy community and party system explain the overall trajectory in each policy, also confirms it. Finally, the ideas of the policy community, and hence its influence in Scottish policy, were apparent before devolution in the workings and policy decisions of the Scottish Office. There were often the same people and the same arguments as before devolution, but with Scotland's new political autonomy they matter much more, and their arguments and role in developing the policy ideas for a left-leaning government have led Scotland to place a distinct bet on professionalism to run its health service.

4
England: markets

Customer satisfaction has to become a culture, a way of life, not an 'added extra'.
(Tony Blair 2002)

Most states that have decentralised, no matter how different the powers of different regional governments, have established a consistent tier of regional government. The UK stands almost alone in tailoring its degree of regional devolution to the pressures from each region. Scotland, reflecting its high degree of mobilisation, won a strong Parliament; Wales, with a much lower degree of mobilisation, won a weaker Assembly; and England largely continued to be governed as before – that is, by the UK government elected in UK general elections. The famed flexibility of the UK constitution shows. The devolution settlement is draped across the landscape of territorial political mobilisation, from the peaks of Scotland, with its Parliament, to the lowlands of the East of England, where a Conservative majority is reluctant to let its regional chamber call itself an assembly at all (Sandford and McQuail 2001). It is for that reason that many expect to see more change – more and different devolution as the shape and political mobilisation of the various parts of the UK change. It also means that scholars have a form of control case in the study of comparative UK politics. England is still governed by the parties and institutions that governed the whole of the UK before devolution. The rebalancing of policy advocates and agendas in Northern Ireland, Scotland, and Wales since devolution is particularly visible, since in England we see the substantive continuation of the politics that used to rule them. Strikingly, for all that the four systems are moving on their trajectories (as their different party systems and policy communities predict), England is the most radical.

England's bet is on markets. English radicalism is directed at the core of the NHS model, namely, the idea that the government should directly own the health care system, contract with or hire the professionals, and direct it. Northern Ireland, Scotland, and Wales are all experimenting with different policies for an NHS that is still run by the state. England is pursuing a focus on management and the use of market logics with a determination that continues its trajectory of the last two decades and might surprise observers who expected different polices from a declared social democratic government. In the likely outcome, trusts, 'foundation hospitals', private providers, and various mixtures are all contracted by the state but have the flexibility to modernise and improve health services while maintaining an even level of quality and a focus on one task – health services. English policy combines the ends of social democrats with an intense commitment to market reform and corporate rationalisation. A government worried about the threat from its right routinely opts for market reform policies that promise to squeeze better value out of the service because the market reformers are better funded and more able to articulate their claims to provide what the public wants.

Inheritance

England is the part of the UK most clearly dominated by London – by the economic power of the South East of England, and the many networks that concentrate power and money in that city. England is distinguished by this centralisation of its elites in London and by its sheer size. With approximately 85 per cent of the UK population and dozens of cities, English society is complicated and diverse and presents a major challenge to a Secretary of State who wishes to manage any part of its public services. It also has a politics like no other part of the UK, with a strong market-liberal intellectual infrastructure, a Conservative party that is a serious contender for a majority, and a lively left–right debate about the relationship of state and market.

English politics

When I say history, I mean the history of Britain, and when I say Britain, I mean England, and when I say England, I mean places not too far from London. (Parson Thwackum, in Tom Jones, Henry Fielding 1740: cited in Sandford and McQuail 2001)

British political administration is concentrated spatially as well as numerically. The labels underneath the two slots in the capital's letterboxes capture the spirit perfectly – 'London' and 'All Other Places'. Basically, if you are not in (or within easy reach of) London, you are politically nowhere. Success in political administration depends on the judgements of your fellows and to be judged you must get to London. (Heclo and Wildavsky 1974:7)

The bulk of analyses of 'British politics' or comparative analyses of 'the UK' are really analyses of England. Analysts' propensity for this is reasonable, given the size of England, diversity of the UK, its centralisation until devolution, and the analytic complexity of explaining a state with no single party system and the shadowy politics of territorial offices. Richard Rose, expert in the politics of Northern Ireland, Scotland, and Wales, wrote in the 1989 preface to his UK politics text *Politics in England* that the book has that title 'because England is central in the United Kingdom . . . Where differences cause friction, Scots, Welsh, and Ulster people are expected to adapt to English ways. What is important for England will never be overlooked by any United Kingdom government and politicians who wish to rise in government must accept English norms to do so. One can thus write about British government and English society' (Rose 1989:vi).

England, unlike Scotland or Wales (let alone Northern Ireland), has historically sustained the Conservative party. While the Conservatives enjoyed impressive mid-twentieth-century successes in Scotland (including the only absolute majority of votes, in the 1955 election), they have been historically weak outside England. On the other hand, Labour, from the days that the Scot Keir Hardie won Labour's first seat in Wales, has tended to depend on Scotland and Wales for electoral sustenance. Four Labour governments since 1945 have been dependent on the presence of Scottish and Welsh MPs at Westminster (Table 4.1).

England also lacks a serious tradition of political nationalism, which is why it is governed directly by the UK Parliament 'Westminster' (and why it might be unstable; Hazell forthcoming). English political nationalism has historically been subsumed into British, pro-Union nationalism, or taken largely literary forms (Colley 1992; Kumar 2003). It is easy to interpret the Conservative party as an English party, and the party has often been seen as such in Scotland and Wales. The Conservatives' focus on such campaigns as defending the Union and opposition to European integration, combined with their governments' insensitivity to the politics of Scotland and Wales and their dependence on English votes, have given them an image as an English nationalist party, but it is highly doubtful whether this is accurate today. Rather, they

Table 4.1. Labour government majorities dependent on Scottish and Welsh Labour MPs, 1950–74

Year	*UK Labour majority*	*Scottish and Welsh Labour MPs*
1950	5	64
1964	4	71
1974 (Feb.)	Minority government	64
1974 (Oct.)	3	64

Sources: Butler and Butler, 1994; Political Science Resources website, www.psr.keele.ac.uk/area/uk/uktable.htm.

are a conservative party with strong market-liberal inclinations that have their dominant electoral base in England.

The consequence of these two factors – the existence of a strong right-wing party and the absence of a nationalist-Unionist debate – creates a politics and party system focused heavily on right–left issues organised loosely around redistributive politics and the role of the state. In turn, this means that England of the four polities is the only one to maintain a serious, far-reaching and politically important debate about the state in society; it is the only one where a change of government could lead to a major change in the structure and extent of the welfare state (the election of the Conservatives in 1979 did just this).

The size and administrative structure of England gives it a different set of problems and possibilities. England is far larger and more complicated than any other part of the UK. England has eight regions; all of them have larger populations than Northern Ireland and all but one have a larger population than Wales (Table 4.2). Scotland's Health Minister depends on fifteen health boards; Wales has around 50 organisations total; and Northern Ireland around 19. England has 28 strategic health authorities, 302 primary care trusts (PCTs), and 274 acute and other trusts, making a total of 604 major NHS organisations (excluding agencies of various kinds). This also means that the ability to make and superficially implement policy that the greater resources give to the Department of Health are usually balanced out by the impossibility of knowing about, let alone successfully 'running' the complicated English

Table 4.2. Regional/national populations of Great Britain and Northern Ireland, 2001

Region/Nation	Population (millions)
North East	2.5
North West	6.7
London	7.2
South West	4.9
South East	8.1
East Midlands	4.2
West Midlands	5.3
East of England	5.4
Yorkshire and the Humber	4.9
Wales	2.9
Scotland	5.1
Northern Ireland	1.7

Sources. The Office of National Statistics; General Register Office for Scotland; Northern Ireland Statistics and Research Agency.

NHS. Repeated efforts to do so, backed as they are with coercion (such as star ratings), not only fail to win useful degrees of managerial compliance but also fall foul of professions (Givan 2003). They are further undermined by evidence of apparent political fiddling at the top, for example promoting the hospital that serves the Prime Minister's constituency (McLellan 2003).

This means that the managerial, political, and professional infrastructure of England is more bureaucratised than those of Northern Ireland, Scotland, and Wales. In Scotland, the top officers of fifteen health boards are the keystone of the health service. Managers and professionals who have worked in different systems comment appreciatively on the simplicity of administration when the board chief executives and the NHS Scotland chief executive can sit in a room, or go to a party – 'I was at a party last night' commented a Scot who had worked in England 'and got a tremendous amount of work done. You could never see so many people and chat with them in a few hours in England' (3–15). Wales, writes a former CEO of NHS Wales, 'is an ideal size, not least because one can get key opinion leaders into one room' (Wyn Owen 2000:2). 'Chats' and face-to-face interactions, with trust and mutual judgement at work, are a particularly salient characteristic of the British style of government (Heclo and Wildavsky 1974) and are naturally easier in the smaller capitals. To the great extent that the English policy community is integrated, it pays the price in disconnection from its services far from London.

Without such easy, informal, and potentially trust-building advantages of small size, the English public administration has developed broad-based rules to be applied to its many trusts and health authorities and a bureaucracy to enforce it. This means that the centre's monitoring problems are far greater; distance from London, intricate local networks, and the faults of health data systems combine with the intrinsic complexity of health services to make it very difficult for the Department of Health to 'run' health services in Birkenhead, Berwick, or Penzance. The result is more bureaucracy in the health services, more instability at the interface between local and UK politics, and more problems for a centre that aspires to control the health system and feels, as one Downing Street policy maker has put it, 'hardwired' to the frontline.

On the other hand, the size of England and the relatively high status of the Department of Health as a major spending department mean that the civil service policy and administrative capacity at the disposal of the Secretary of State responsible for health far exceeds that of the devolved administrations. The Department of Health has far more high-level civil servants than any of the old territorial offices or new devolved governments (Table 4.3). Before devolution, this meant that the small health departments of the devolved administrations would often come close to copying English policy. The

Department of Health, but not the Scottish Office, Northern Ireland Civil Service (NICS), or Welsh Office, had the capacity to delve into complicated areas from inner city dental services access to the impact of new discoveries on the need for dermatology beds in hospitals (the Scottish office at least could usually find willing clinical elites). The decisions of the government can be turned into policy and implemented far more quickly and with less hazard in England. Compare two surprise reorganisations fiercely criticised by those charged with acquiescing: the abolition of Welsh health authorities (Chapter 5), and England's abolition of regions and mergers of health authorities (a programme called 'Shifting the Balance'). Both decisions were launched with little consultation and to the surprise of those affected (Milburn 2001). The difference is that the Welsh, with their small inherited policy capacity, were still struggling with organisational design eighteen months later, while England's 'Shifting the Balance of Power' programme was largely operating within eighteen months (the text explaining the ideas and programme came out in July 2001, only two months after the surprise announcement; Department of Health 2001b). This expert civil service cushions both the Secretary of State in England and the English NHS from potential policy disasters. On the other hand, it lowers the cost of adventurous, and potentially disastrous policy (Greer 2004a). It is also highly debatable whether this skilled Whitehall department, for all its expertise in policy design and legislation, has any better ability to implement policies directed at changing professionals and complex organisations such as hospitals.

Under unified UK governance, England was decisive in choosing the government that was responsible for the politics and policy of the entire UK. Northern Ireland, Scotland, and Wales were bound by formal and informal Cabinet unity to enact policies based on those of the Cabinet. This almost invariably reflected the policies chosen by the 'UK' departments, which were based in London and responsible for England. The Secretary of State at the Department of Health, therefore, was the leader in developing UK policy and the territorial offices, transmitting the policies with greater or lesser change to the rest of the UK. As a consequence, the politics of the NHS were English politics, and Chapter 2's history of NHS organisation is primarily a discussion of English health policy decisions. The 1974 reorganisation, the 1983 introduction of general management, the internal market, and the politics of pragmatism in 1997 were all driven by problems, politics, and policy ideas from London. Their basic design came from the Department of Health and its political masters, and the autonomy of the three territorial administrations was only in implementation and details.

The English health system, however, brought its own distinctive evolution into UK politics and policy communities. Three characteristics stand out

Table 4.3. Health service civil servants by grade and region, 1996/7

Department	Grade 1	Grade 1a	Grade 2	Grade 3	Grade 4	Grade 5
Scottish Office	1	–	2	4	1	19
Welsh Office	1	–	–	4	–	14
Northern Ireland Office (including NICS)	1	2	3	7	4	28
Department of Health	2	1	5	21	19	75

Note: Figures for Northern Ireland, Scotland, and Wales include relevant central services.

Source: *The Civil Service Year Book*, 1997 (1996 for SO).

in the development of English health systems. First is the dominance and difference of London, second is the more complex ecology of health politics that England inherited in 1948 and that still influences it, and third is the distinctive policy community bred of right–left political competition.

Health in England is like most other sectors; London is atypical, troubled, and a powerful influence. Historically, London has always been the centre of innovation in English medical practice, and its great teaching hospitals – rather than the universities as in Scotland – dominate medical education. The great hospitals also afforded access to the lucrative and high-status London private practice market, i.e. the famous medical specialists of Harley Street. Harley Street presaged, and possibly invented, a key part of the bargain between public service and private gain that still drives medicine in the South East of England (and to a limited extent elsewhere). Posts at the great teaching hospitals were interesting, high-status, and, relative to the cost of living in London, unremunerative; they conferred professional status rather than a desirable quality of life. The status that came with affiliation to such a hospital made it possible for a doctor to begin to attract private practice which, unlike the hospital, was lucrative. The hospital provided a form of quality control in return for the labour of promising young doctors (Peterson 1978; Hollingsworth 1986; Rivett 1986:6–19). To this day, it holds that a wholly private doctor unaffiliated with the NHS is suspect, for the simple reason that the highest-status hospitals are almost always NHS hospitals. Patients who face serious complications in private hospitals tend to be quickly sent to NHS facilities.

The buildings of Harley Steet, first rated in 1753, are no longer suitable for most medical interventions and private beds have diffused to private hospitals and wards of NHS hospitals, but the logic still obtains, above all in London and the South East. Likewise, the interaction of status, wealth, and London also holds; London's combination of lucre and medical advance is an appealing prospect that ensures that doctors come despite NHS salaries, which in the expensive capital city are unpleasantly low (they do deter others, such as nurses, from working in the capital). The logic of UK-wide public sector wages is in good part to prevent the dominance of London. The minimum pay required to have any nurses or teachers in London at all affords them a good and comparatively cash-rich life in relatively low-cost Manchester or Norwich, and the result is redistribution to the areas outside London via public sector workers' spending and better public services. A biographer of Bevan relates a conversation between Bevan and Lord Moran of the Royal College of Physicians that suggests this problem with London led to the decision about what would be the basic structure of the NHS itself:

> Bevan: I find the efficiency of the hospitals varies enormously. How can that be put right?
> Moran: You will only get one standard of excellence when every hospital has a first-rate consultant staff. At present the consultants are all crowded together in the large centres of population. You've got to decentralise them.
> Bevan: That's all very well, but how are you going to get a man to leave his teaching hospital and go into the periphery? . . .
> Moran: Oh, they'll go if they get an interesting job and if their financial future is secured by a proper salary.
> Bevan (after a long pause): Only the State could pay those salaries. This would mean the nationalization of the hospitals. (Foot 1975:131)

Such was the influence of London: the NHS would have to break a reinforcing lock of status and money. To a large extent it did; hospitals in the Midlands and North are now centres of internationally important medical innovation in a way almost unimaginable before 1948. When CHI examined its results in 2002, looking for geographic patterns, it found that health services improved the further one got from London (Commission for Health Improvement 2002). To this day, meanwhile, London's legacy of major hospitals, with massive constituencies, high international profiles, and laudable achievement is counterbalanced by their overgrowth. Central London, with a population that is actually quite small and atypical, often either young, wealthy, and healthy, or very seriously troubled, boasts enough medical expertise and infrastructure to serve a medium-sized country. It means that central London is almost the only place in the UK (possibly rivalled by Glasgow) with anything like overcapacity in acute health services; interviewees inside and outside London suggested that only this unusual degree of capacity in the immediate environs of Westminster Palace, and hence possible competition, could have convinced governments that the NHS could sustain an internal market (3–16, 6–2, 5–4).

If Scottish health care had a legacy of police in the Enlightenment sense – of a connection between policing, forensic and public health medicine, universities, hospitals and local government – England had a more diverse and less integrated ecology of organisations that undermined the ability of medical elites to represent the health system in the same way they successfully claimed to do in Scotland. English hospitals, especially those in London and the other major urban areas, tended to bifurcate between high-status voluntary hospitals, often connected to local universities, and Poor Law hospitals, often more innovative and superior in quality but much lower status. When the NHS was created in 1948, the teaching hospitals were given their own governing boards, reflecting their autonomy and status; these boards remained in place, and the teaching hospitals unintegrated into regional structures, until the 1974 reorganisations. Hospitals themselves were subject to no analysis of overall strategy and goals until the 1962 Hospital Plan (Mohan 2002). This history bequeathed a division in health care that took decades to wear away; a weaker legacy of coordination than in Scotland; and very different local constellations of health services.

Finally, the English policy community is born of its long history of left–right, often class-based, arguments about distribution and the role of the state. England enjoys a livelier and more organised right-wing, economically liberal, and socially conservative set of policy advocates. A plethora of think-tanks including the Adam Smith Institute, Civitas, the Centre for Policy Studies, and Policy Exchange all flesh out new thinking on the welfare state that often calls its presuppositions into question. The equivalent think-tanks on the left and centre-left, such as the Institute for Public Policy Research, Catalyst, the New Economics Foundation, Demos, and the century-old Fabian Society, perforce participate in these debates – something that their devolved equivalents such as the Institute for Welsh Affairs or the Bevan Foundation are not so obliged to do. The press includes more determinedly conservative titles that are willing to take on the welfare state, such as the *Daily Telegraph*, the relentless *Daily Mail* and the more politically mercurial but generally conservative *Sun*, *The Times*, and *Daily Express*. The right–left cleavage in English public policy leads sometimes to the intellectual equivalent of the pursuit of the median, centrist voter; self-declared centre-left institutions such as the Institute for Public Policy Research will advocate market liberal projects such as the privatisation of the postal service (Corry 2003).

Meanwhile, there are also definite losers in this technical world of English health care, dominated as it is by advocates from management, academic policy analysis, and professional organisations. One is local government, which is something of a black sheep in English politics. It is easy to overstate how powerful English local government ever was, or how important. Such overstatements tend to mention the Birmingham of Joseph Chamberlain, but even he was drawn into local politics as a by-product of national politics, tried to become a Sheffield MP while running Birmingham (Marsh 1994:57), and soon enough left local government for national politics. While local governments such as Liverpool pioneered social reforms (Best 1979:60–2), or late Victorian cities built town halls as a symbol of pride (Briggs 1993), the variance in local achievement was so wide as to create pressures for overall standards and central funding. Financial dependence on the centre started to roll back local government autonomy (Harris 1983), the creation of the NHS took away its municipal health systems, and central policy took over some municipal services (such as gas and water) and would later force the privatisation of others (such as public transport). What saved local government was the respect for local autonomy characteristic of Britain until the 1980s. In this 'dual state', the central government often refrained from using its power and generally accepted a qualitative difference between it and local government rather than a hierarchical relationship (Bulpitt 1983).

The worst blows came starting in 1979, when the new Conservative government set out to control what it saw as spendthrift local authorities. At the same time, some local governments proved their cause's own worst enemies; far-left 'entryists' took over some high-profile councils and parts of the Labour party; they then, improbably, tried to use municipalities such as Liverpool as bases from which to create a socialist Britain (Seyd 1987). As they did with Scotland and Wales, the Conservative governments violated the old understandings of the 'dual state'. They made policies for local government and avoided consultations with it (the obsession with controlling local government eventually led them to the policy and political disaster of the poll tax, or community charge; Butler, Adonis, and Travers 1994). In the ongoing UK tension between seeing local government as a form of democratic polity and seeing local government as a device for locally sensitive service delivery, the Conservatives voted firmly for a view of local government as a form of service delivery – and judged it inadequate at that. As a result, the central government undertook to constrain local government's spending and activities. Local governments responded by seeking to subvert their new regulatory regime, both levels of government went to the courts, and the result was that centre–local government relations in England were soon a spider's web of complicated legislation and judicial decisions (Loughlin 2000).

The Labour government of 1997 was made up of politicians who were determined to avoid any association with what they saw as Old Labour local government and who were equally determined to demonstrate that they could modernise public services. This reduced the ability of local government to act as an articulate part of the policy community. As it lost power and status, it also lost its ability to articulate policy advice or be seen as capable of mobilising advice and acquiescence. Several interviewees at the top levels of health policy in England and the UK have commented that they wanted decentralisation, and perforce English regions, simply because it would be easier to balance the centre with new governments than try to revive local government (0–3, 5–4). In short, the local level in English government is often mute.

Organisational distinctiveness

Strictly speaking, there is no English organisational distinctiveness; England was the 'UK' policy that Northern Ireland, Scotland, and Wales might vary. In 1997, however, the English White Paper *The New NHS: Modern-Dependable* began to mark out a clearly English health policy (Department of Health 1998b). Like the other White Papers, *The New NHS* was brought in to dispatch the Conservatives' internal market and establish a replacement that would reduce divisions within the service, placate unhappy professionals and employees, and demonstrate Labour's credentials as a sober and modernising force. In England, the model was of the purest pragmatism: *The New NHS* explained that 'There are some sound foundations on which the new NHS can be built. Not everything about the old system was bad. The Government believes that what counts is what works' (§2.5; also the interpretations in Ham 1999; Klein 2000).

What the government apparently found to have worked was the basic structure of acute care, with its basis in the trusts; faith in the importance of local tacit knowledge as a basis for planning decisions; and the concept of purchasing (or commissioning: 'we prefer to use the word commissioning – it is a softer word and captures the relationships we want' 0–2). Thus *The New NHS* abolished individual GP fundholding but kept commissioning; district health authorities were now instructed to corral their GPs into locally defined primary care groups that would advise on local area needs and service delivery and guide commissioning decisions. The result would be a more unified system that would entrench primary care at the centre; the White Paper envisaged the development of the primary care groups into full commissioning bodies, primary care trusts, which could also provide services directly to their local areas. This design preserved whatever gains had been made in the importance of primary care, and above all strengthened the basic trust structure of the NHS. The NHS remained, and increasingly became, an ecology of firm-like administrative units.

Policies and politics

England's distinctive political attribute, in the UK, is its left–right axis of party competition. Its electoral system and parliamentary government ensure that two parties dominate, and its political history means that they are left and right wing respectively. As a consequence, England's political debates put the operation and even existence of the NHS in question. Labour argues that it must hold the NHS to a high standard to save it from public disappointment, since public disappointment could lead to a change away from the NHS model of health care. It also acts as if it is in hostile territory, working hard to control the media and thereby earning itself a reputation as a party led by 'control freaks' (Kavanagh 2001). For New Labour, 'modernisation', with an ally in power and with expanded funds, is imperative if the NHS is to survive. The Conservatives, meanwhile, are indeed experimenting with ideas for shifting to some other form of health services provision and will even consider breaking the NHS's cost advantage as the only real buyer of health care in the UK through programmes such as 'patient passport' – essentially a voucher programme (announced at the 2003 party conference).

An English policy community, where management analysts, managers, and corporate rationalisers exercise considerable influence over the flow of policy ideas, directs English health policy agendas toward the management and organisation of health services. What, asks Labour, can be done with the NHS organisation and management to defend it and improve public satisfaction with its services? What, ask the Conservatives, would it take to improve the satisfaction of target voters with health services, whether via the NHS or not? The English NHS has tremendous support in public opinion. The political challenges and institutional problems with trying to change health services organisation to a new model would be staggering, as the Conservatives in government found with even their smallest interventions. Nevertheless, the English political debate can imagine the NHS to be under threat, and perhaps even doomed to be replaced by something else that is better suited to modern society. The public might not agree with this prophecy, but politics is defined by the frequency of self-fulfilling prophecies.

The policy community

The sheer size of England means that it has a much larger health policy community. England's strong centre-right/right policy advocates also give it a different orientation, with more market reformers and corporate rationalisers vetting and discussing ideas. English health policy is not just focused on how to run the health services; it is also focused on whether the government should be running something like the NHS in a recognisable form. Thus there are regular debates about new forms of financing the NHS in England, overviews of health policy include discussions of it, and even advocates of a NHS owned by the state and funded through general taxation have to defend their support for this financing model, whether they are policy analysts (Harrison and Dixon 2000:73–91) or political (Gordon Brown's commissioned report by Derek Wanless; Wanless 2002).

In comparison to devolved policy communities, the English health policy community includes a broader and larger infrastructure of corporate rationaliser and market reform thought. It also includes an extensive academic and professional policy infrastructure dedicated to working out ideas and techniques for public service and health service management. There are specialists in health service management throughout the UK, but their largest numbers and their most prestigious and important institutions are located in England and broadly work on English questions. The output of research institutes, think-tanks in London, and the major academic centres are focused on English research sites and policy questions. Within the civil service, new public management lessons were driven by the centre on the behalf of the government from 1979 onwards, including after Labour came to power, and the result is that the Whitehall departments have new public management skills and instincts better inculcated than the territorial offices. As the private sector became more involved, above all through PFI, the large contracts and the impetus were both in the centre and the incentive was to invest in relationships and knowledge at the centre of the English (UK) departments. This focus on the use and development of health services management dovetails with the overall penetration of new public management ideas in English public administration and supports the logic of managerialism and market reform. Politicians and officials seeking advice and acquiescence will work with the sophisticated, well-resourced, and well-established management cadre and its policy advocates.

Politics: institutions

The UK central state – Westminster and Whitehall – is one of the world's most famous, most studied, and most imitated forms of governance. Students of England's government can benefit from analyses of Westminster and Whitehall dating to Bagehot if not before. Thus little introduction is needed here. Essentially, Westminster is a model of a government that concentrates power and accountability. Power in the UK flows through it; accountability flows up to it; its first-past-the-post system creates a tendency to two-party politics with an attacking opposition; and its Cabinet government gives party leaders the patronage needed to enforce strict party discipline (McKenzie 1964:635). Whitehall, for decades, was the classic model of a nonpartisan, professional civil service. The civil service, nicely treated by Campbell and Wilson (1995) is 'one part occupational classification and three parts state of mind' (Heclo and Wildavsky 1974:382). It still runs much like the liberal professions Abbott studies (Abbott 1994). It has control over its own entry, selection, and promotion procedures; the judgement of civil service peers is key to personal advancement; and policy formulation and analysis are its domain of professional expertise. The Westminster model might be undermined by two developments of late – European legal regimes that constrain Parliament's autonomy, and devolution, with its potential to fragment parties by breaking up the great chain of patronage leading from the Prime Minister to the constituency parties. The Whitehall model certainly has been undermined over the last two decades, when politicians have sought to reduce the constraints civil servants put on policy, bring in trusted special advisers, and turn the civil service into specialists in 'delivery' who operate in ways borrowed from the private sector. Internal documents of the Department of Health have described it as a 'department for delivery', which is not a traditional self-image for a major department of state. When Secretary of State Alan Milburn combined the posts of NHS Chief Executive and Permanent Secretary of the Department of Health, it was the Chief Executive (Nigel Crisp) who took the new combined job.

The environment shapes the ideology and strategy of UK governments. First, the UK governments are more likely to be single-party than the others; first-past-the-post elections, unlike the various proportional representation schemes of the devolved countries, tend to create two-party politics rather than shifting coalition politics. Then, UK governments have degrees of autonomy not available to the devolved countries. The two kinds of constraints that limit Northern Ireland, Scotland, and Wales – regulation and finance – do not apply to the UK, since it writes the legislative rules and sets tax rates while enjoying a wider range of trade-offs between its English and UK services and priorities. The UK government, also, has exclusive access to EU policymaking; unlike the devolved countries, it can affect its European regulatory environment.

Politics: the party system

People have to know that we will run from the centre and govern from the centre (Tony Blair, cited in Hennessy 2000:476)

England's party system has a major anomaly compared to the rest of the UK: it has a strong Conservative party. The size of England, and its propensity to vote Conservative, mean that this party, which has always had its core mass support in England, is one of the two major UK parties. The English divide between Conservative and Labour has defined UK politics for a century, despite the fact that the Conservatives have been in decline in Scotland since the 1950s and were never strong in Wales. Although it is unusual for a part of the UK to have a serious Conservative party, the part of the UK that has one is a very big part – 85 per cent – which makes the Conservatives an important force across the UK.

Analyses of British politics that focus on the left–right debates about the role of the state are useful insofar as they apply to England, even if they misrepresent the rest of the UK by portraying it as a two-party system. The English party system spreads parties along a left–right axis with Labour on the left, the Liberal Democrats in the centre (with a leftward tendency) and the Conservatives on the right. The centrist voters that all pursue are in the middle. There is very little in the party system to draw parties towards the extremes; when a party does shift toward an extreme (as happened with Labour in the early 1980s) it is because of the activists within the party and their efforts. The main reason that English parties can be so relaxed about guarding their rears while moving toward the centre is that there are no important small parties akin to the Scottish Socialists or Greens on the extremes to peel off voters. Even when England is in a three-party pattern, as it has been for much of its democratic history (Heclo 1974:38), competing parties tend to be in variously defined centrist positions (like that presently occupied by the Liberal Democratic Party) rather than on a clear ideological end of the spectrum.

Without a left-libertarian party flanking Labour, the only price it pays for centrist policies is low turnout in constituencies it would probably win anyway (first-past-the-post systems, by creating a tendency to two-party politics, have this potential anywhere, since they make life harder for small parties on the left and right of the major parties and allow major parties to trade off abstention among their further wings for new centrist voters). The same holds for the Conservatives; the difficulty of starting new parties ensures this situation will probably continue.

In such a party system England's Labour politicians have considerable incentives to invade Conservative 'territory'. There lie new voters, and so long as Labour faces no assault on its leftward flank it is free to continue trying to collect new voters there, or to pursue policies that offend its left-wing electors but that it judges wise policy investments that will pay off later in terms of better public services or other successes. The result is the remarkable situation of 1997 onwards in which Labour, a self-declared social democratic party with some very left-wing members, staked out policy stances on issues of taxation, private sector involvement in the public services, or foreign policies and wars that were markedly to the right of Liberal Democrats – a party partly created by people who left Labour on the grounds that it was too left-wing. This has been a winning electoral formula for Labour under Tony Blair.

Combined with a policy community that focuses on NHS services and debates their management, industrial organisation, and financing, the result is that English health politics looks like none other. Labour politicians have an incentive to try to balance their commitment to the NHS with policies that will win more right-wing voters over to it, or at least to Labour. This means that they seek out new techniques that will improve the NHS's through-put and effectiveness as a service provider rather than turn it to some other goal; and improving its effectiveness as a service provider is exactly what managers and management policy advocates, who dominate the policy stream, do best. 'Shifting the Balance of Power', a set of radical organisational changes, for example, came about in the 2001 general election campaign and was rumoured to be a policy chosen for no reason save to pre-empt a possible Conservative move to abolish health authorities (0–3, 0–6). If it was in part a pre-emptive move to stop the Conservatives, it was still effectively an operation conducted on their territory. New Labour spends so much time on Conservative electoral territory that many of its policies are adaptations to the special demands of that terrain.

The first 'New Labour' government

John Major, campaigning as a Unionist, had tried during the last days of the 1997 campaign to use opposition to devolution to win votes, telling voters they had '72 hours to save the Union'. Blair and Labour responded that they rather had '24 hours to save the NHS' (Butler and Kavanagh 1997:111–12). The Labour campaign, and its slogan, certainly won a large majority but also caught the party's sense that the NHS needed saving rather than administering. The first Blair government (1997–2001) entered with both an overwhelming overall majority and a majority of votes in England. This was partly due to the electorate's irritation with the misadventures of the Major government; it was also due to the ability of the Labour leaders under Tony Blair to forge the party into a powerful device designed to defeat Major. Labour was an extremely effective party with its popular Prime Minister and a winning formula based on party discipline, centrist policy, and determined media management. This centrism and centralism, combined with its tendency to start arguments about public services from market reforming premises, would later cause problems, but in 1997 there was great hope. The hope came not just from the change from a weakened governing party to a self-described 'new' party but also from the chance given to policy advocates of many stripes to work with a new politics. New Labour offered a new governing party with a different ideology and strategy. Policy advocates specialising in topics of little interest to Conservatives or making arguments that contradicted Conservative ideology saw new possibilities of success.

TERRITORIAL POLITICS AND HEALTH POLICY

Table 4.4. Seats won at general elections by the three main UK parties since 1945 by nation

	Scotland			Wales			England		
	Con.	Labour	Lib.	Con.	Labour	Lib.	Con.	Labour	Lib.
1945	27	37	0	4	25	6	167	331	6
1950	31	37	2	4	27	5	253	251	2
1951	35	35	1	6	27	3	271	233	2
1955	36	34	1	6	27	3	293	216	2
1959	31	38	1	7	27	2	315	193	3
1964	24	43	4	6	28	2	262	246	3
1966	20	46	5	3	32	1	219	286	6
1970	23	44	3	7	27	1	292	217	2
1974 (Feb.)	21	40	3	8	24	2	268	237	9
1974 (Oct.)	16	41	3	8	23	2	253	255	8
1979	22	44	3	11	22	1	306	203	7
1983	21	41	8	14	20	2	362	148	13
1987	10	50	9	8	24	3	358	155	10
1992	11	49	9	6	27	1	319	195	10
1997	0	56	10	0	34	2	165	328	34
2001	1	55	10	0	34	2	165	323	40

Note: In 1983 and 1987 all SDP/Liberal Alliance seats are listed together; from 1988 the Alliance became known as the Liberal Democrat Party.
Sources: Butler and Butler, 1994; Political Science Resources website, www.psr.keele.ac.uk; United Kingdom Election Results website, www.election.demon.co.uk; The Electoral Commission, Election 2001: The Official Results.

The result was that the first Blair government had a remarkably clear field for the development of policy. With its huge majority (167) (Table 4.4), feeble opposition, and wave of public goodwill, it had all the formal opportunity to make major changes to British public policy. It certainly made major changes in the structure of the UK. It is hard to say what is more striking – that a single government made changes such as creating the devolution settlement, half-reforming the House of Lords, introducing European human rights law, reshaping local government in England, creating the Greater London Authority, and introducing freedom of information and data protection law, with more changes in their second government such as the creation of a supreme court (Morrison 2001), or that its leaders almost never mention their record of constitutional change in public (Bogdanor 2001). In public policy, however, it was at first markedly more timid. In health services, for example, its motto was at first 'what works', and then subsequently an often very unpopular 'modernisation'.

In all probability there are two reasons why the party was not more radical. First, the Labour party had a blemished record of government – of bad luck, policy and party management failures, and electoral punishment. Blair, his Chancellor Gordon Brown, and others in the press and party were acutely conscious that Labour had never been in office for two full consecutive parliamentary terms. They attributed it to the party's tendency to 'lurch from profligate post-election boom to fatal pre-election bust' (Stephens 2001:186). Proving Labour was a responsible party that could govern and win re-election was an important value to them; previous Labour disasters spurred them to the centre. In Labour's self-analysis, attacks on the party as high-taxing left radicals were crucial to its earlier defeats, and so it set out to prove itself on the grounds of stewardship – in fact, to prove itself at stewardship largely defined by liberal thought more identified with Conservatives. 'For too many of our 100 years', Blair told the 2003 Labour conference, 'we have been a well-intentioned pressure group' (Eaglesham 2003). It is not an accident that one of the major accounts of Labour is titled *Safety First* (Anderson 1997), even if leading New Labour figure and Blair confidante Peter Mandelson preferred the more stirring *The Blair Revolution* for his book (Mandelson 1996).The most obvious form of such self-discipline was the remarkable decision to abide by the planned spending commitments set by the Conservatives for the first two years of Labour government. Britain's first centre-left government for nearly two decades chose to spend within expenditure limits that the departing neoliberal government had set, and that then-Chancellor Kenneth Clarke found 'eye-wateringly tight' (Atkinson and Elliott 1999). Public spending actually fell as a percentage of GDP in Labour's first two years.

A second reason for not being more radical was that Labour faced serious questions about the stability of the UK welfare state. The resilience of public support for institutions such as the NHS over the previous decades might have caught the eye, but so did the daily attacks on the public services in the right-wing press. With a mobilised press, numerous think-tanks, and an opposition party to the right of Labour, there is almost automatically a debate about the form and existence of the welfare state in England. New Labour activists could argue, and routinely did argue, that the welfare state had to be able to prove itself if it were to be able to justify new investment – that it had to modernise itself, respond to a changing society, and be run for the benefit of consumers rather than producers, if it were to be able to survive. More simply, Labour wanted to avoid the old tag of tax-and-spend and its potential to discredit the whole welfare state, and sought to do it by forcing the welfare state to give it visibly better value for money. Blair began a 2002 Fabian pamphlet: 'It is always harder to be critical about your own work than somebody else's. So it is with the reform of the public services . . . [but] we know in our hearts that if an ideal, no matter how worthy, fails to meet the challenge of the times it becomes a diminished ideal. So let us start with a blunt truth. Our public services, despite the heroic efforts of dedicated public servants . . . are not all of the quality a nation like Britain needs.' At the end he concluded that 'Only by meeting this urgent challenge of revitalising our public services can we realise Labour's historic values. Strong public services have always defined New Labour's purpose . . . It would be a betrayal of our Party's past achievements and values if we were to falter in the task of reform. For reform is the surest route to social justice' (Blair 2002:1, 34).

The basic formula continued to work in the 2001 general election. Labour was re-elected on a nearly stable vote, with the same army of back-benchers. It continued its practice of launching 'pre-emptive strikes' into Conservative territory, returning with votes and policies (on issues such as patient choice in the NHS, abolition of health authorities, or tough crime policies). The Conservatives remained disorderly. The Labour government promised to focus on public service reform, as did its internal opposition; very substantial amounts of new money (intended to raise NHS spending to a European average for health spending) gave grounds for optimism.

On September 11 2001, Blair had been planning to give a contentious speech to the Brighton TUC conference in defence of PFI (as a modernising reform) when he was called back to London to respond to the terrorist attacks in the USA. This day proved a turning point for Blair as for many others. Afterwards, Blair would often give priority to foreign affairs and risk his career for policies opposed by much of his party. The 2001 attack on Afghanistan was the subject of much debate, but Blair began to face real internal challenges and public criticism when he decided to be the only major world leader to side with US President George Bush and play a leading role in the contentious invasion of Iraq in 2003. The invasion – and a dangerously large parliamentary rebellion coupled with a major Cabinet resignation – damaged Blair's standing with activists, members (many of whom left), the increasingly left-wing unions, and many backbenchers. This in turn made the government more vulnerable to left-wing attacks on social policy issues. The Iraq vote made subsequent rebellions on issues such as foundation hospitals possible, since the left within the Labour party could increasingly act on its suspicion that Blair's government was no kind of Labour government. David Hinchcliffe MP, Labour chair of the Commons Health Committee, called the ideas Blair enunciated in the 2003 conference 'ideas from the dustbin of Margaret Thatcher' ('Westminster Hour', BBC Radio Four, 28 September 2003). Rebellions multiplied and grew (Table 4.5) (Cowley and Stuart 2003). In 2003 the party remained strong, with an overwhelming majority, good public opinion for the middle of

Table 4.5. Significant rebellions in the second session (November 2001–July 2003) of the 2001 Blair administration

Date	Size of rebellion	Issue
September 2002	56	Iraq
January 2003	44	Iraq
February 2003	121	Iraq
March 2003	139	Iraq
March 2003	17	Fire fighters' strike
April 2003	30	Criminal justice
May 2003	33	Trial by jury
May 2003	65	Foundation hospitals
July 2003	62	Foundation hospitals

a second term, and a fragmented opposition, but with an angry and empowered left and many exposed positions.

Policy outcomes

Despite the centralism of the regulatory scheme in English health services administration, the English health policy agenda is best summarised by its bet on markets. This has come to be called 'the diversity agenda' and is attached to the 'choice' agenda for patients and a basic NHS structure built on markets. The diversity agenda focuses on providing a service that is free and universal at the point of service – but not necessarily provided by the state. It could include more autonomous 'foundation hospitals', private firms contracted to provide 'fast-track' treatment centres, importation of foreign surgical teams, export of patients to other EU countries, and greater use of the for-profit and charity sectors for provision. Such a project, with its combination of pragmatism, public administration techniques borrowed from elsewhere, and belief in market reform, does not have coherence in its design, its vision, its development, or its outcomes, but does have coherence in its reflection of the ideas coursing through the English policy community and the debates generated by the English party system.

Organisational form

Organisational change, by and large, is a qualitative phenomenon, but it can also be a quantitative phenomenon. England, compared to the other three health systems of the UK, has more organisational change. Before devolution it was not sheltered by territorial offices and distance from London. It felt change more acutely and probably became more accustomed to it. Since 1999 the pace of change has become dizzying. The 1997 reorganisation set out in *The New NHS* lasted until 2001, and even appeared to be buttressed by an *NHS Plan* that appeared to accept most of the organisational structure, focusing instead on its goals and introducing a 'modernisation' agenda with a Modernisation Agency to drive it along (Department of Health 2000b). However, in the run-up to the 2001 general election the Secretary of State, Alan Milburn, surprised many by announcing a programme of changes known as 'Shifting the Balance'. Poetically, he did this at the ceremony launching the Modernisation Agency (Milburn 2001). The programme entailed abolishing the health authorities (or, rather, merging them in groups of three into new strategic health authorities – SHAs) and the regions of the NHS Executive, which was being merged into the Department of Health. The primary care groups, always intended to become primary care trusts (PCTs), were hurried along into trust status. 'Shifting the Balance' was originally a speech, and documents on what it meant came out for months after (albeit with some signs of hurried preparation; the consultation document proposing the new 'North West London SHA' had a table of contents filled with references to the 'North West Midlands SHA'). Before the last guidance and instruction was out, and before the old district health authorities were dissolved into SHAs, the government had already advanced to a new concept – 'foundation hospitals', which were vaguely based on Spanish models and in reality more akin to trusts with new powers. In implementing 'Shifting the Balance' the Department found that the regions could not be wholly replaced and created four directors of health and social care, each with a region (they could not be called health and social care regions, since that would suggest regions had not been abolished). By the end of 2002, these too were set to be eliminated.

Meanwhile, relations with the private sector started to impinge on organisational form, as the government continued to experiment with the 'diversity' agenda in which patients and parts of the health service contract with the private sector, or foreign governments, for acute care. Foundation hospitals legislation has now passed Parliament and the 'diversity' and 'choice' agendas are to be implemented, but there is no reason to expect that changes will not continue. Diversity also includes efforts to stimulate NHS management. After a (hotly contested) *British Medical Journal* article suggesting that California Health Maintenance Organisation Kaiser Permanente is better value than the NHS, the government began to franchise failing trust management to the managers of successful trusts and American Health Maintenance Organisation managers were brought in to run a few small parts of the English NHS (Feachem, Sekhri, and White 2002; see also the extensive online debates on the *BMJ* website).

Even if there is not to be much diversity (i.e. introduction of non-traditional, non-NHS providers), there is to be patient choice – an agenda with potentially immense effects for the NHS that had been decided and was being piloted in 2003 (Coulter 2003; Department of Health 2003b). The patient choice agenda includes the ability to go overseas (a reaction to a European Court of Justice decision that could be presented as a problem requiring further patient choice formalisation). Patients will be able to select where they would like to have an operation from several area hospitals (as enabled by information technology that was contracted in 2004), thereby increasing their satisfaction and redistributing resources according to patient flows. The implementation of choice will be difficult (Appleby, Harrison, and Devlin 2003), but its importance to the government is as a way to increase efficiency and provide services to an electorate supposedly prone to abandoning faith in the old NHS (and Labour).

As if these changes were not enough, Labour also began to experiment with devices to reallocate professional roles and diminish professional autonomy over issues such as rota. 'We are changing the terms of trade between doctors and the state . . . this is a departure from the postwar conspiracy of silence between doctors and government. The doctors were quiet about underfunding and rationed care . . . [and so] there was no challenge to doctors' one person connected to the government explained in September 2003. The government developed its quality agenda but also, dangerously, tried to reallocate staff by expanding the role of nurses (in prescribing) and allied professions in order to use medical staff more efficiently. These changes are perfectly reasonable to those who think of trusts as firms, with chief executives allocating tasks to achieve customer satisfaction efficiently, but constitute an existential threat to the professionals, who see themselves losing their control over their work to managers and ministers. Professionals and much of the public see managers as unqualified to intervene in medical work and division of responsibilities, while the role of intuition and individual context in medicine means doctors are reluctant to lose regular contact with patients and low-level tasks (doctors' claim to be the apex of the medical professions also rests partly on their ability, in theory, to do most of the tasks that they assign to others; Abbott 1994). This led to a highly contentious consultants' contract that was rejected by doctors in the first round on the grounds of its giving too much power to managers they trusted too little (Smith 2003) (reflecting the different trust levels in the system, the Scottish consultants narrowly voted to support it).

As a result of this remarkable set of changes, the analysis of England's outcomes in health services organisation require that two questions be answered. First, what explains the English trajectory of focus on management, trusts, and commissioning? And second, why does England reorganise so much, given that there is broad acceptance that reorganisation is counterproductive and likely to waste much of the new money going into the NHS?

The English political stream is dominated by the particular party system that New Labour must navigate, and its strategy for doing so. New Labour has been widely criticised for 'targetitis' and an overreliance on media announcements, including constant targets and new schemes, such as a 2001 campaign for better hospital food, that are often worthy but whose announcement looks like an effort to 'capture a media cycle' (www.betterhospitalfood.com). Such complaints come with exposure to almost any sort of politics, but there is ample evidence that New Labour in opposition developed a style of permanent campaign that it took with it to office and which marked a dramatic quantitative, if not qualitative, change in central demands on the NHS. The public administration consequence is a hyperactive policy style and, sometimes, major disruptions caused by the government's need for an announcement. Making policy at the speed demanded by a twenty-four-hour media is over time an unhappy task – unhappy for the policy makers and unhappy for the objects of the policies (Greer 2004a). Thus the particular strategy of New Labour is partly to blame for the frequency of organisational change.

However, three of the UK governments are currently Labour-led or Labour and all face tough media scrutiny, so this explanation alone is not enough. The difference is that New Labour in England faces a substantial opposition across a left–right divide and a much smaller degree of consensus about the nature and structure of the health services. This means, in turn, that Labour is particularly open to rationalising ideas that promise a 'modern', customer-friendly, non-producer-dominated health service. Its media and political strategies, geared to an environment it perceives as hostile to governments in general and centre-left governments in particular, then demand *more* policies than anywhere else and so accelerate the pace of change.

The policy community, meanwhile, is able to supply Labour with a constant stream of ideas marketed to fit its preoccupation with 'modern', new policies. It is the policy community, moreover, that explains why England is the site of the greatest triumphs of market reform thought in UK health policy. This policy community has led to the adoption of policy logics that think of a health service as an ecology of firms (trusts), each dealing with each other in contracting relationships and subject to a regulatory and supervisory regime. Internally, each is a classical organisational form from business – a hierarchical pyramid with a responsible chief executive and, probably, a board at the apex.

The policy community that provides this is both focused on management and dominated by students of management (and economists, in a way no other system features). The corporate rationalist solution is a separation of management decisions and policy from the Secretary of State – meaning that the BMA and a sympathetic independent commission have now both concluded that what the NHS needed was Griffiths' dream of an autonomous executive management board (Futures Group 2002; Beecham 2003). Most debates about health services in England take place within a corporate rationalising framework, and focus on what managers should do or how they should be organised. This is unremarkable until one crosses a border into, for example, Scotland, and hears conferences where the arguments are not about how managers should organise care, but rather about how professional networks should organise care. The Modernisation Agency, which is supposed to spearhead improvement by diffusing best practice, redesigning services, and supporting 'new ways of working', directs most of its activity towards managers through training or through diffusing strategies for them rather than professionals. Tellingly, and in a reflection of the tensions that led to the crises over the consultants' contract, its 'new ways of working' programme focuses on altering professional demarcations, changing staffing rotas and requirements, and developing new incentives to change staff and professional behaviour. This is wholly unobjectionable, indeed basic, management, but in the health services context the decision to opt for management by managers (and the implied substitution of professional dominance with managerial hierarchy) is a contested choice.

Governments also get advice from, for example, civil service officials who might have rotated in from the Department of Transport (where, to the extent that it controls transport, it does so through a web of quangos, contractors, and semi-public corporations), the variously named department responsible for local government (which rigidly enforces the obligation local authorities have to tender much of their work),[1] the Department of Work and Pensions (much of whose workforce is in the semi-detached Benefits Agency), or even the Ministry of Defence, which has PFI contractors for many activities close to combat. The UK – or England – is routinely highlighted in international comparisons as the country, along with New Zealand, that most enthusiastically embraced new public management. A contract-based system based on negotiation among firm-like entities (or firms) to provide a specified service is, after twenty years, very common in English public administration. New public management still has radical potential, though: 'What [critical MPs] Frank Dobson and David Hinchcliffe realise is that foundation hospitals are a minor issue. It's really about the withdrawal of government from direct services and provisions. As long as ministers are accountable for running the services we will micromanage and set targets – all the pressure groups press for central intervention' explained a former minister in the

department in June 2003. In other words, advice, acquiescence, and acceptance largely structure the English policy community in a way that produces
a policy stream of management, market ideas.

Public and private

Relations with the private sector is the most distinctive issue in English policy
and one in which England diverges sharply from the choices of the rest of the
UK. All parts of the UK have chosen to integrate the private sector through PFI
and even expanded it relative to what they inherited from the Conservatives;
constraints come from either a decision to placate important unions (in Scotland
and Wales) or the small size of the projects (in Northern Ireland and Wales). In
England, not only has PFI become the chief form of health service (and other)
capital investment; the government also constantly experiments with new ways
to involve the private sector more closely in the NHS services.

The 'diversity' agenda is of a piece with New Labour thought (and the
ingrained English affection for new public management) that argues the ends,
not the means, are what matter. If the government's goal is to provide high-
quality primary care at a good price, there is no principled reason why it
should not be provided by Boots the Chemists rather than by a traditional GP,
and there is no reason why capacity increases should be through traditional
capital investment rather than contracting private-sector, or French, facilities.
The English private hospital sector has not done especially well out of this,
but there is a concordat with them in which the government promises to work
with them to solve government problems (Department of Health 2000a).
England has embraced PFI in a way no other part of the UK has done and
has been able to develop a PFI sector in a way that smaller Northern Ireland,
Scotland, and Wales cannot.

Medical referral networks probably constrain implementation of the
diversity agenda. Doctors work under conditions of tremendous uncertainty
and need to use tacit judgements and contextual evidence (if not, they would
not need to be so highly trained); they reduce the uncertainty by working in
networks with other doctors whom they trust and with whom they have had
good experiences and can work closely. They are highly reluctant to advise
patients to move outside these networks; there is already enough uncertainty
about the medical trajectory of any one patient without introducing the possibility of ill-fitting or poor doctors. Doctors are therefore reluctant to refer
to specialists they do not already know and trust (and specialists are often
reluctant to use each others' radiologists' X-ray pictures), so they are not likely
to enthuse to their patients about the prospect of treatment by an unknown
doctor, whether across town or across the Channel. Patients' consumerism is

still very easy to overestimate – patients broadly do rely on doctors for guidance – so it is unlikely that enough patients will shop for even easy elective surgery to disrupt the NHS or solve the government's capacity and waiting problems, while the coordination between medical professionals appears to be far superior to the coordination between different formal organisations.

What drives the government to repeated efforts to embrace the private sector, and do so publicly? As with other parts of the English agenda, the answer lies in Labour's position in the English party system, which structures the solutions it will entertain, and the policy community that it inherited. The party system means that Labour feels problems with the NHS – such as waiting lists – acutely, and the policy community surrounds it with policy doctors proposing more new public management. If it wants to modernise the NHS so as to win over the centrist and centre-right public to the NHS and to Labour, then it must be seen to be resolving problems of waiting lists. The immense (by political standards) lead times required to increase medical staffing or build infrastructure fight with the need for quick solutions. Failure to cope with the problems carries the threat of the Conservatives regaining their position as a strong party based on the right. On the other hand, including the private sector on Labour's terms is a pre-emptive strike against the opposition, since it leaves them little else to offer.

That 'modernisation' and 'diversity,' i.e. corporate rationalisation and market reform, should be the particular way in which Labour 'governs from the centre' reflects the strength of new public management in the policy stream. There are abundant specialists in health service management who are extremely sceptical about PFI and are responsible for lively debates (as well as firm opposition from unions, above all the GMB and UNISON). They are countered, however, by a broad swathe of advocates in policy communities far beyond health who work on a contracting basis. To the kinds of Treasury civil servants who once suggested that the intelligence services work on a contracting basis (with 'customer' departments 'paying' for the kinds of intelligence they needed), contracting with the private sector for PFI appears practicable (Hennessy 2000:441). To the small groups of policy advisers working in Number 10 and the Treasury, new public management and new media management combine to make private sector forays appealing. Policies that use the private sector clearly govern from the centre; they might not have (yet) noticeably worked in health but have become the basis of policy areas such as telecommunications, local government purchasing, and the railways; and they offer immediate solutions to unpleasant headlines about capacity. Immediate policies to respond to problems related to capacity matter, especially to a party staking its fortunes on NHS spending. One of Blair's least flattering public experiences during the 2001 campaign was an encounter with a Birmingham woman complaining of inadequate capacity for her cancer-suffering boyfriend (Brogan 2001; an event happily, for Blair, overshadowed by his Deputy Prime Minister John Prescott punching an egg-throwing local at a campaign stop in Rhyl).

New public health

> Perhaps we should just get rid of all these public health departments in Portakabins and those pamphlets nobody reads and spend the money on television buys. (English policy discussion, September 2003)

The logic of market reforming thought comes from economics and thus from the same, Smithian, source as the logic of division of labour. In Adam Smith's example, the pin factory becomes more efficient when each person, rather than make each pin, carries out only one of the tasks that produces a pin, does so well, and builds up skills while producing more parts. Division of labour – specialisation – and markets come together and mutually reinforce each other so that overall needs are satisfied by the interconnected specialists. This means that the greater the specialisation in a health system, and the greater the reliance on 'firms' and 'markets' with their presumed incentives to excel at core competencies, the less likely it is that decision makers in health services will want to engage with police, local government, the voluntary sector, the bus company and the regional government office in pursuit of better population health through joint working on wider determinants of health. A hospital trust that responds to its clear responsibilities to its contractors to provide services within the centre's regulatory framework should be, if the system works, positively disinclined to divert resources and attention to its role in broader population health outcomes. Only if the government either demands through regulation that the service produce population health outcomes, or makes funding through PCTs contingent on it, will it even produce an extra set of incentives – and a policy outcome could well remain elusive. What is certain, though, is that to the extent that the organisational structure of the 'diverse' 'new NHS', appropriately 'modernised', with its balance shifted, has actually come into being, it will not respond to homiletics from junior ministers about population health. Having fashioned an already very medical, treatment-focused organisation into an ecology of yet more focused organisations, governments should not be surprised that they each make one part of their pin and show little interest in the overall welfare of the town in which the factory is located.

The result is that England has taken new public health far less seriously than any other part of the UK, persistently focusing on lifestyles (Hunter 2003:31–100). Several interviewees reported that senior politicians thought of public health as 'womens' work' (0–4, 5–2, 6–2). Wales has made new public health a centre of its health policy; Scotland has tried to improve its statistics while still focusing on health care; and Northern Ireland is a good environment for ground-level new public health advocates to work. England is working in the opposite direction and shows a positive lack of interest in *new* public health. To the extent that there is a new public health agenda, it is driven by local-level managers and leaders, funded by grants such as Health Action Zones (mostly part of the Treasury-driven social inclusion agenda), and powered by the ability of local-level managers and leaders to circumvent organisational incentives (Greer 2001a; Greer and Sandford 2001). Defending the widely criticised decision to shift regional directors of public health into government offices for the regions, the Department of Health pointed to the extent to which the tax and benefits regime, rather than the NHS, dominates social inclusion and thereby public health (Department of Health 2001a:21–4).

The problem is that Labour arrived in office in a party system that does not reward new public health work. The Conservatives, rhetorically and in many policies, focus on efficient public services, oppose the 'nanny state', and are sceptical of efforts to reduce social inequality or otherwise engage in 'social engineering'. Few of their voters are likely to be won over to Labour by new public health, and fewer still are likely to be won over by new public health rather than better health service waiting times. There is no left-libertarian party like the Scottish Socialists or Greens snapping at English Labour's heels and obliging it to tackle reinforcing ill health and social exclusion, so public health is not a vote winner and neglecting it is not much of a vote loser. Furthermore, while reducing inequalities and decreasing social exclusion and its consequences appeals to the Labour left, public health's salience was greatly decreased by the rarity of problems (rather than widely acknowledged conditions).

The policy advocacy community in England is split, as in Scotland and Wales, between the health services' public health specialists and local government's non-medical public health specialists. Neither public health nor local government has much prestige, and a large part of the NHS public health workforce had, during the internal market, been drained off to supply crucial population knowledge for contract negotiations, and had suffered deskilling in public health work (Tuohy 1999). The Department of Health's public health section and its broader policy contacts are also more fragmented than Scotland (when the Department moved from its famously squalid quarters in London's disagreeable Elephant and Castle to an attractive new building well positioned on Whitehall, it left important parts of the public health function behind in 'the Elephant'). The result is that the role of public health in the overall health policy community is much weaker than the groups interested in health services and management, and new public health advocates' position is weaker in England than in the rest of the UK. They were marginal since their allies, like local government, were marginal (in contrast to Wales), and their position as part of medical elites was more tenuous than in Scotland – and the position of medical elites in English policy debate is a good deal less important than in Scotland.

The public health function itself underwent a series of reorganisations that many public health practitioners found unhelpful. In 1997 the institutional home of public health was fundamentally in the district health authorities and in the NHS regions. 'Shifting the Balance' abolished both of these tiers and left SHAs and the regional directors of health and social care with exiguous public health responsibilities. PCTs were instructed to provide public health as part of their duties to community health, and the public health teams from the old NHS regions were moved into the government offices for the regions, the better to engage in joint working (Department of Health 2001b:5, 13, 18–21). The White Paper on regional government then suggested that elected regional assemblies should have public health functions, but did not propose to turn the public health teams in the government offices to them, suggesting that the result would be duplication (Sandford 2002). The PCTs, new, hurried, and caught between service-focused central demands and all the local politics pushing them in different directions, tended not to invest in public health. The House of Commons Committee on Health argued that this was happening, the government responded with a stiff speech to PCTs from a junior minister, and the PCTs by all accounts nonetheless continued to diverge widely in their attitudes toward public health or new public health. The public health teams in the government offices, meanwhile, had an opportunity to work with other departments such as the Department for Environment, Food, and Rural Affairs or Transport, but lost connections with the NHS ('I'll miss my friends' commented one regional director of public health just before the transfer; Greer 2001a) The shift effectively turned regional directors of public health into lobbyists for new public health in government offices dominated by field branches of other ministries. The shift to PCTs was not helpful to public health, but the regional public health teams had the potential to develop new public health work (at the expense of opportunities to do old public health work, which is more closely linked to the health services).

Overall, then, new public health has made little headway in England. It does not benefit from any partisan logics drawing politicians' attention: public health, after a long period of neglect in the shade of health services (including incorporation as a set of contracting specialists), is not strong enough to influence the health policy agenda or influence the problems that arise (the main reorganisation was rather a spirited use of a problem, terrorist threat, by an enterprising chief medical officer, to create a large new health protection organisation targeting communicable diseases: Department of Health 2002). Rather, the history of new public health since 1997 is best understood by looking at changes in NHS services organisation, since the key event was 'Shifting the Balance of Power', in which public health functions were an afterthought (0–6) and which effectively marked the end of serious government attention to new public health. Advocates of a policy focused on health rather than health care can enumerate the arguments as to why public health fared so poorly in England – but they can at least take heart from events in Scotland and Wales.

They might also be able to take heart from English mid-level governments in the regions and London. The most intriguing developments are those in the English regions and Greater London. Three northern regions (the North East, the North West, and Yorkshire and Humberside) are due to hold referenda in 2004 on the creation of elected regional assemblies. These regional assemblies would be able to have a role in public health, even if the obvious, and attractive, option of transferring NHS strategic public health teams from regional government offices to the new assemblies is not in the proposals. The role of the proposed assemblies in health resembles that of the Greater London Authority (GLA), which has been working in public health since its creation (Greer and Sandford 2001; Sandford 2002). The GLA, like other organisations that have a health role and interest but no health services responsibilities, focuses on developing the health component of its other policy areas. This has led to health impact assessment and networking through the London Health Commission (LHC), an informal organisation of key actors such as the NHS supported by the GLA. As ever, it is difficult to evaluate such work, although the difficulties are as much a consequence of excessively short timeframes for evaluation and weak methods as a lack of impact. At a minimum, evidence from ongoing research suggests that the LHC and GLA are increasing the connections necessary for service integration and the overall awareness of potential health gains from different policies in London's extremely fragmented, competitive environment. If the English elected regional assemblies come into being, their combination of a health competency and no distracting health services agendas might turn them into new public health advocates as well. They would share the clarity of focus that comes from a lack of control or responsibility for health services and would thereby show the benefits of intergovernmental division of powers. Governments or quasi-governments without policies, in other words, made a good fit with public health advocates who have policies but no support from the stronger levels of government.

Quality

England and Scotland are the two parts of the UK where there has been significant work and government focus on quality improvement, evidence-based medicine, and clinical governance. The two regions differ dramatically in the way that they do it. Scotland's model is close to professional self-regulation, with professional elites occupying a position at the apex of its quality improvement mechanisms and heavily involved, while in England quality improvement is much more a political tool of the centre. Thus, the question for England must be why quality improvement became such an issue (unlike in Northern Ireland or Wales), and why the chosen solution took a regulatory form that concentrated power in the Department of Health rather than in professional elites. The answer is that crises – quality problems as frightening as a medical mass murderer in Manchester and grievously incompetent paediatric heart surgery in Bristol – made quality much more of a problem for a quasi-market whose regulatory institutions were being built at the time.

Quality became part of the overall regulation of the NHS in England. Walshe (2003) appropriately discusses most quality issues in England as forms of regulation. Quality assurance primarily took place from 1998 through two agencies, CHI and NICE, as well as the Audit Commission and National Audit Office (peripherally), older, more restricted bodies (such as the professional regulators of the General Medical Council) or smaller and less important ones. From 2003 the NHS combined various agencies into the new CHAI, the Commission for Healthcare Audit and Inspection. The initial impetus for quality was the need to demonstrate that the NHS was good value for money. This was a constant from the Conservatives, whose calm and consensus-oriented White Paper *A Service With Ambitions* had begun to emphasise the quality of treatment and whose developing interest arose at about the same time as in other countries (Department of Health 1996). To demonstrate the usefulness of the NHS to the presumably sceptical voters who had shifted from the Conservatives to put Labour in power, the Labour party needed to show that the NHS was good value, and that included good quality as well as value for money. Quality also has the virtue of seeming impartiality, which would release the government from rationing decisions (Syett 2003). Ministers and managers, outclassed in public by professionals, could enlist science on their side in battles over rationing. Labour politicians interested in giving the public the receipt showing good value for tax money began to want to include a guarantee (the Conservatives, before, were responding to the imperative to demonstrate to a sceptical public that they cared about the NHS and its patients at all; Klein 2000:194).

At the same time, the English policy community supplied multiple policy advocates with ideas for health services quality improvement. England is a major centre of what is called the 'evidence-based medicine' advocacy coalition, which has a major institute in the Cochrane Collaboration in Oxford (even if the work and research of its leader, A. L. Cochrane, is associated with Wales and a panel study he led of the Welsh town of Caerphilly). The quality movement is diverse, and only in recent years have various terms and smaller projects (consensus conferences and reduction in practice variations, clinical governance, technology assessment, clinical audit, evidence-based medicine) rhetorically and organisationally come to unite as 'evidence-based medicine'. In Scotland, the Scottish Intercollegiate Guidelines Network (SIGN) focused on developing and diffusing best practice through a professional-dominated system that would be entrenched in Scotland's White Paper. In England, the government and Department of Health faced no such existing encompassing organised infrastructure of elite professionals engaged in quality improvement. The English White Paper adopted most forms of quality improvement in one way or another, including technology assessment in the form of NICE, but the two key groups empowered by the changes were not so much from health elites as from broader groups represented across British public administration (Department of Health 1998a). These winners were the groups able to articulate regulatory arguments and produce information useful for regulation: specialists in the collection and analysis of data, and auditors (or inspectors).

Data collection came in the form of extensive reporting requirements to the Department of Health that were expected, eventually, to allow the centre to understand the quality of medicine it funded. Patterns in clinical outcomes and service use, interpreted by statisticians, would identify problem areas and possible best practice; if the data became good enough, the whole of England could supply a data set to correlate different types of comparable operation with outcomes (0–5). This data collection, as much as finance, gives trusts very confused incentives since they can be coercive and depend on a measure of self-reporting. Schemes for collecting and using clinical data also face tremendous and possibly insuperable difficulties in implementation: medical records are designed (or organically evolve) to serve doctors and nurses working in conditions of uncertainty and time pressure rather than to inform statisticians, and as a result can make very poor data and tools usable at only one site (Berg 1997, especially 109). This focus coincided with the government's interest in ranking hospitals and providing a form of consumer guide, and with improving NHS data technology (as well as furnishing a hardy answer – more, better computers – with a meaningful question).

The other focus of the quality improvement agenda was more successful, in part because it faced fewer short-term technical hurdles. That was the movement for inspection of the clinical and other services of trusts, coupled with national guidelines, and it provided the ideas that created CHI. This policy brought together advocates of reduced practice variations (as CHI was to develop national service frameworks – NSFs – specifying appropriate care); clinical audit (to stabilise quality and level it up); and the development of commensurable ways to understand what hospitals did that could identify problems. These flowed together into CHI, and would (with more invasive powers and responsibilities, and the feared word 'inspection', redolent of schools' tough regime, added) also make CHAI (Klein 2000:210). The core activities of CHI visits to see if the resources, training, and clinicians are providing good care in general, while maintaining a positive relation with the professions. Maintaining a good relationship with medical leaders, and relying on their elites and activists to develop NSFs, of course, is not the same thing as being led by them.

It is hard to generalise about the approximately thirty organisations involved in regulating, inspecting, or trying to influence the activities of trusts and professionals. They range from the relatively friendly approach of the National Patient Safety Agency, which concentrates on trying to persuade, to the relatively tough audit and inspection work of the National Audit Office and Audit Commission, which in their different ways are charged with making sure public money is 'well' spent and which can cause poorly rated managers or organisations real problems, or the classic regulators such as the General Medical Council (concerned with bad doctors). The impetus to create these organisations, however, is essentially regulatory. In a system that is now to be composed of trusts in a quasi-market, the use of market mechanisms and the lack of management mechanisms in theory both call for regulatory agencies. Most markets do, after all, contain low-price, low-quality producers, but the government cannot be thought to permit that in its NHS.

The result was that the new quality improvement mechanisms became a keystone in the new structure of regulation that was to free the government from direct responsibility for running the health service. With quality assured and technology evaluated, the PCTs and trusts could negotiate and contract for best value and not spend on unwise technology or unwittingly purchase bad care. Political control was assured since the new agencies did not set their own priorities. Scotland's quality improvers would point out their independence compared to England (3–13, 3–21).

Some serious problems also arose – problems that regulation could be thought to solve. The problems were major scandals, above all the focusing events in Bristol. Thanks in good part to a campaign by the satirical *Private Eye* it emerged that doctors in Bristol had been performing paediatric heart surgery, with appalling results, and without any supervision that would have caught the misrepresentation of results and overall poor practice. Poetically, the data collectors at the Department of Health, responsible for collecting meaningful data on almost every clinical procedure in order to better control and improve the system, received a whistleblower letter which was filed and not acted upon until after the scandal had emerged (Public Inquiry into Children's Heart Surgery at the Bristol Royal Infirmary 1984–1995, §85). While this might be expected to cast doubt on the strategy of ensuring quality through the central activities of the Department of Health, it was counterbalanced by the ability of advocates of the existing strategy to suggest that the solutions, more information technology, were already in train. There were no available, plausible, policies presented in time to counter the proposals that redoubling effort would work. Reviewing the effects of 'Bristol', a CHI official explained that 'since Bristol – and all you need to say is Bristol, we all know what it means – there has been a real push to improve our quality improvement mechanisms and clinical governance . . . CHI is a key part of this' (0–2). Subsequent scandals, including problems storing corpses at a Bedford hospital and unauthorised organ retention at the Alder Hey hospital in Merseyside, kept the government willing to listen to and enforce solutions suggested by its quality improvers; the government's need for reassurance partly seems to have explained why it chose the head of the Bristol inquiry to head the new CHAI.

In short, England has an important and growing quality improvement regime but its political context has led to the adoption of different policies from the policy stream. While in Scotland the professionals organised themselves before there was a political drive for quality, in England the size and diversity of the health services had prevented any such overall organisation. The Labour government wanted to guarantee quality as part of its self-described campaign to rescue the NHS (especially in the eyes of those voters 'borrowed' from the opposition), and also sought a regulator to decrease the worries that competition would lead to a race to the bottom in quality rather than institutional innovation and improvement. The combination of data collection with the more important CHI/NICE/CHAI regime promised to solve these problems, and was a flexible enough policy to have more political force after scandals emerged.

Conclusion

The core logic of Labour's activity in English health policy is fairly simple. While facing the same problems as Scotland and Wales, England has adopted policies that emerge from the interaction of its policy and political streams rather than the problems themselves; indeed, the political and policy debates explain how problems seen as pressing in Scotland, such as bad diet, are nearly invisible in England. Governing with votes 'borrowed' from the Conservatives, and a determination to be centrist, English Labour makes health policy by using new public management and other tools associated with neoliberalism to 'modernise' a health service enough to convince the public that they should support equal, high-quality public services and the party that produces them. This strategic position in the party system coincides with an English policy stream shaped by management, and to a lesser extent new public management, and which accordingly is more than able to have extensive, sophisticated, valuable debates wholly within the parameters of markets and reliance on management. Advocates of other views are both less appealing to a party that uses the opposition's weapons to hold the opposition's territory, and also have nothing like the dominance in advice, acquiescence, and acceptance that they have in Northern Ireland, Scotland, and Wales. As problems arise these advocates are less likely to make their ideas heard and therefore less likely to see it adopted.

This extends even to involving the private sector, to the outrage of unions (who, like left-wing voters, have nowhere else to go) and trying to increase managerial control over professional autonomy through the new contract – an effort which led to an outraged, overwhelming 'no' vote from doctors. Perhaps the most visible demonstration of the impact of policy communities on agendas, and of England's distinctiveness, lies in the different responses to a 2003 European Court of Justice decision allowing patients to receive treatment anywhere in the EU, thereby opening up the prospect of cross-border patient choice. This decision created great excitement since it has the potential to disrupt the basic control over patients' movements. But the responses to this seemingly objective pressure were very different. In England, this became both another policy sold by advocates of patient choice, diversity, and markets, and via their arguments a problem that needed to be solved (i.e. formalised and integrated into NHS policy). In the rest of the UK, there was silence combined with some planning for an increase in UK patients treated abroad.

English policy outcomes do appear to be divergent because of the interaction of ideas from England's distinctive policy community and the political strategies fitted to its distinctive party system, and the adoptions of different policies reflect the jostling of policy advocates. The policy outcomes also carry on from the pre-devolution legacies, thereby confirming the hypothesis that inherited policy communities matter in shaping post-devolution policy trajectories. English experience since devolution also provides strong, suggestive evidence that the old 'UK' policy community, like the 'UK' departments and 'UK' Parliament, is an English, metropolitan social institution.

Labour in England is working in an environment unlike that of Labour in Scotland or Wales. It must fight a right-wing party in a policy environment shaped by the revolution that party created over two decades. The result is that it accepts broad assumptions of English health policy, such as firm-level thought, and then goes on deliberately to use 'right-wing' policies such as private sector involvement in order to hold territory it took from the Conservatives in 1997 and forge a new pact between all but the most determined Conservative voters and the welfare state. As its chosen mechanism, the English government has repeatedly put its bet on markets.

Note

1 Between 1997 and the start of 2004, officials responsible for local government affairs cycled through membership in the Department for Environment, Transport, and the Regions (DETR), then the Department for Transport, Local Government and the Regions (DTLR), and then the Office of the Deputy Prime Minister (ODPM).

5
Wales: localism

[Welsh Health Minister] Jane Hutt says the patient is a citizen, not a patient or a serial shopper. (National Assembly for Wales policy maker)

Not for the first time, Wales is radical and underreported. While England, Northern Ireland, and Scotland discuss and differ about health services, Wales has tried to change the agenda entirely. England, Northern Ireland, and Scotland are all marking out positions on the best way to run health services through varying mixtures of markets, hierarchies, managers, and professionals. By contrast, Wales has shifted its focus away from squeezing the most out of the health services to changing the social determinants of health and integrating democratic politics and community into the health system to an extent rare among the health systems of the advanced industrial countries. By (low) international and UK comparative standards, Wales is the most likely to have tried to enact in policy the arguments of those who focus on 'health' rather than 'health services' – public health, wider determinants of health, health inequalities, and primary care, rather than health services. To do this, the NHS of Wales is adopting both explicit population health goals (such as the reduction of inequalities and the development of healthier communities) and an organisation that puts the focus on local area service integration with local government in order to produce overall population health. The Welsh bet is on localism.

What caused this to happen? What allowed this agenda, advocated by academics and analysts around the world, but ignored in most systems, actually to become a keystone of policy in one place? Post-devolution health policy in Wales is best explained by the strength on the ground of groups that are relatively weaker in England, Northern Ireland, and Scotland. In Scotland, devolution gave more latitude to the leaders of its health system. These insiders' well-articulated agenda and influence on policy ideas gave Scottish policy its distinctive profile. The same persistence of insiders is even more marked in Northern Ireland, but Northern Irish insiders tend not to advocate major system-wide policy change, and Northern Ireland's politicians, when they have the opportunity, do not do so either.

In Wales, however, the insiders were relatively weak and fragmented and the way was clear for the entrance of new groups into health policy. Wales is not well endowed with medical elites, a strong and articulate management or academic management studies infrastructure, or the officials, business-people, and advocates who sustain market reforms. In the breach, groups that are marginal elsewhere exercise much more influence in the policy community and over the flow of ideas. Local government, advocates of primary care, and advocates of new public health all have much more influence in the policy communities of Wales and are more likely to make their ideas heard and influence the perception of costs and benefits of policies. Wales before devolution was a case of permissive managerialism, in which the permissive structure had long permitted an unusual and precocious managerial focus on local population health. Wales after devolution pursued a localist health policy, which coincided in much of its logic with the policies of its past but which varied dramatically in style. In the replacement of insiders and per-missive managerialism with new policy advocates and localism, Wales might be the system in which the democratising effects of devolution mattered most.

Inheritance

Wales presents a very different political landscape from England or Scotland. It is historically a highlands country. The same inaccessible hills that have allowed the Welsh to preserve their distinctiveness have also made it difficult for them to build strong economies or institutions of politics and civil society. The casual traveller, crossing in and out of Wales by train (its rail network, such as it is, radiates from Shrewsbury in England), cannot but notice from the window of a train crossing the border that the beautiful and often forbid-ding green hills are Welsh while the accessible, fertile plains historically worth conquering are English. Liverpool in the North and Bristol in the South long dominated much of Welsh life, but are both in England, and English. Wales's land and location made it fragmented yet distinct, preserving its nationhood while never developing a single core area that could build the nation. This dif-ference from the national histories of other parts of Europe explains how major works on Welsh identity can combine the certainty of national identity with fundamental questions about its meaning: consider the titles of major public intellectuals' books about Welsh national identity such as *Wales! Wales?* or *When Was Wales?* (Smith 1984; Williams 1985).

Scotland's central belt is a densely populated, economically and socially vigorous centre for most of Scotland's population, and therefore a geopolitical, cultural, economic and social base for an independent civil society, and a coherent state until 1707. Wales, by contrast, is gifted with almost too many small population and urban centres for state formation or geopolitical survival in the high-pressure environment of medieval and early modern Europe. Over the country's history, it has been dominated by Glamorgan, Gwynedd, Anglesey, Pembrokeshire, Carmarthenshire, and the North East; each of these areas was able to build enough economic and social strength to assume a leading role in Welsh life at some point but none could ever come to dominate in the way the South East came to dominate the development of England or the central belt the development of Scotland. With no such centre, it was hard to organise Welsh society or defend it against the English crown, which subjugated it centuries ago. The problem, as John Davies puts it, 'was not so much too many mountains as too many plains' (Davies 1993:97–8). Only since the explosive nineteenth-century growth of Glamorgan and South Wales and the decline of rural areas and the North has the country developed a firm centre of population and cities that dominate its civil society.

Even South Wales was not without its own rise and decline. Once it had some of the great nineteenth-century boom towns. American-style histories of resource booms created such Valleys towns such as Pontypridd and Merthyr Tydfil, and the ports and steel towns such as Llanelli and Newport. Like many other great nineteenth-century boom towns around the world, they descended into incredible economic breakdowns in the first half of the twentieth century and now live on with little of their old, extraordinary vitality. Cardiff and Swansea's growth in the nineteenth century meant Bristol no longer dominated the South as Liverpool dominated the North. Cardiff was first dubbed Wales' metropolis in 1873 and much later emerged as Wales' capital in the 1960s when the Welsh Office moved there (Davies 1993:439). The placement of the capital in Cardiff, replacing the city's declining industrial and port economy with a public sector one, opened up new gaps between Cardiff and the rest of South Wales without closing the gaps between South Wales and the rest of the country. The undeniable shift of the population to an English-speaking, industrial existence in South Wales, in a country with wide cultural and socio-economic variation, has led to fierce polemics about Welshness. Each part of Wales has its own model of its identity, from the English-speaking, industrial culture of the valleys to the Welsh-speaking farms and quarry towns of the North, with all manner of variations in between.

The consequence of this historic fragmentation and inability to assemble a counterweight to the sheer scale of England was a Wales with a much weaker set of 'Welsh' organisations. Wales has historically been, and for many purposes still is, part of a unit called 'England and Wales' (for a useful history of its

administrative status to 1980, see Foulkes, Jones, and Wilford 1983) Its educational system, professional structures, legal system, and media have been
mostly part of a larger arena dominated by England. Westminster passed no
Wales-specific legislation between the seventeenth century (when Wales lost its
separate structures of government) and a ban on Sunday pub openings in
Wales passed in 1881. In policy terms, the result is a smaller set of inherited
policy communities and insiders compared to Scotland, and consequently
more room for changes in their composition. There are no Welsh royal colleges of medicine; Wales depends on the London-based Royal Colleges, which
are not known for sensitivity to Welsh politics or agendas. Likewise, despite
the honourable history of the University of Wales, Welsh academia is broadly
similar to and integrated with English academia (Morgan 1995:31–2). Given
this lack of high-profile, articulate, and regional organisations, Welsh policies
are less dominated by them and offer more openings to more diffuse and
lower-status groups such as local government.

Political autonomy, as territorial offices hint and devolved administrations
show, breeds an autonomous set of policy communities (Keating and
Loughlin 2002). Such policy communities must nevertheless be built on a
social base, and Wales lacks much of the social bases of the policy communities in England and Scotland – above all the professional elites, management
cadres, professional policy analysts, corps of civil servants, and university-
based experts. As a consequence, the bases of Welsh policy communities
differ, reflecting a Welsh history of powerful grassroots distinctiveness and
weak Wales-wide organisations and spokespeople.

Territorial office politics

From the late nineteenth century, when activists set to work creating a
modern civil society across fragmented Wales, the country entered a slow, but
clear, virtuous circle. Greater willingness to assert distinctive Welsh interests
and identity as a nation on a par with others eased the construction of more
durable political and social institutions, which in turn reinforced the distinctiveness of Welsh interests and identity. Starting from a well-known identity
and basic social differences from England (such as the language and
entrenched nonconformism), over a century the Welsh through determined
collective action built institutions that identified and nurtured clear Welsh traditions in an increasingly large number of activities. As there came to be more
freestanding Welsh institutions on a par with England, they could form the
base for yet further expressions and mobilisation of Welsh distinctiveness. One
such institution was the creation of a Welsh Office.

The idea of a Welsh Office had long floated around in Labour politics for decades but had not prospered. Herbert Morrison argued in 1946 that 'Wales could not carry a cadre of officials of the highest calibre and the services of English high officials would no longer be available' (Morgan 1981:377), while Aneurin Bevan famously asked whether sheep were different on different sides of the Welsh border (Morgan 1995:451–2). In 1964 Welsh activism and political mobilisation within Labour finally had institutional impact when the incoming government of Harold Wilson fulfilled its manifesto commitment to create a Welsh Office in Cardiff, under its principal advocate, the elder Labour statesman James Griffiths. To the extent that there had been Welsh administrations before, they were not clearly Welsh; during the Second World War the home for the department with Welsh education responsibilities was Bournemouth (Evans 2000:121). Minister of Housing and diarist Richard Crossman was sour about the development: 'Another equally idiotic creation is the Department for Wales [sic], a completely artificial new office for Jim Griffiths and his two Parliamentary Secretaries, all the result of a silly election pledge' (Crossman 1975:117). Wales Office competencies were wide but initially mostly confined to 'oversight' rather than responsibility for powers. Whitehall departments initially remained the key players in Welsh public policy and viewed the new office with suspicion (Deacon 2002:22–5).

The creation of the new office proved fortuitous for the government, which almost from then found itself facing increasing Welsh national mobilisation. Welsh language activism (spearheaded by the Welsh Language Society, founded 1962) and a reinvigorated Welsh nationalism (led by the nationalist party Plaid Cymru) put the existing settlement under increasing pressure throughout the 1960s (McAllister 2001). The victory of Plaid Cymru's Gwynfor Evans in a 1966 Carmarthen by-election was a shock to the whole UK political system (Morgan 1981:376–400). Years before the SNP made its modern breakthrough in 1968, the Welsh nationalists had won a Westminster seat and shaken Welsh and UK politics.

This direct nationalist threat led to Labour proposing devolution for Wales as well as Scotland in 1979. If in Scotland the referendum failure was a hard-fought battle (inside Labour as well), in Wales it was a rout for devolution (Jones 1983; Jones and Wilford 1983). The comparatively devolutionist North West – Gwynedd – mustered 21.8 per cent in favour. The least enthusiastic region, Gwent in the South East, voted only 6.7 per cent in favour. Wales overall voted 11.8 per cent yes and 46.5 per cent no (Jones and Wilford 1983:138–9). The reason, in good part, lay in the structural weakness of Welsh national mobilisation. Wales lacks a strong, mobilised set of regional organisations that are a natural, powerful, constituency for autonomy, as in Scotland. Welsh national movements, and their avatar Plaid Cymru, have historically been hampered by reliance on Welsh-speaking rural areas and difficulties in the vote-rich Labour heartlands of the South.

Almost twenty years of Conservative rule, unpopular in Wales, then shifted the balance in favour of devolution as much as in Scotland. Support for devolution jumped in every region of Wales, sometimes by almost 40 per cent from 1979 to 1997 (Balsom 2000:153, 159), but the inherent problems of resource mobilisation in a country with a weaker civil society remained and continued to restrict Welsh devolutionist movements relative to Scotland. When Labour returned to office in 1997, once again committed to devolution for Scotland and Wales, the 'yes' campaign in Scotland was powerful and almost unopposed while the 'yes' vote in Wales was in danger until the very last minute, when pre-dawn returns from the last district, Carmarthen, gave supporters of devolution a victory by a tiny margin (Andrews 1999; Jones and Balsom 2000). The final vote totals were very close, and put a question mark over the new National Assembly for Wales (NAW): 559,419 votes in favour (50.3 per cent) versus 552,698 votes against (48.7 per cent) (Balsom 2000:153).

The Welsh Office therefore remained the centre of Welsh politics, policy, and administration until 1997 (the literature on it is small: see Thomas 1987; Griffiths, D. 1996; Deacon 2002). Unlike its Northern Irish or Scottish predecessors, it had to hew a distinctive Welsh policy arena out of the unified England and Wales organisations, policy regimes, and Whitehall departments responsible for policy until its creation. The substantial institutional and policy inheritance from the days of Welsh administrative unity with England naturally limited its ability to promote change. If the Scottish Office gained powers as the UK welfare state expanded, building itself into the governance of Scotland as the welfare state grew, the Welsh Office by contrast assumed powers and oversaw differentiated policy as the welfare state underwent its ordinary legislative modifications. This meant it collected regional offices that traditionally looked to London and lacked any habit of policy making or coordination between themselves (Rose 1987:162–3). What the Welsh Office did successfully do was acquire powers over an increasingly large number of areas and deepen them over time (Deacon 2002:37–8). This included the 1968 transfer of health and 1974 absorption of the Welsh Hospital Board, which was the first big spending policy area that the Welsh Office gained and which by the time of devolution had enjoyed the most time to diverge. The Welsh Office staffing figures showed the change; its civil service (excluding health service employees and similar workers) jumped from 225 in 1965 to 2,035 in 1997 (Deacon 2002:109).

However, the Welsh Office was still a small and politically weak department that ranked poorly in the Whitehall village. Its junior ministers were only rarely promoted, and its Secretaries of State rarely went on to another Cabinet post, making the Welsh Office resemble an apprenticeship programme with no job at the end (Deacon 2002:46–52). It was relatively weak in the number of high-level civil servants in its various functional areas (see Table 4.3). Even given that the Welsh Office was more policy-focused than some of the big spending departments in Whitehall, its staff were still junior and spread across more areas of responsibility than their colleagues in Whitehall. It rarely had a bill and instead was challenged mostly to produce secondary legislation (Griffiths 1996:163; Deacon 2002:5–9).[1] 'In implementation it was no better or worse than any other Whitehall department – it was a perfectly good administrative machine but had no tradition of policy formulation or analysis' said a NAW adviser (4–6). 'They assigned [a civil servant] to make sure we didn't do anything too creative' remarked a health reformer in management (4–16).

The Welsh Office excelled in three, low-status but vital aspects of Whitehall activity. First, it prevented political and policy problems through occasional interventions (to support industry, for example). Second, it lobbied Whitehall and Westminster; one of the first achievements the new Secretary of State for Wales claimed was the relocation of the Royal Mint to South Wales (Morgan 1981:389). Third, it changed policy at the margins so that it would work better in Wales. The result was a form of permissive managerialism that put the emphasis on stability and permitted considerable autonomy to its managers so long as they minimised visible problems. Its legacies – a largely unmanaged system and weak policy formulation capacity – would shape the policy community and potentials of the National Assembly for Wales.

Organisational distinctiveness

The result of this comparatively late administrative delegation to the Welsh Office, and the lack of impetus or capacity for policy formation, was that there was limited organisational distinctiveness in Welsh health care. In the multi-tiered 1974 organisation, the Welsh Office had the functions of the regions in England, in much the same way that the Scottish Office took on the functions of a region in Scotland. The organisational outline, however, was the same. The Secretary of State for Wales, like his counterparts in Northern Ireland and Scotland, signed *Working for Patients* (Secretaries of State for Health; Wales; Northern Ireland; and Scotland 1989). The Welsh Office did implement the internal market, converting district health authorities into purchasers who sought acute services from trusts, while there was a much weaker move to fundholding than in England.

The real distinctiveness of the Welsh health service lay in its development of a managerial policy orientation and capacity that had no equivalent in the rest of the UK. Permissive managerialism allowed quite a striking policy orientation in Wales. This was an unusual degree of attention to service integration and the determinants of health outcomes – so unusual that it stood out in the UK of the 1980s. Encapsulated in a document titled *Strategic Intent and Direction for the NHS in Wales*, this focus on improved health gain ('to add years to life, and life to years') (Welsh Office, Welsh Health Planning Forum, 1989) was possible for two reasons.

The first was the near-total lack of interest in the topic in Westminster and Whitehall and the Welsh Office's weak capacity to control its managers. The combination gave both Secretaries of State with an interest and managers with an agenda room to move. It had already led to divergence in the form of the 1982 All-Wales Strategy for People with Mental Handicap, which was driven by an interested Secretary of State for Wales. This set nationally determined outputs for mental health services and demanded public involvement while bringing in large sums of money for schemes that could show they were genuine examples of service integration between local government and health.

The other reason for a focus on improved health gain was stability in lower cadres and the unusual, leadership-inspired, health gains focus of the senior officers in the Welsh health service (4–3, 4–5, 4–6, 4–14, 4–16). The 1983 Griffiths letter and the consequent introduction of a managerial cadre in Welsh health services had dramatically different effects from those the Thatcher government expected. In the case of Wales it meant that the Welsh health service management cadre could be developed by an enterprising group (led by John Wyn Owen, head of the NHS Wales) who built institutional bases outside Welsh Office direct control (including an agency called the Welsh Health Common Services Agency, WHSCA, which centralised functions such as purchasing and thereby offered a resource-rich, autonomous, central, management platform from which to effect change). This movement, the most prominent Welsh divergence, culminated in the *Strategic Intent and Direction* and its organisational embodiment, the Welsh Health Planning Forum (protagonists discuss it in Longley and Warner 1999; Wyn Owen 2000). In 1996, just before the appointment of John Redwood as Secretary of State, the National Audit Office (NAO) reviewed the project. Recognising that seven years was too soon to see health impacts, the NAO report examined the extent to which the *Strategic Intent and Direction* had changed planning and service delivery. It found that most of the hospitals and about half the GPs had made changes, especially to planning, even if the impact on service delivery was less striking (National Audit Office 1996). In the context of the 1980s, this was dramatic and dramatically different from the policies pursued in the rest of the country. With the Welsh Office largely interested in preventing unusual headlines or disruptions and the management corps relatively new and unified by this agenda, it was possible to implement the strategies. Over time these strategies and the leadership style of the management cadre brought in during the 1980s created a legacy of joint working in Wales. With that legacy came a slow increase in the ability of many professionals and managers to imagine health as an outcome to which health services contribute, rather than health as a product of the health services.

The implementation of the *Strategic Intent and Direction*, then, in a part of the UK accustomed more to vague oversight than to policy change and implementation, fixed core ideas and perspectives in parts of the Welsh management, public health, and academic health communities. One member of this group, still working in Wales, commented in late 2002 that the implementation was so effective that Wales still has what he called a 'Japanese soldier in the jungle' phenomenon (4–16). Referring to the tales of Japanese soldiers on isolated Pacific islands who continued to fight the Second World War for decades after 1945, he explained that the strategies were sufficiently popular and well-implemented that even after a decade of changes in the Welsh health services he could still find administrators and professionals who thought the strategies were still the basis of Welsh health services. Many interviewees asserted that their perceptions of the feasibility, costs, and benefits of public health and service integration were more positive than those of their counterparts elsewhere because of their experiences with the Planning Forum ('which provided all the partners with a common language'; 4–5) and the associated policies, sometimes dating back to the 1982 mental health strategy. The Welsh policy community developed different perceptions of costs, benefits, and feasibility.

Welsh divergence might have been most marked by the development of this focus on service integration and public health. The true political autonomy of undevolved Wales was most tested by an unlikely figure, John Redwood MP. Redwood, the Wokingham (Berkshire) MP and a leader of the Conservative party right wing was Secretary for State for Wales from 1993 to 1995. Redwood achieved notoriety in Wales for some policies that reflected his faith in capitalism and a smaller government, as well as his enthusiastic Unionism. Reasoning that Wales faced the same policy problems as elsewhere, he stressed that UK, rather than Welsh, policies explained successes in Wales, and made Unionist gestures such as refusing to allow the Welsh development office in Brussels to fly the Welsh flag (Deacon 2002:32–3). Redwood also won lasting fame (notoriety in much of Wales) for returning underspend monies to the Treasury in 1996. This decision, like many others, was in keeping with credible Conservative party views but played very badly in Wales (Deacon 2002:33).

Redwood, sensing and sharing public impatience with managers, publicly set out to reduce their role. He dramatically, efficiently, and with little public support reorganised Welsh local government into twenty-two unitary authorities, producing a map without the problems of his English counterparts but leaving many of his enemies in Welsh local government convinced that the map he created was designed to destroy local government (Deacon 1997). In health, Redwood reorganised the service into five large health authorities in 1995. He abolished WHCSA on the grounds that 'I didn't see why they should be employing economists'. Rather than economists, or WHCSA ('a supply depot' he called it in a 2003 interview), he focused on trying to communicate with ordinary people. This meant efforts to manage 'by walking around', such as asking residents of Merthyr Tydfil whether they wanted to keep their hospital and deciding to keep it on that basis (and thereby winning positive notice from a usually hostile Welsh press that had seen his English colleague in the Department of Health closing hospitals). When Redwood was asked in 2002 how often his policies led him to pay a price in the UK government, he said he only suffered when he tried to use his Wales experiences in issues such as hospital closures to argue for specific policies, such as keeping small hospitals open, in the rest of the UK (4–17). Within Wales, however, Redwood's policies dealt a powerful blow to the organisations that had produced the *Strategic Intent and Direction* and begun to implement it. The cadres moved on to other jobs but remained part of the policy community with those who had been involved as part of the NHS.

When Labour came to power in 1997 Wales received its first independent White Paper on the NHS. *Putting Patients First* (Welsh Office 1998b) shared many aspects of organisational design – above all a teleology of commissioning between trusts – with the English White Paper. Thus *Putting Patients First* shared with England a focus on the development of primary care groups (in Wales, local health groups) as commissioning vehicles with a local remit. Within this broad pragmatism, Wales varied in its increased localism and shift away from a focus on health services. The White Paper made all the local health groups conterminous with local government and instructed them to work with local government in designing services and commissioning. It also, when taken with the equivalent public health White Paper (Welsh Office 1998a), made it clear that Welsh divergence from the other UK systems would lie in its demand for integration between the NHS and other services and a local population focus. Simply, to the rhetoric about this point that all the White Papers employed, the Welsh policy makers added marginal organisational design changes intended to produce more localism and integration between services.

Summary

Welsh health policy before devolution was in many ways driven by the same high-profile policy goals as England, but its implementation was far less supervised and very different. Its new cadre of specialised managers turned out to be dominated for the first ten years by advocates of service integration rather than managerial oversight. Top-down management was not the style of the Welsh Office, which was called upon primarily to avoid problematic headlines by both easing the implementation of UK policies and by smoothing relations with managers. Rather than try to impose policies, diverge from English policy, or engage in performance management, the Welsh Office concentrated on avoiding problems.

Welsh health politics and administration was less pressured than its equivalents in England (where top-down management was accompanied by real top-down coercion) or in Scotland (where clinical technocrats often tried to enforce their views through the professional organisations or the Scottish Office). The unusual alignment of Welsh health policy meant that there was more of a predisposition to service integration and new public health concerns than seen in other parts of the UK (Hunter and Wistow 1987). Among the small Welsh policy community, much of which was in the civil service, management corps, or the few academics associated with the Welsh health service, there was a much stronger tradition of local joint working. The resulting policy community was able to suggest and design a set of health policies for the National Assembly that not only varied from the rest of the UK but even inverted its agenda, turning overall population health promotion and localism into the centre rather than a rhetorical ornament.

Policies and politics

The distinctive features of Wales are its party system, which pits left Welsh Unionist Labour against a farther left, more nationalist Plaid Cymru in a way similar to Scotland; and its institutions, which directly and indirectly constrain the National Assembly. These features shape the Welsh political community. On the one hand, there is incentive for Wales to be distinctive and to the left of England, and on the other hand, there are great difficulties in developing and implementing innovative policies because of an overall legal position that constrains the National Assembly's autonomy, internal structures that muffle partisan competition, and a civil service unprepared for the demands now made on it.

The policy community

One major source of health policy 'insiders' is in the elites of clinical medicine and research. In Wales, compared to England or Scotland, these elites are poorly organised to affect Welsh policy. Scotland has its own Royal Colleges. Wales shares all of them with England – and some have very weak infrastructure in Wales: one manager sighed that 'they think that we're close enough that they can come out from London for the day' (4–22), while a NAW interviewee said that 'they are weakly organised here, and seem to be a force for reaction' (4–6) (see also Table 2.4). The insider clinical and medical research elites are also less numerous and important in the operation of the medical system. Wales has fewer universities than England or Scotland and only one full-scale high-level academic medical centre (in Cardiff). The Welsh academic health policy community is small; it is possible for the National Assembly to occupy nearly every important academic working on health policy. 'It's not our traditional orientation but now everybody's pitching in' explained one senior Welsh medical academic in November 2003. Small numbers and poor organisation mean that clinical medical elites have trouble mobilising the advice, acquiescence, and approval that would give them the ability intellectually to direct and influence policy streams.

Politics abhors a vacuum. Without well-organised clinical elites, a powerful academic and think-tank network, or an entrenched focus on management and markets, the Welsh policy community is more open to groups whose low status excludes them from a decisive role in the health politics of other areas. The most important such group is local government. Local governments' role in the Welsh Labour party is difficult to overstate; it is the school for its politicians, the core of its local organisation, and provides the local base for its politicians while enjoying, in many areas, intense symbolic power as a long-term Labour bastion (Tanner, Williams, and Hopkin 2000; see especially Williams 2000 for the origins and mythology). Local governments throughout the UK are interested in having some say in health services, but in Wales the promise of improved service coordination combined with local governments' power of approval are enough to bring health services within reach. When the chair of a local health board in South Wales was asked why local government would want to be involved in health services, he smiled and made an expansive gesture: 'It's the keys to the castle!'(4–19). A second important group, which is more powerful than elsewhere because of its role in the Labour party, is the trades union movement. The trades unions in Wales are better linked with the Labour party in the heartland Labour areas where they play a major role in the internal politics of constituencies and the party organisation, and where there is little electoral gain to taking on unions (as in parts of England).

Better Health, Better Wales, the 1997 White Paper on health, made it clear that the Welsh health system would be expected to work towards the target of improved population health and do so with help from local partners. *Putting Patients First* and *Better Health, Better Wales* both built in localism and focused on the wider determinants of health (Welsh Office 1998a, 1998b). This was easy to miss amidst the general pragmatic tone of the 1997 health papers, but it reflected the structure of the Welsh health policy community charged with designing detailed policy and implementing it. The interlocutors of the Welsh Office – the management cadre, the academics, and the professionals on the ground – had all been working within, and were shaped by, over a decade of Welsh population health strategies before the Redwood interlude. Even if the direct legacies of the movement leading up to the *Strategic Intent and Direction* had been eroded by turnover and reorganisation, that situation could be counterbalanced by the strength of other groups involved in local population health strategies: groups that lacked influence in a UK government but were strong in the new Welsh health policy arena relative to their rivals. Most of the policies being sold were and are localist and focused on population health outcomes.

Politics: the institutions

The ability of Wales to take its own path is circumscribed by its particular, constrained constitution, its unusual legislative politics, and its problems with implementation (for analyses, see Rawlings 1999, 2003; Burrows 2000; Patchett 2000). The National Assembly for Wales is basically a fairly common type of regional government, with administrative autonomy but weak legislative powers akin to those of French or 1980s Spanish regions. Like the Scottish Parliament, it inherited its basic powers from the Secretary of State for Wales and the Welsh Office. The autonomy it inherited, however, was far more circumscribed. The major legal difference is that Wales, unlike Northern Ireland or Scotland, does not have primary legislative powers. Instead, it has secondary legislative powers. While these powers tend to be about implementation, they are specified in the Westminster primary legislation and their scope correspondingly varies widely. Secondary legislation, and the National Assembly powers, can be circumscribed into almost nothing or given wide latitude by broadly written Westminster legislation. Legislative changes must gain the support of the Secretary of State for Wales, a UK Cabinet minister not responsible to the National Assembly. Then they must gain the parliamentary time necessary to be enacted.

The structure of the Welsh settlement both exacerbated the problems this design caused and flatly limited the National Assembly's powers. The

Scotland Act's list of powers was a negative list – it specified the (considerable) powers of Westminster and then left any other powers, including 'new'
powers, to the Scottish Parliament. By contrast, the Wales Act 1998 specified
Welsh powers in great detail. To do more would take Westminster legislation
(Rawlings 1999; Patchett 2000). The result is that Wales has a roving veto
player, in the shape of the Secretary of State, who is capable of vetoing
changes that happen to require primary rather than secondary legislation as
specified in primary legislation. Even under the most harmonious of circumstances the National Assembly, when it wants primary legislation, must
compete for time in Parliament with English initiatives that are much more
likely to win votes for the UK government. The National Assembly, seeking
more autonomy, therefore convened a commission to investigate the need for
greater powers (known as the Richard Commission after its chair, Ivor
Richard) (Hazell 2003b; Osmond 2003) and in the mean time tried to reg-
ularise its relations with Westminster (Patchett 2002).

   Like the Scottish Parliament, the National Assembly for Wales is elected
by a mixture of constituency first-past-the-post voting and regional proportional representation seats (of the total of sixty seats, twenty are elected in the
five proportional representation regions). This increases the representation of
smaller parties; while Labour dominates the constituency seats (and the first-
past-the-post Westminster seats) in Wales, the smaller parties can capture list
votes (Table 5.1).

   The National Assembly is also an unusual experiment in government – a
sort of hybrid between British local government structures on the one hand
and a typical legislature on the other. Unlike the Scottish Parliament or
Westminster, which are fairly typical parliaments with a government commanding a majority and an opposition party, the National Assembly is a 'corporate body'. In this model of government, legitimised by its use in UK local

Table 5.1. Electoral results for the National Assembly for Wales,
1999 and 2003

	1999	2003
Conservatives	9 (1/8)	11 (1/10)
Liberal Democrats	6 (3/3)	6 (3/3)
Labour	28 (27/1)	30 (30/0)
Plaid Cymru	17 (9/8)	12 (5/7)

Notes: The first number in parenthesis is the total of constituency seats; the second is
the total of regional list seats. In 2003 one ex-Labour independent, John Marek AM
of Wrexham, won a constituency seat.
   Sources: Osmond, 2000; Constitution Unit and Institute of Welsh Affairs, 2003.

governments, the main decisions are made by and in the name of the whole, with a great deal of policy work done in committees, such as that responsible for health and social services, and the ministers responsible for departments sitting as members of the committees. The ideal was that it would promote cross-party working and pragmatic, cooperative politics rather than partisanship. It did not fare well (Rawlings 2003).

The problems with such a structure quickly outweighed the benefits of its resonance. Almost immediately, it came under pressure from many politicians' preference for a clear-cut Westminster-style model. As a result, there has been a steady shift to terms reminiscent of a government; for example, the use of the title 'First Minister' (which is the same as 'Prime Minister' in Welsh) to describe the head of what came to be known, after some changes, as the Welsh Assembly Government. It also suffered under the strain of hiding partisan differences. Working as a corporate body allows the government to present its decisions as unanimous and still take partisan credit, while trapping opposition and coalition partners alike. In the Health and Social Services Committee, for example, minutes tended not to record the party of the Assembly Member (AM) who made a point, thereby effectively muzzling any party's objections to a policy (4–15). It became difficult to identify the sources of a policy or of opposition to the policy. Politicians inside and outside government found that the corporate body structure muddied accountability and visibility in a way they did not like. The result was the slow, systematic erosion of the corporate structure and increasingly prominent party divides reflected in practice.

There is a second, less predictable, choke-point in Welsh policy making, namely the policy development and implementation capacity of the civil service. The Welsh Office from which the National Assembly for Wales inherited its policy capacity had been little used to making policy and was never engaged in serious policy divergence across all fronts (Griffiths 1996; cf. Deacon 2002). This meant that it was more suited, culturally and in staffing terms, to a relaxed administrative and firefighting role. After devolution, though, the National Assembly began to formulate and demand real change across a variety of policy fields and the burdens on the Welsh civil service began to show. The civil service was understaffed relative to its new roles, and the successive Welsh leaders' determination to avoid the negative publicity of increasing the headcount in the bureaucracy meant that it was difficult to hire more civil servants. To some extent this lack of sheer capacity could be remedied by building in parts of the public administration that had not been part of the Welsh Office; the Health Promotion Authority for Wales, a quango, was merged into the Welsh Assembly Government's health team – with the result that the National Assembly civil service had a new infusion of dedicated advocates of population health and new public health ideas. Reshuffles at top ranks, meanwhile, were in part attempts to create a culture of policy formulation and delivery rather than administration and coincided with a worrisome series of appointments process problems. The speed of policy work in Wales slowed markedly. The mechanics of health services organisation took a long time to work out, while work in more peripheral policy areas virtually ground to a halt, with no medical research strategy for the first five years of devolved Wales (4–7) – and this was despite the intense workloads of many civil servants.

Politics: the party system

Wales has a long history of overwhelming votes for a particular party – enthusiasms not often shared by England. Wales since the initiation of modern democratic politics was at first a bastion of the Liberal party, and subsequently shifted to support Labour (Field 1997). At its 1906 peak, the Liberal Party won thirty-four of Wales' thirty-five seats, with the only other seat held by Keir Hardie, Britain's first Labour MP and still connected to the Liberals (Morgan 1995:60). Since the nineteenth century the bulk of the Welsh population has lived in South Wales, above all Glamorgan, where it was attracted by the tin, coal, steel, and transport booms of the nineteenth and early twentieth centuries. This industrial heritage created not only many of the population centres of modern Wales (catapulting towns such as Cardiff, Newport, Neath, and Merthyr Tydfil from insignificance to major urban status), it also created a powerful and solid working class in the area. The new towns of industrial South Wales, built around one or two industries, owned by a few who employed many in often appalling conditions, were almost tailor-made for the development of a strong labour movement (Morgan 1981:59–90; Davies 1993:398–509; Lewis 2000). Such a movement did grow, developing a strong tradition of community organisation and self-help (Thompson 2003) as well as strong leftist politics. The working classes of South Wales were the first to abandon the broad Liberal coalition and elect the Scot Keir Hardie, for Merthyr Tydfil, in a 1900 'psephological accident' that accurately anticipated the future – and gave Labour a Westminster seat it would not lose again (Hopkin 2000:57). Wales went on to produce some legendary Labour politicians and even local governments (such as Merthyr Tydfil, which kept school places mostly free during the 1930s depression, or Bedwellty, whose councillors were suspended in the 1930s for spending more on poor relief than the Ministry of Health permitted: Morgan 1981:236).[2] Further east, the voters of Ebbw Vale elected the Labour hero Aneurin Bevan, who was the Minister of Health in the 1945 Attlee government that created the NHS across England, Scotland, and Wales.[3]

To this day, Wales has large swathes of Labour territory and its Westminster delegation, aided by the first-past-the-post electoral system, is almost overwhelmingly Labour. In South Wales, the party also historically has dominated the local governments, and apart from redoubts such as Plaid Cymru-leaning Gwynedd and Liberal-tending border areas, Labour is the strongest party. This long-term historic dominance also gave Labour the other characteristics of locally dominant parties, some of them undesirable (cf. Key 1950). Charges of factionalism, incompetence, and poor administration swirl around local governments that Labour has dominated for decades (memorably, in 2002 the Merthyr Tydfil Council neglected to fill out the form needed to be properly constituted and narrowly escaped having to hold new council elections; 'Blunder sees whole council disbarred', BBC Online 20 February 2002). The safety of many Welsh parliamentary seats, meanwhile, is a standing temptation to select MPs by factionalism, parachutes of loyalists from headquarters, or time served in Labour. Local government is consequently very well connected with the Welsh Labour leadership. In longstanding Labour areas – with firm Labour control over local government, the Westminster seat, and the National Assembly seat – there are often close connections between the small number of politicians who dominate the area. The Welsh Local Government Association and the biggest trades unions are some of the strongest interest groups in the new Wales and much stronger than their siblings in the rest of the UK. The local authorities also face a government that has relatively little electoral need to distance itself from local government.

The main opposition to Labour is Plaid Cymru, the Party of Wales (the English descriptive clause was added to improve the party's relations with anglophones). The Welsh and Scottish party systems thus resemble each other in their basic faultline. Rather than being predominantly left–right conflicts, they combine a conflict between the centre-left and the left with a conflict between devolutionists proud of their national identity and nationalists interested in significantly increasing their political autonomy. Plaid Cymru's base lies in rural, Welsh-speaking areas such as Gwynedd, but it has made successful forays into Labour heartlands, memorably capturing valleys Labour heartlands such as Rhondda Cynon Taff local authority. This means Labour's incentive is to pursue, at least occasionally, policies that are distinctively Welsh and free it from the tag of being dominated by Westminster, and to pursue policies that respond to Plaid Cymru's challenge on its left.

The other parties – the Liberal Democrats and the Conservatives – are much smaller and more erratic. The Conservatives, as in Scotland, survive predominantly because of proportional representation in the Assembly, and the Liberal Democrats because of their strong electoral bases in areas such as thinly populated mid-Wales. The Liberal Democrats are centre-left like

Labour and have been devolutionist for over a century. This cluster of parties on the devolutionist/nationalist and left/centre-left ends of the Welsh party space is of a piece with the Conservatives' weakness. Wales, like Scotland, really has no competitive right-wing party and governments therefore face little or no threat from the right; Plaid Cymru and Labour are the key parties, and the Liberal Democrats the occasional coalition makers.

As a consequence, Welsh Labour politicians have a positive incentive to favour policies that are to the left of England and to make this known strategically at times. There appears to be relatively little support for the Conservative policies, or the more rightist politics associated with them. This alone would predict Welsh policies to the left of England. Furthermore, as in Scotland, Welsh politics values Welshness. Labour and the Liberal Democrats, particularly, are vulnerable to accusations of not fighting hard enough for Wales. As First Minister Rhodri Morgan put it – to known irritation in London – Wales will put 'clear red water' between a leftward-trending Wales and a rightward-trending England (Constitution Unit and Institute of Welsh Affairs 2003:3).

The first Assembly

Welsh politics combines a party system that promotes distinctiveness and a degree of leftism relative to England as well as institutional and organisational weaknesses that make it risky to develop new policies. Combined with the lack of a powerful, pre-existing and self-consciously Welsh set of regional organisations, this means that Wales' start at devolution was rocky.

Welsh devolution was in many ways a creation of the remarkable figure of Ron Davies, a charismatic Welsh Labour politician who had campaigned hard within the party (to persuade it of the merits of devolution), then in Whitehall (to win powers for the new Welsh government), and then in the referendum. Davies, then Secretary of State for Wales, was likely to be the first leader of the new Welsh devolved administration until a strange sex scandal led him to step down from his post and from the race to lead the Labour party in Wales. In what was widely reported as a 'stitch-up', the Labour leadership successfully imposed Alun Michael, an MP for South East Wales, as the new leader (for participants' analyses, see Flynn 1999; Morgan and Mungham 2000). This took place after the constituency candidates had already been selected. As a result, the new prospective leader of Wales had to sit for a less prestigious list seat in a completely different part of Wales (mid-Wales), and narrowly escaped failing to win. The result was an uproar and a First Secretary of the National Assembly widely seen as a stooge of the Labour leadership in London.

These events also appear to have damaged Labour's electoral prospects in

Wales – contrary to expectations, Labour did not win a majority (Mungham 2001; Trystan, Scully, and Jones 2004:4–6).[4] Michael attempted to govern in a minority, forming shifting coalitions with different parties to promote Labour's agenda. Attempting this in an envenomed party atmosphere and a brand new assembly was difficult. The coverage of the new First Secretary was unkind and both public opinion and many articulate parts of the Labour party began to sympathise with his defeated, populist opponent Rhodri Morgan. After an accident-filled nine months (from the May 1999 elections to February 2000), Michael was forced out (and later reappeared as a junior minister in Westminster).

The proximate cause of his departure was intergovernmental relations. Wales was to receive EU regional aid for its large poor areas under Objective One, but the EU funding required matching grants from the state. The Treasury in London and Wales had been arguing for some time about who would provide the matching funds. Michael's inability to win Treasury matching funds gave the opposition the chance to force a vote of no confidence, and with a Labour abstention Michael fell (Osmond 2000:39; Morgan 2003). He resigned as leader of Labour and was replaced quickly by the more popular Rhodri Morgan. This marked a change in a number of ways. Morgan formed a coalition with the Liberal Democrats, thereby stabilising Welsh government. The vote of no confidence also marked a break with the previous reluctance of Plaid Cymru to attack for fear of undermining the infant National Assembly. Finally, the new leadership of Wales had little interest in hewing a line close to that of the UK government. The UK government had done Rhodri Morgan few favours and Morgan, by contrast, had already demonstrated that being distinctively Welsh and to the left was a winning combination within the Welsh Labour party and in the Welsh electorate.

The 2003 National Assembly elections left the Welsh Labour party with a majority of one – it has thirty AMs in a sixty–member Assembly with a voting total of fifty-nine once the (Plaid Cymru) speaker was elected to post and ceased to vote. Three days after the election, First Minister Rhodri Morgan told his party and the BBC that there were going to be limits to family-friendliness in the new Welsh politics: 'Nobody must become ill, you can't go on skiing holidays – nobody must break a leg – you can't get pregnant, you can't be on paternity leave' ('Morgan urges "iron discipline"', BBC Online, 4 May 2003).

Policy outcomes

Welsh health policy outcomes, in the UK context, are coherent and relatively radical. Their coherence reflects the dominant coalition in Welsh health policy communities, which is made up of public health and primary care advocates (in the professions, universities, think-tanks and management corps), local government, and unions, while their radicalism lies in the fact that almost nowhere else are these groups' preferred policies enacted. The story of post-devolution Welsh health policy is of the change that happened when Wales ceased to be harnessed to the policy debates of the very different English political system. Given the different weights of the participants such as market reformers, new public health advocates, and professionalists, it was likely that localist, new public health ideas would appear often and prominently on the agenda, and lead Wales to diverge.

Organisational form

The dominant thrust in post-devolution Welsh health services organisation is localism: the creation of a locally responsible health service that formulates its understanding of needs in local communities and in partnership with local government. This goal, its policy benefits, and its justification in terms of democracy and even socialism, are all focuses of debate in Welsh policy-making circles. The implementation of the localist agenda, however, is producing a very different outcome – centralisation of health services planning and control is as marked an outcome as is delegation of planning and control.

The coalition agreement between Labour and the Liberal Democrats that Morgan signed at the start of his time as First Minister had specifically said that the health services needed some time to settle down and that reorganisation would not happen soon. Relatively quickly, however, Labour reversed course and announced a 'Structural Review of the NHS' that would recommend abolition of health authorities and reform of the rest of the NHS. The Liberal Democrats accepted the breach of the agreement with resignation since Labour seemed bent on it, but were, like many, mystified by the decision.

The new Welsh organisation came into life on 1 April 2003 (Lloyd 2002) (Figure 5.1). It built on the pre-devolution legacy of twenty-two local health groups, each one conterminous with a Welsh unitary local authority. The UK government had made these effectively consultative groups beneath the shadow of the five health authorities created by Redwood. The National Assembly Minister of Health and Social Services, Jane Hutt AM, opted to turn the twenty-two advisory local health groups into twenty-two local health boards (LHBs) with commissioning powers. This meant constructing twenty-two commissioning bodies (for a Welsh population of 2.9 million) with populations ranging from 55,983 (Merthyr Tydfil) to 305,340 (Cardiff), and close connections with (including representation from) local government.

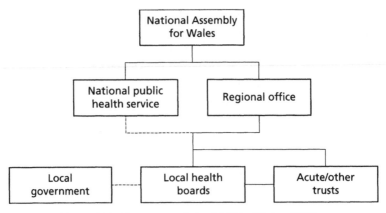

Figure 5.1: Structure of the NHS in Wales, 2002

Each LHB shares with the local authority a duty to formulate a health and well-being strategy for the local population.

Putting forth the consultation document, Hutt stressed that the plan would demand 'new approaches. These will be based on new and dynamic partnerships within the NHS and between NHS Wales, local government, the voluntary and independent sectors and the communities they serve' and was intended to be 'simpler . . . accountable . . . and have a stronger democratic voice in the way it is governed' (National Assembly for Wales 2001b). In the plenary debate on the plans, the Labour AMs relentlessly focused on the advantages of local community involvement (Assembly *Record*, 27 November 2001:73, 96). A Welsh Assembly Government adviser expanded on it: 'it is philosophically driven by a form of distributive socialism . . . Labour wants to be strong at the centre and at the local level, and clear intermediate layers. Prior to the reorganisation, there was weakness at the centre, at the local level, and a thicket in between' (4–6).

Other Assembly Members were more critical and pointed out that the results of the consultation were being closely held by the government; they cited evidence of interest group and stakeholder opposition in the debate (Assembly *Record*, 27 November 2001:83–5, 90). Given that the results of the consultation itself had not and still have not been publicly released in useful form, we can only rely on these opposition (Conservative and Plaid Cymru) AMs' interventions in the plenary for assurance that, as Plaid's Ieuan Wyn Jones said, 'I am not aware of a single organisation that wholeheartedly supports the Government's plans' (Assembly *Record*, 27 November 2001:90). At least , said one interviewee, 'in what's been a rough ride, local government's been consistent – the Minister could call on them. Local government has four places on the new LHBs, which is a big prize' (4–6). Or, perhaps, 'it's a local government association coup' remarked a more critical observer (4–4). Whether the reorganisation was a coup or a blow for distributive socialism, it was explicable in light of the systemic regularities in the Welsh Labour party and post-devolution Welsh policy communities, both of which strongly represent localism, local government, the public sector, and public sector ideals.

The problems created by this decision to reorganise on a localist basis amounted to serious local capacity issues, exacerbated by Hutt's insistence that the (uncosted) proposals be 'cost-neutral', i.e. not cost more than the previous arrangements (Assembly *Record*, 27 November 2001:123). Wales, instead of five commissioning teams, now required twenty-two. This led naturally to three kinds of solutions played out during the roughly two-year planning phase of the reorganisation. First, aspects of the system were centralised; Wales now had a central commissioning service for rare or capital-intensive services, a unified public health corps, and central control of smaller, crucial services once carried out by health authorities, such as the upkeep of the lists of physicians in the NHS. Second, the National Assembly created three regional offices with responsibility to coordinate and develop economies of scale between different LHBs; it hotly denied that they would become revived health authorities. Third, it encouraged LHBs to solve their own capacity problems by merging operations with each other or developing close partnerships; most notably rural Powys, with no high-level hospital services, merged its LHB and providers.

The result is a system in which across much of Wales complicated, complex tasks are recentralising under functional pressures and scepticism about the LHBs' capacity. Localism, as actually implemented, seems to be a form of needs identification under central tutelage – according to an official involved in implementation, almost a mechanism for increasing public, or at least local government, participation (4–11). Local government and local communities entered the health service to a far greater extent than anywhere else, with the constitution of the LHBs, but key health services remained in the hands of health specialists (managers and professionals) and withdrew, or were withdrawn, from the LHBs' practical remit. As the structure came to life and health professionals continued to worry, the National Assembly encouraged local experimentation with joint working out of both nervousness and hope.

Why had the Welsh government done something radical, untested, stressful, and probably beyond its administrative capacity when it had promised the public and its coalition partners that it would do no such thing? First, a distinctive Welsh response to the policy activism coming out of England seemed imperative. The result had already been the Welsh health plan (National

Assembly for Wales 2001a), which both answered any criticisms that England had a plan and Wales did not, or that a great deal of money was coming into the health system and the government had not declared how it would spend it or why. The problem was that this plan did not give the party an easy-to-deliver policy outcome; problems of waiting lists and output figures that refused to change remained. 'I asked them why they did it' explained an analyst, 'and they said that they couldn't work out where the money was going but it seemed to disappear at the health authority level' (4–5). The government needed some sort of radical policy change to deal with the sense of malaise, mark out its own policy direction, and to be seen to be acting on health policy.

The problem was a health system that looked stagnant, and Labour was interested in distinctively Welsh, left-wing action. The Welsh policy community strongly represents local government (through the Labour party as well as directly), while public health and primary care advocates loom larger and have experience with local joint working. Equally, operating twenty-two LHBs both allows managers to continue in post (relative to the shakeout that would have come with Wales-wide commissioning) and gives them the remit to work with local communities for better health. Several interviewees in Cardiff Bay and Welsh health policy suggested that the intervention of managers and the NHS Confederation explains Hutt's last-minute tilt from unified commissioning to the creation of twenty-two commissioning bodies after not only Plaid Cymru but also Labour's coalition partners, the Liberal Democrats, had prepared press releases taking credit for the expected shift to Wales-wide commissioning (4–15). Local government and to a lesser extent health service managers combine imposing powers of advice (on local conditions and the health system, respectively), acquiescence (in any policy involving partnership), and approval (in local government's political power). Against a backdrop of Welsh involvement in joint working and a policy community predisposed to it, there was little to stop these two powerful groups from developing the strategy. The result was a widespread suspicion that the reorganisation was a simple compromise between the desire of the powerful Welsh Local Government Association to control health (win the keys to the castle) and the interest of the NHS Confederation in preserving a management function and management (4–3, 4–4, 4–6, 4–10, 4–15).

The result is a system based on local area needs assessment, and commissioning with the centre encroaching. This reflects the combination of a party system that puts a premium, for Labour, on leftward tilts and Welsh distinctiveness, with a policy community that diminishes the influence of corporate rationalisers, market reformers, and medical professionalists relative to community and public health advocates. Its slow recentralisation (the eventual degree of local autonomy remains unclear) reflects the old problem of Welsh Labour – the combination of local government power, intellectually and politically, with local government's spotty record and the problems that most observers expected of trying to improve a health service by turning five quangos into twenty-two quangos. When the National Assembly called in Derek Wanless, author of a report on NHS spending for the UK Treasury, to advise on a report on Welsh hospital services, the results were not encouraging about the governance of Welsh hospitals. There is a real danger that implementation problems and building threats to the acute sector will upend the policies that the Welsh have chosen (Review of Health and Social Care in Wales 2003).

New public health

Wales's advanced public health policy and intense political focus on the wider determinants of health outcomes is of a piece with its locally based, community-oriented health service, and so its public health policy is just as shaped by Wales' distinctive policy community. Wales takes new public health more seriously than the other three jurisdictions of the UK, with more money dedicated to reducing inequalities, efforts to use organisational form to promote new public health, a privileged position for its public health corps in the new organisation, and real ministerial pressure on the development of public health strategies that cut across government borders and integrate multiple public policies to defeat complex causes of ill health. The rhetoric of this strategy (and much of the implementation) hinges on, and is justified by, ill health and inequality. The Welsh population, like those of Scotland and Northern Ireland, suffers more illness than it might and, as the Wanless team suggested for both Wales and the UK, acute services will never be able to cope with the cumulative effects of unhealthy lives (Wanless 2002; Review of Health and Social Care in Wales 2003). Furthermore, there are serious inequalities of morbidity, mortality, and chronic conditions across Wales; the health statistics of poor Valleys communities and their Vale of Glamorgan neighbours vary dramatically (Welsh Assembly National Steering Group on the Allocation of NHS Resources 2001). The strategy also fits with the broad shift of focus Wales has made since devolution away from health services to health outcomes, and which was presaged in Wales' pre-devolutionary health strategies and policy variation.

The most noticeable form of this policy shift is in the rhetoric of policies and the definitions of roles. The rhetoric of the Welsh NHS is very different from that of the other three UK systems. Documents such as the health plan discuss health outcomes and the causes of poor health before discussing the policy tools necessary to attack these causes (consider the subtitle of the plan: *A Plan for the NHS with its Partners*: National Assembly for Wales 2001a). The health services are a major such policy tool, but only one, and they are often only at their most effective when linked with other services such as social work or the police. As well as this, Wales (along with the Greater London Authority, which is not distracted by having any health services) is the leading UK jurisdiction in health impact assessment, i.e. evaluating any policy for its health impact and health potential as recommended by the World Health Organisation and the Acheson Report (Greer and Sandford 2001; Breeze and Hall 2002).

In addition to this rhetoric and policy direction from the centre, there is real money by the low standards of public health spending. The NAW 2002–3 budget states plans to spend a total of £46 million in 2004–5 on health improvement and health promotion, making public health 1.2 per cent of the health budget – a good total for the UK, considering the immense sunk and new costs of health services in any NHS budget. In this case it takes the form of the Inequalities Fund, a £6–7 million annual budget item for the reduction of health inequalities (much of which goes on health promotion targeted at coronary heart disease). In addition to new, specific health promotion and inequalities spending, the National Assembly, like the Scottish Parliament, commissioned a report on inequalities. Its chosen consultant was Professor Peter Townsend, an internationally known expert in the relationship between poverty, inequality, and health, who produced a report on how better to use the NHS in Wales to reduce health inequalities (Welsh Assembly National Steering Group on the Allocation of NHS Resources 2001). This actually led to changes in the distribution of new funding within Wales, in an attempt to diminish inequality.

New public health is the prime justification of the reorganisation. On the one hand, the organisation of health, with its emphasis on local service coordination and control, is justified by and part of the Welsh public health strategy. Many of the determinants of health outcomes are in the hands of local government and the Welsh reorganisation was intended to harness local government with the NHS to improve health overall rather than run health services.[5] On the other hand, the core of public health work will not be delegated to the LHBs. Rather, the reorganised NHS Wales builds in a unified public health corps, placing the public health specialists of the old health authorities in one Wales-wide body. This unification stands out compared to the seemingly wilful destructiveness of England's reorganisation of public health, which has fragmented and constantly shifted public health offices around from organisation to organisation. The new Welsh structure creates one body with shared information and organisation and possibly some insulation from many of the day-to-day problems of commissioning and service management that can occupy public health specialists. One participant in Welsh health policy making observed that it is unfair to judge Wales by short-term service-based criteria since the true goals of Welsh health policy are much longer-term and centre on wellness (4–5).

Documents prepared before and in the first years of devolution, including one by a group descended from the old Welsh Health Planning Forum including Jane Davidson, who went on to be NAW Minister of Education, had focused on the need for Wales to work on its wider determinants of health (Monaghan, Davidson, and Bainton 1999). Policy academics at the University of Wales colleges in Bangor, Cardiff, and Swansea, and the University of Glamorgan's Welsh Institute for Health and Social Care have all argued for a focus on the wider determinants of health. Other research institutes advocated the same, including the Nuffield Trust, from London, and the Institute of Welsh Affairs (IWA). The latter greeted the NAW with a 'handbook' with themed chapters, including one on health co-authored by, *inter alia*, John Wyn Owen and Mike Ponton; the former was the leader of the innovative Welsh NHS in the 1980s while the latter was Chief Executive of Health Promotion Wales and went on to become Director of Health Service Policy and play a major role in *Improving Health in Wales* (Jones *et al.* 1998). This policy community put health inequalities and wider determinants of health to the fore. It included advocates such as Jane Davidson and Mark Drakeford, future National Assembly special adviser and an author of the 'social services' chapter in the IWA book (Drakeford, Butler, and Pithouse 1998). As a result, when a Labour government was seeking a health policy that would respond to left-wing threats (and be visibly Welsh, an important attribute even for the reputedly Blairite Alun Michael), the availability of new public health issues and policies was greater and the competition from advocates of a focus on health services less.

Public and private

English health policy makes a point of incorporating private provision into the NHS, whether through the 'diversity' agenda that contracts services to the private sector or through PFI. Scottish and Northern Irish health policies use PFI extensively (despite Northern Ireland's small projects, which attract little interest) but have pointedly avoided incorporating private health provision such as private hospitals. Again, Wales stands out, if not as starkly. PFI is not being expanded as rapidly as a policy and its operation is being restricted in new contracts to such an extent that it might not deliver any expected savings. Most importantly, the 'Welsh way' in PFI involves preservation of the status, pay, and treatment of staff transferred from the NHS to the private sector contractor. This eliminates a significant reason why governments pursue PFI, namely the possibility of replacing expensive public sector union workers with cheaper and less organised private sector labour. It has accordingly changed the calculus trusts use when deciding whether a PFI would be beneficial (and outraged managers whose projects were being negotiated when the announcement was made) (4–23). Asked to define the 'Welsh way' in PFI, one NAW interviewee summarised the differences as scale and said that 'building versus staffing contracts are sharply divided – we make a point of extending the groups [considered] 'clinical staff' who aren't transferred – the porter and the laundry stay in the NHS and are not transferred.' (4–6). Welsh interviewees point out that they are building non-PFI hospitals, including a wholly public sector new build in Porthmadog. While the National Assembly has not made a point of its decision to eschew much closer engagement with the private sector (probably to avoid irritating the UK government), it has marked out a clear choice of traditional NHS direct provision.

Politically, rejecting expansion of PFI entails rejecting what appears to be something for nothing – an influx of capacity and investment, albeit at a future price. Other politicians in the UK have opted for PFI on these grounds, even if they agree that the PFI hospitals entail high transaction costs and very long-term budget commitments. The Welsh party system, with Plaid Cymru critical of PFI, gives politicians their usual incentives to shift left and away from England (or, as in this case, stay where they are, and watch England shift away from them).

Despite this incentive, the Scottish Executive, which shares a similar party system and an opposition critical of PFI, has opted to increase private provision in public facilities. Wales, by contrast, has a policy community that is sharply hostile to the expansion of a private role. This differences traces back to the strong position of unions and local government in the Welsh political system and Labour party, and, secondarily, to the strength of public health and primary care advocates rather than traditional health service managers. Localists in local government and unions, in largely Labour Wales, are tightly intertwined with each other and with their Labour representatives. Increased private provision is a direct blow to unions, especially UNISON, because cost savings and changes in work practices with a transfer to the private sector tend to involve either drastic reductions in union protections and wages or a shift to a largely non-union workforce. Localists and unions accordingly oppose private provision, and their powers of approval (their key role in Labour politics), combined with their roles in giving advice and securing acquiescence, means that they have to be consulted on such issues and are more difficult to ignore. Their presence shapes estimates of the feasibility and desirability of projects, and greater private sector involvement is something they are likely to criticise. Without the argument that the English party system offers, namely that the whole concept of public provision is under attack from a right-wing opposition and its milieu, and without many market reform advocates working in Wales, the pressure is to listen to the strong union and local government voices within Labour.

Quality

The Welsh quality outcome is as striking as Wales's organisation and new public health outcomes, but for the opposite reason. While Wales has enacted public health and organisational policies with resonance and rhetoric that differ in fundamental and marked ways from those of the rest of the UK, it has not meaningfully worked to establish a quality agenda of its own or to promote quality agendas overall, and when it has moved it has been in a debate about English auditors. Wales is still under the inspection regime of England (with NICE doing technology assessment and CHI, now CHAI, doing quality inspection visits and implementing National Service Frameworks). Welsh plans to establish its own audit and inspection agency are not driven by health concerns, and there has been no autonomous push by clinical elites or the National Assembly to improve quality through either control over professionals or efforts to induce them to improve their own clinical governance. Insofar as there is a problem recognised in the political agenda, it is the presence of essentially English auditors and inspectors in Wales, since Wales has different priorities and is sensitive to criticism.

In Scotland, the three independent Royal Colleges and the clinical medical elites clustered around organisations such as SIGN have been able to establish an independent quality agenda, sign up the Scottish Office, and then consolidate it with an autonomous, and professional-dominated, set of Scottish quality organisations in 1997 and since devolution. By contrast, neither Wales nor Northern Ireland has such strong, organised, medical elites. As a result, it seemed quite reasonable to the authors of the Welsh devolution settlement to leave audit and quality tasks in the hands of UK – effectively, English – agencies such as CHI, NICE, and the Audit Commission. The alternative would have been a drive to establish an independent Welsh audit capacity, and the investment required to remedy Wales's lack of capacity, when viewed by the existing Welsh Office policy makers, seemed excessive. Meanwhile, within Wales, the professionals of the country's one tertiary, teaching hospital, were left to participate in the larger English arena, and the former Chief Medical Officer of Wales, Dame Deirdre Hine, went on to run the Anglo-Welsh CHI.

After devolution political dissatisfaction with the work of the UK agencies, particularly CHI and the Audit Commission, began to grow. These agencies occupied the uncomfortable position of being seen as outsiders while having a remit based on critique and suggestions for improvement – unkindly, replacing their Welsh operations could be seen as shooting the messenger. There was an entrenched sense in the National Assembly that independent Welsh institutions would be better, almost by definition, than ones shared with England. Part of the problem was that there was a case against using English audit – the Audit Commission, particularly, came under criticism for applying the wrong standards, while CHI, griped one NAW policy maker, would pass trusts 'where you should put a mark on your leg yourself to make sure they don't amputate the wrong one'.

The mixture of motives is necessarily unclear, and the public salience of quality is very low even as the legislation advances. The pre-eminent health quality policy is the decision to shift to graduate nurses, which is a measure of the effectiveness of lobbying nurses (another group that is often marginal when market reformers or medical professionalists are strong). A distinctive, unified, Welsh health audit might also be desirable (particularly as England continues with its service focus and demanding performance management regime) but there is only a small constituency for it. There is a small overall Welsh policy community, encompassing a few think-tanks and academic research centres, which sustain policy ideas for devolution. The proposal for a separate Welsh audit capacity, like proposals to create a unified Welsh public service corps (combining the civil service and local government officials) or a Welsh degree structure (WelshBac.) are kept alive by the activities of these groups, and are available to solve problems that can seemingly be solved by more devolution. Any sense that NHS Wales is being bruised by regular reports by people who do not understand what it is trying to do is enough to make audit a problem for the National Assembly (a July 2002 Audit Commission report on the public services in Wales, which was justifiably critical, created a two-day political storm) (Audit Commission 2002). The focus is on auditors rather than a drive to improve quality for regulatory or professional purposes.

Conclusion

Welsh health policy's guiding themes – new public health, localism, and trust in the public service – stem from a policy community dominated by believers in, and workers in, local public services. If Welsh policy outcomes appear therefore to be markedly different from those of the rest of the UK, it is because these groups' influence is increased by the relative weakness of their rivals. Competing projects, diagnoses, policy problems, and understandings of the world are weaker in Wales because of the relative weakness of parts of its civil society, including the press, academic and management corporate rationalisers, and academic medical elites. In this way the age-old characteristics of Welsh civil society – its distinctiveness and its relative lack of complex regional organisations with considerable resources – have shaped not just the nation but also the policy communities. Wales's coherent health policies reflect the ideas in the health policy community.

A lesson emerging from Wales is that lack of capacity can undo the best-intentioned reforms. There are a few areas where the local government, LHB, and National Assembly are in tune and working well, but more where there have been problems that inexorably draw power back up to Cardiff. It will be some time before the civil service, managerial corps, professionals, and politicians of Wales have the collective expertise to replace five appointed authorities with twenty-two locally accountable units. By then the system might well have congealed into a highly centralised health service with a great deal of local bureaucracy – or been reorganised again. That would be a sad outcome. Wales should, at least, carry the lesson that capacity building is vital and difficult, for without administrative and policy capacity, the best of ideas may perish in the execution.

The development of Welsh health policy is intimately tied to dynamics that have shaped Wales over much of its history. The shape of Welsh civil society is something that the Welsh have created, often through sheer force of will. Wales's university system, its one academic medical centre, its think-tanks, and its press have all been clear and well-documented cases of collective action by a people whose identity was strongly felt but organisational resources weak. Wales lacks equivalents for many of the proud old organisations that dominate policy in England and Scotland – and most other countries. This civil society accordingly does not resemble others, and neither does the Welsh policy community that since 1997 has had its day in the sun.

The result is that Wales has again embarked on an internationally important experiment in health policy formation. Wales has broken with tradition and tried to focus on prevention. The result, seen by a sceptic, might be a 'local government coup'. It might fall prey to the small and constrained organisational apparatus that the National Assembly inherited. But it is radical as health policies go.

Wales also confirms the hypothesis that regardless of outside threats, debates, and pressures, the crucial interpretive and problem-solving work of politics is done locally and by politicians and policy advocates conditioned by their institutional histories and interrelationships in Cardiff Bay. Welsh policy outcomes have been broadly in line with the composition of the policy community and party system; they can be explained individually by the interaction of politics and policy that they create, and are similar to pre-devolution decisions. The Welsh bet on localism reflects the impact of devolution, more than elsewhere in UK health policy. Scotland's insiders and their agendas loomed larger when Scottish health policy shifted from being marginal variations in the Scottish Office to being a full-scale health agenda for a highly autonomous polity. The policy elites of the UK largely turned out since devolution to be the policy elites of England. But in Wales, the shift from permissive managerialism to localism is striking in its impact and new politics. Wales has shifted, with devolution, from government by a territorial office concerned with stability to a new government: a government that has opened up and interacts with a policy community to produce a novel, if extremely challenging, policy agenda.

Notes

1 Deacon (2002:100–1) quotes a 1990 Department of Health medical officer responding to the Welsh Office's Deputy Chief Medical Officer for Wales who had raised concerns about the Department's handling of BSE ('mad cow disease') in Wales: 'I am surprised you feel it necessary to put so much effort into challenging the views of colleagues at DoH who are more senior, more experienced in the area, devote a higher proportion of their time to the topic and have frequent access to the real experts in the field' (cited in the *Western Mail*, 27 October 2000).

2 Merthyr Tydfil would continue with such bouts of resistance; in 1970, when the new Education Secretary Margaret Thatcher discontinued the provision of free school milk, Merthyr Tydfil developed such subterfuges as excluding milk, but providing free milkshakes out of the education budget instead.

3 Abertillery, another valleys constituency, held a recount in 1945 just to confirm that the Conservative candidate had done so poorly as to lose the deposit candidates must put down (Morgan 1984:42).

4 On the night of the first devolved elections in 1997, a BBC producer in Cardiff expressed it succinctly. Watching the election night BBC broadcast from (comparatively boring) Edinburgh while Wales underwent a political earthquake, the producer repeated the words 'Wrong place! Wrong place!' (Trystan, Scully and Jones 2004:4n.5).

5 'Local health boards and local government will be required to work together to produce and implement local health and wellbeing strategies, moulding an integrated approach . . . They will also facilitate a combined and concerted attack on the causes of ill-health and the inequalities that they cause and will promote a vigorous health improvement agenda' said Hutt in the 27 November 2001 plenary debate on the topic (Assembly *Record*: 74).

6
Northern Ireland: permissive managerialism

[England] can be quite cynical. Do away with the market one day and bring it back the next. We look on that with contempt. (Northern Irish policy maker)

In everything I've done, Northern Ireland is delightfully behind. In the Scottish Office you were on the tails of England – frequently the Department of Health would drop it on you with no warning. It was always nice then to ring Northern Ireland and find out that they didn't know and weren't the slightest bit bothered about it! (Scottish policy maker)

Of the four systems, Northern Ireland is the one in which devolution should have mattered most: after almost thirty years of 'direct rule' by part-time ministers from London and no accountability to voters, any area of policy had probably diverged from what the population would seek. Instead, after the Belfast Agreement and a referendum created the devolved Stormont Executive and Assembly to govern the country, if anything policy change slowed down. Policy outcomes – consistency and lack of change – carried over from before devolution.

Northern Ireland's health policy remains, essentially, permissive managerialism. The essence of permissive managerialism is a combination of minimal policy activity (such as quality improvement, new public health, or acute care redesign) and an emphasis on running services with a minimum of fuss in the middle of a civil war. If these essential managerial goals are accomplished, then local health services can have considerable latitude to develop their own cultures and focus on different issues. The reason for this choice of health policy lies in Northern Ireland's small size and history of high political conflict and policy stability. Like Scotland, it is dominated by its insiders and, more than Scotland, it has most of the same insiders as before 1998. The difference between the insider systems lies in what it takes to be an insider in Northern Ireland versus Scotland. Scotland's strong, organised, high-status medical elites long ago staked out a claim to speak for the system from a position of knowledge, legitimacy, and superior ability to foresee developments in medicine. With such medical elites comes a serious agenda focusing on issues such as quality and clinical networks. By contrast, Northern Ireland's insiders are those who are necessary to keep the system running – mostly a mixture of managers from various organisations and civil servants. Their influence reflects not just Northern Ireland's small size but also its easygoing culture, inherited from direct rule (when British ministers were otherwise occupied) and, before that, the conservative, effectively one-party Stormont regime. These decades of direct rule produced an ingrained disrespect for local politicians and a health policy community built around those who could keep the system running in very challenging circumstances – and, if possible, do something to attack social causes of conflict. In Northern Ireland that meant managers and a few officials, rather than the determined advocates found in Scotland's policy community.

Why didn't the arrival of a devolved assembly replace permissive managerialism with something else? Northern Ireland's unusual history and political structure has created politics that almost eliminate the potential pluralism of devolution – neither formal institutions nor the structure of politics create a pluralist political sphere in which advocates of different policies can contend. Northern Ireland's institutions are a unique experiment in formal consociationalism pasted on to a Westminster government. The institutional design of devolution lures parties into government by granting them great executive powers in their departments and little formal accountability to the Assembly or the public, and then makes collective decisions nearly impossible. The Northern Irish party system is remarkable because the Unionist–nationalist cleavage obliterates right–left cleavages; two Nationalist and several Unionist parties compete to best and most vociferously represent their communities. Informally, the long historic legacies of direct rule have led to an unusual political system long accustomed to minimal political accountability for policy. In this vacuum insider groups such as the civil service, voluntary sector, and professions dominated policy making because of the importance of their advice, cooperation, and legitimacy and the essential demand from London that the public services should not add to the difficulties of the life of a Secretary of State for Northern Ireland. The result of this situation is that devolution has had far less impact on Northern Irish public policy than in Scotland and Wales: the party system creates little or no incentive to have policies at all and fits well with a small and generally conservative policy community.

The degree of real policy change was consequently minimal in 14 October 2002 when the Secretary of State for Northern Ireland suspended the Assembly amidst recrimination between Unionist and nationalist camps and among Unionists (November 2003 elections subsequently produced an Assembly too divided to elect its First and Deputy First Ministers, meaning it could not operate). It is no accident that the policy legacy of Northern Irish devolution was so small. The political stream very rarely intersects with issues connected to health (or any other policy), since the salient issues are all of constitutional and sectarian politics, while the health policy stream, atrophied by decades of single-party or direct rule, is dominated by a conservative civil service. Northern Ireland has no shortage of politicians but few of them need to pursue policy solutions and, reflecting the political drought, there are few policy advocates to propose them.

Inheritance

The characteristics of Northern Irish politics and policy are inheritances of almost thirty years of direct rule and the five decades of devolution before the Troubles. The interaction of the existing civil service and policy communities with the mechanisms of direct rule gave a particular cast to participation in Northern Irish policy making – limited potential for expansion of conflicts, tightly knit policy communities, little pluralism, a tendency towards log-rolling distributional politics, and a circumscribed agenda largely driven by (outsider, London-based) professional organisations and broad UK-wide public policy directions. Stormont (1922–73) copied policy from Great Britain in a combination of Unionist ideology and the laziness of a conservative dominant party. The logic of the conflict made parties that mobilised organisations for various preferences regarding constitutional politics and severed them from a role in policy. As a result they never developed the institutional mechanisms to formulate policy or handle voters' policy preferences. This created a political system in which parties did not play a role as conveyor belts between the population and the political system. Instead, at any given time they were preoccupied with group rights and constitutional politics, and as many as half of them, Protestant and Catholic, would be working to undermine the regime. All that was left was a sense among the public that public policy was made by unaccountable elites.

Stormont politics

Northern Ireland's existence is predicated upon the social and political divides that have run through at least the last four centuries of Irish history.[1] Power had largely been in the hands of a British-affiliated group of Protestants, including a landholding elite dominant across the island, and also, in the prosperous northern province of Ulster (particularly in its north-eastern counties), a broad swathe of industrial and agricultural workers. In Ulster, sectarian division between the Protestant majority and the Catholic minority became an integral part of the society. This was periodically reinforced by violent conflict and constantly reinforced by residential segregation, employment and social discrimination, regular symbolic practices such as Protestant marches, and the development of two poorly integrated sets of social institutions – Protestant ones centred on theoretically secular economic, civic, and political institutions, and Catholic ones built on the foundation of the Church's extensive organisation.

Northern Ireland was born in 1920–22, when the Anglo-Irish Treaty that ended the Irish wars of independence created two Parliaments, one in Belfast and one in Dublin, which were intended to be roughly parallel and have similar status within the Commonwealth. The decision to partition the island grew out of the fierce resistance of Protestants in the North East to any participation in an Irish state (which would be perforce Catholic-dominated). When Irish home rule was legislated just before the First World War, these Protestant loyalists and Unionists armed, threatened mutiny in the mainland British armed forces, and with the support of the Conservatives threatened the basic stability of the British regime. In the South the majority Catholics demanded home rule or more. The outbreak of war saved the UK from greater regime crisis, but a failed uprising in 1916 led in the South to a classic cycle of guerrilla provocation, state repression, further guerrilla mobilisation, and further repression, until the Irish countryside was largely out of control in 1918–19. In mostly Protestant North-East Ulster, by contrast, Irish nationalism was weaker and milder, and Unionists continued to demand 'exclusion', or the separation of Northern Ireland from the rest. This they had probably already won before the war, and after the war it was certain.

The government in London, exhausted by the four years of war in Europe, threatened by state breakdown from the Rhine to the Bering Straits, economically in deep difficulties, and already committed to substantial autonomy for Ireland, did its best to wash its hands of the problem by establishing the two Parliaments. The South descended into a civil war between the two major factions of republicans. In the North Unionists recreated an Irish state in the six counties (of Ulster's original nine) that the Protestants could dominate. This epoch, from 1922 to 1972, is known as Stormont, named after the complex of buildings in Belfast, dominated by a grandiose legislature, from which Northern Ireland was ruled. The Stormont regime built a Protestant ascendancy, almost completely excluding Catholics from meaningful social, political, or economic roles, while restricting power to a narrow elite among Protestants.[2]

During the years of devolution, Northern Ireland's Parliament exercised considerable authority over most aspects of social policy, including tax-raising powers. Stormont was an unusual creature (Wilson 1955b; Lawrence 1965; Calvert 1968; Birrell and Murie 1980; Whyte 1983; Hadfield 1989:95–124). Whitehall made few efforts to control the Northern Irish Parliament; a convention in Westminster ruled out parliamentary discussions of devolved matters, and the Home Office staff responsible for Northern Ireland were few and would remain in their positions for decades. London had formal powers to override decisions, but Stormont called its bluff immediately. London objected when the Stormont government abolished proportional representation in local government elections in 1922, thereby further disenfranchising Catholics and, more importantly, heading off any splits or progressive movements in Protestant areas. In response, the government in Belfast threatened to resign and the Cabinet in London backed down, as it was unable to see any alternative political forces that could take power. After that there were no significant challenges to Stormont's autonomy until the eruption of the Troubles (Birrell and Murie 1980:5–30).

Northern Ireland's structure of politics diverges from those of England, Northern Ireland, and Wales because the Unionist–nationalist cleavage obliterates the left–right cleavage. Parties compete within religious communities to best represent, or fight for, that group; there are few crossover voters in a system dominated by the logic of enemies (Rose 1971; Ruohomaki 2001). Northern Ireland had been designed to guarantee a Protestant majority (which is why historic Ulster was shorn of three of its counties, Cavan, Donegal and Monaghan – their inclusion would have brought it close to religious balance).

Formally, the Stormont government was a typical Westminster system with a government elected out of a Parliament that was itself elected by a first-past-the-post system and aided by a nonpartisan civil service. However, the structure of politics and electoral rules meant that there would always be a Protestant majority and no big crosscutting parties; first-past-the-post Westminster systems could hardly be better designed to oppress in a society where one-third of the population is permanently at odds with the majority (gerrymandering served the same goal in local government). Reflecting the impossibility of getting elected in most places and the meaninglessness of being a Catholic in Stormont, the Nationalist Party often failed to run, leaving seats uncontested.

The demographic dominance of Protestants, the first-past-the-post Westminster system, and the dominance of the Ulster Unionist Party (UUP) of Protestant political organisation (through links with elites from the Orange Order to the industrialists of Belfast) made Northern Ireland a one-party state with a 'political system which belied the political', in Arthur's phrase (Harbinson 1973; Arthur 2000:47). Its policy shifted from exclusionary and deeply conservative only when that was necessary to head off a threat to Protestant electoral unity from the left or right. The government focused on parity with the UK as a political plank, seeking to establish the same standards for the welfare state as in the UK as part of its Unionist ideology (in contemporary language, it wanted to eliminate 'lee-way', or gaps between Britain and Northern Ireland, by pursuing a 'step-by-step' policy of imitating each of Westminster's steps; Wilson 1955a:187–8). Thus Northern Ireland established a health service in 1948 alongside the UK NHS, with much the same organisation and the same guiding principles of free care in a nationalised service. Social security and other benefits likewise kept pace with the UK, despite the significantly lesser financial capacities of the Northern Irish government. This era, and Unionist ideology, enshrined parity as an important political goal in Northern Ireland and established many very similar structures. An immediate consequence of these high standards, combined with Northern Ireland's increasingly debilitated textile and engineering-based economy, was massive fiscal reliance upon the UK Exchequer (Birrell and Murie 1980:10, 19).

Such politics created a distinctive policy-making process with three key characteristics: its closed list of participants (excluding most Protestants as well as any Catholics); its constricted agenda and reliance on the UK for ideas; and its focus on distributional politics. They all emerge from a single-party system operating against a deeply sectarian backdrop. First, the one-party-dominant regime created little incentive for policy innovation. Ministers were only barely accountable for policies under their control, since the UUP, to the extent that it fought political battles in these years, tended not to fight on specific issues. Therefore, poor performance was less of a worry – and the measure of performance was distributional gratification to a degree that surprised arriving direct rule ministers (Lord Windlesham 1973:270). Second, as a consequence of this, policy was mostly imported from Great Britain by the civil servants. Even if there was very little constitutional-level contact, the Northern Irish quest for parity and lack of policy capacity meant Stormont spending departments were in close touch with their Whitehall counterparts. They needed to know what steps to take in order to pursue their 'step-by-step' policy: 'We'd hear about something across the water – and take a look at it' was one retired civil servant's analysis of the policy-making style (2–7). Third, the constricted policy-making circles were largely made up of groups that benefited from the institutional status quo and which tended to opt not to change distribution of resources, or at least not to reduce each others' resources or autonomy. These groups were there for advice, acquiescence, and approval, not because they aggregated followers. The result was a stable set of alliances among elites in control of health policy, with little pressure from the atrophied political system. The eruption of constitutional politics in the late 1960s did little to change this, as it vaulted over issues such as the organisation of health care.

Major health system reforms of the last years of Stormont appear to be counter-examples. Like the reform plans being mooted at the time in Great Britain (but ultimately unsuccessful there), they combined health and social services in single organisations. Social services was one function taken from small, underfunded, and often sectarian local governments and granted to subregional boards, thus establishing Northern Ireland's distinctive combination of health and social services in the same structure and creating the possibility of a real continuum between acute, primary, and social services (Birrell and Murie 1980:191–261). Also like the plans in Britain, which focused health care administration on the district and regional levels, Northern Ireland's changes set up four boards roughly equivalent to the district health authorities in England, while like Wales and Scotland the functions of an English region were combined with those of a health department. This approach simply adapted a common template and took advantage of Northern Ireland's small size and the need to do something about its local government. Northern Ireland responded to a UK-wide sense of the need to reform the territorial organisation of public services with a particularly innovative blueprint first published as a 1969 Green Paper on local government reorganisation, which had significant effects on health care (Government of Northern Ireland 1969:8–11) and was adopted by Stormont in December 1970 as the regime desperately tried to 'modernise' while progressively disintegrating (Hennessy 1997:184–9).

The reason for the reorganisation, however, had less to do with good health and personal social services than with the systematic discrimination by local governments, which was one of the factors causing the Troubles. Northern Ireland's social services, thoroughly politicised and sectarian, had to be changed – since they were a major cause of Catholic grievance, according to the important Cameron Report (Commission appointed by the Governor of Northern Ireland 1969:56, 91, 93). Political events, driven by events unrelated to health policy, forced the reorganisation of local government and a reduction of its powers, and advocates of integrated care seized the opportunity this created. While the Cameron Commission and Catholic resentment focused on housing and jobs, the policy response was to strip local government of most functions as part of the various last-ditch measures to head off civil war. The problem of conflict created by sectarian government, including local government, led to a discussion of proposals for the reduction of the powers of the local governments. This discussion took place in the early 1970s when advocates for integration were particularly strong across the UK (those advocates' ideas also explain the short-lived area health authorities in England's 1974 reorganisation, created entirely so that something would be conterminous with local government and assist service integration; Greer forthcoming-c). There was a two-stage process: first local government reform, thanks in good part to Cameron, became a major policy response to the problem of Northern Ireland's conflict. This created a new problem, since it demanded a new structure. In the Macrory Report and consequent reorganisation, health and social service integration in area boards was policy that tackled the problem of designing new structures for the services stripped from local government with 'technical content' (Review Body on Local Government in Northern Ireland 1970, paragraphs 70–7; see also Government of Northern Ireland 1969). Major reforms, in this window of opportunity, could happen that could not happen in those parts of the UK where life and local government were more normal, but the influence of service integration advocates in health policy was a result of the idea that local government reform would help solve Northern Ireland's conflict rather than an interest in improving health policy.

Direct rule politics

Health policy, though, was hardly forefront in Northern Irish politics in the late 1960s and early 1970s (Norton 1996; Hennessy 1997; Rose 2000:171–234). Stormont collapsed in 1972 after the disastrous policy of interning suspected militants enraged (and mobilised) Catholics, and the killings of 'Bloody Sunday' in Derry in 1972 galvanised opinion – and the Irish Republican Army (IRA). Prime Minister Edward Heath, in the aftermath of the events in Derry and the IRA's sanguineous response, tried to take over security policy from Stormont. When it refused, he announced on 24 March 1972 the suspension of Stormont for one year. The optimistically named Northern Ireland (Temporary Powers) Act 1972 vested the powers of Stormont in a new UK Cabinet minister, the Secretary of State for Northern Ireland, who was able to legislate with little Parliamentary oversight. At the time the structure was thought temporary; first the government negotiated in secret with the IRA, and then designed a new devolved government for Northern Ireland (known as Sunningdale, after the Civil Service College premises where the negotiations were held). A distant ancestor of the Belfast Agreement, it tried to build a moderate devolved government on the partnership of the UUP and Social Democratic and Labour Party (SDLP), and collapsed when the Unionist rank and file and most leadership abandoned the effort (Hennessy 1997:221–6).

After the collapse of Sunningdale, it became clear to British policy makers that there was no immediate prospect of Northern Irish self-rule. Given that Britain did not opt to pull out (much to the relief of Dublin), there was little alternative to establishing a more durable and formal set of mechanisms for governing Northern Ireland (Hadfield 1989:125). This structure, known as direct rule, lasted through to the start of devolution in 1999 and remained at hand, ready to reinstate if the Secretary of State for Northern Ireland saw the need (Hadfield 1989; Cunningham 2001:125–140). Direct rule is thus an important epoch, for the policy-making habits and structures of direct rule persisted and shape the information, connections, and policy frameworks of those who now make policy under devolution. Most of the political actors in today's Northern Ireland began their careers in the last days of Stormont, but made their names under direct rule.

Formally, direct rule was of a type with territorial office rule in Scotland and Wales. The biggest institutional innovations of direct rule was the establishment of the Northern Ireland Office (NIO) in Whitehall around the Secretary of State for Northern Ireland. The NIO, despite being largely composed of Northern Ireland Civil Service (NICS) officials on secondment, looked to most Northern Irish civil servants as if it were 'up in the stratosphere, dealing with security and high politics' but came with establishment of the system whereby the Secretary of State and junior ministers were the executive and the effective centres of power (2–4) (Bell 1987; Carmichael 2001). Within the NICS, the change was remarkably smooth, the civil servants demonstrating that for all the informality of Stormont they remained distinctively Whitehall-model civil servants (Carmichael 2002). The NICS became formal even by Whitehall standards. Formalisation was an adaptation to decision making by part-time ministers from the mainland that worked by funnelling decisions through extensive paper consultations rather than conversation and 'steers' as was the case under Stormont.

However, informally, the situation was made very different from the Scottish and Welsh Offices by the near absence of political accountability of the Secretary of State (arguably because there was no polity to hold him or her accountable). Northern Ireland under direct rule was a type of vice-regal politics in which the separation of government and the vote was nearly total. The Northern Irish parties were excluded from political office in their administration, and were – with the occasional exception during periods of UK minority government – unable to affect Northern Irish policy. Neither their complaints about constituents nor their policy preferences necessarily had force in the way that the complaints of a UK governing or opposition party might. This was a problem shared by those who voted for small UK parties (the SNP, Plaid Cymru, Liberals, Social Democratic Party, or Liberal Democrats), but at least those parties competed with UK parties on similar issues, and their pressure could force big parties to pay attention to issues or change policies. In Northern Ireland, politicians did not necessarily pay any price for unpopular policy. The structure of Northern Irish politics, the necessary condition for these events, also crippled any discussion of or accountability for policy. The symbolic, sectarian structure of Northern Irish politics meant that parties did not win votes based on their policy ideas. The result was a politics that broke the basic relationship between votes and political performance. This disconnection between Northern Irish voters and Northern Irish policy meant that policy making slipped into the hands of the civil servants and to some extent the providers (in health, the health services and professions) (Connolly 1990; Connolly and Loughlin 1990:125–36). So long as the officials and managers maintained and operated the system without undue fuss, they were generally left alone, and even if Northern Ireland officials and ministers reflected Whitehall the mirror tended to be smudged. 'When there was a reshuffle, or a new Permanent Secretary in London', remarked a former civil servant, 'I'd meet them when I went down and ask if they could keep us up to date, just by copying things to us. They'd copy us everything for a while, and then it would start to arrive every few weeks in big packets, and then they'd forget entirely' (2–7).

Northern Ireland did not have the numerous and sophisticated professionalists of Scotland to take advantage of a policy-making system that gave knowledgeable and legitimate insiders such strength, and its unusual political setting meant few other social groups, with the partial exception of the voluntary sector, could play a role in policy (as happened in Wales; Chapter 5). Meanwhile, policy was also overshadowed by the Troubles. The extent of civil conflict meant that many divisive political issues, whether of normal governing or of Margaret Thatcher's conviction politics, did not seem like good things to place on the agenda. As one interviewee put it, discussing the relative lack of conflict between the government and unions in the 1980s: 'we could convince Thatcher that we had enough conflict here already, without introducing more' (2–7). The chief virtue of a Northern Irish civil servant or manager was not policy advocacy but the ability to manage public services smoothly and try to cope with serious social problems in the middle of a major civil conflict.

At the same time, Northern Ireland enjoyed a very high level of funding; while much of that went on security, it also went on social policies intended to relieve the conflict by striking at the obvious social and economic problems that lay behind the worst sectarianism. Thus Northern Ireland led the UK in its administration's sensitivity to the interlocking forms of deprivation and did valuable experiments in relieving it (leading to the leisure centres strung across Belfast, and much better quality public housing than seen in Great

Britain). The *Guardian*, at the height of Thatcherism in 1986, observed Northern Ireland's divergence from UK social policy and dubbed it the 'Independent Keynesian Republic of Northern Ireland' (Bardon and Burnett 1996:146). An English junior minister in the NIO ceased to take his parliamentary colleagues on tours of deprived areas in Belfast – rather than the misery, they noticed a quality and quantity of social provision not visible in their constituencies (Bardon and Burnett 1996:148). Under direct rule, there was little incentive for the ministers to look for fights, and in areas on a knife-edge there was a positive disincentive to disrupt the status quo. When ministers did, they necessarily did stir up extra trouble, because the immediate local response was to ask why ministers 'from across the water' were making unpopular changes. The Northern Irish social service structure began to assume a rather antique look.

The ministers and civil servants of direct rule often saw their problem as one of how to govern a society without the benefit of the links that normally funnel information and demands upwards. They settled upon two broad strategies. One was to select regular interlocutors – high-profile professionals, important managers, and politically astute representatives of various social sectors. They would meet with these insider groups to keep in touch and use them as informants on the political and practical problems of the system. A second was to continue, and if anything increase, a Stormont habit of close connections between government and grassroots (or parish-pump) groups. Thus, ministers on their days in Northern Ireland, and civil servants constantly, would meet with any manner of groups. Triangulating between the elites of the health and social services system and the demands of various delegations, civil servants and ministers could guess the likely effects of and responses to initiatives that were travelling slowly across from London.

Policy implementation, already influenced by the overriding goal of stable services amidst conflict, reflected yet another set of distortions. The state in Northern Ireland is profoundly distrusted by many. Not only were Catholic areas suspicious of the state (even if health and social services workers largely escaped the violence), but many Protestants, especially loyalists, were ideologically suspicious of state action. Over time, the whole society's faith in public authority eroded, along with society's political links to the increasingly militarised, mystifying, and unaccountable direct rule system. Thus it was reasonable to expect that policy might be better conducted through charities and voluntary sector organisations that would know an area's needs and win greater trust from residents. Such a policy of reliance on the voluntary sector also offered a prospect of using it to build a stronger non-sectarian civil society.

At least a strong, dynamic voluntary sector was built (which drew in many people who in a more conventional political system would have gone into politics). The sector reflected the problems of political recruitment, state–society relations in a climate of distrust, and the extensive Northern Irish social issues budget intended to help resolve the conflict at its roots. In other words, the direct rule administration and voluntary sector were made for each other. The legacy was a strong and capable voluntary sector infrastructure with good policy and advice links into the administration at many levels. The professionalisation of the voluntary sector also led to a distinction being drawn between the perceived middle-class professionals of the sector and the 'community' sector. The community sector activists were more directly sprung from the troubled areas and claimed a better connection to them. The problem was that given the social disorganisation and bigotry common in many Northern Irish communities (especially those most needing social services), the community sector was itself tainted by incompetence and bigotry.

This distinctive policy-making process, born of the disconnection between state and society in Northern Ireland, was suited to administering a neglected system with a minimum of political oversight. It supplied adequate amounts of the desired sort of information to the civil servants who oversaw its operation, and it allowed the various groups – managers, civil servants, physicians and other professions allied to medicine, and others – to coexist in relative stability. It was markedly corporatist and weak on policy change and democratic participation, but the demand to democratise the existing political structure in Northern Ireland was weak compared to other demands, such as the demand for its abolition.

Organisational distinctiveness

The most impressive distinctive attribute of Northern Ireland's health system since the Macrory Report's implementation is its integration of health and social services (Figure 6.1). There are two major claims for it: that it provides a 'continuum of care', which means that it improves coordination among the service providers; and that it improves planning and coordination by giving one organisation responsibility for the whole of care. Neither of these benefits worked as well as expected, because the problems in both cases were caused by more than the lack of formal organisational identity.

First, integrating health and social services failed to eliminate all the problems of service coordination on the front lines. Two professions can only share a domain without serious conflict if one is clearly subordinate (Abbott 1994). This allows medicine to coexist with nursing and the allied health professions. Social work, the main profession involved in social services, is an institutionally weak profession that is not subordinate to medicine (and has a well-

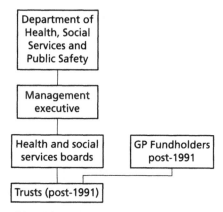

Figure 6.1: Structure of health and social services in Northern Ireland, 1973

worked-out analysis of its domain, one that involves claiming many areas that physicians formally or informally claim). This means that the gap between health and social services is qualitatively different from normal rivalries in medicine – whereas nurses, doctors, and allied professions are all jockeying for position, it is within a single domain which is dominated by medicine, and where doctors dominate. By contrast, social workers and doctors do not share problem definitions, understandings of appropriate responses, or even necessarily outcomes. They suggest radically different courses of treatment, and have no inbuilt way to settle the issue because it is not clear which profession is 'on top' and which is 'on tap'. In turn, it is not agreed whether a given patient's problem is a given illness, or a lack of independence. As a consequence, the professionals tend not to coordinate, and instead compete to impose their definitions of the problem. Given the overwhelming status, resources, and visibility of medicine, the result is that the social services professions usually feel that they are treated as inadequately valued supplementary help for doctors – that they are solving doctors' problems such as bed-blocking rather than using a range of tasks, including medicine, to help patients gain and enjoy more autonomous lives.

The same instability (i.e. professional competition) and imbalance (i.e. medical power), working on a different level, account for the failure of integration on the planning level. The problem of social services when they were under local government was inadequate funding from local governments that were incapable of or unwilling to allocate sufficient funds for staff and facilities. Moving social services into the health and social services boards created a different problem, since it made social services a direct rival of medicine (above all, hospitals) for limited funds. This is a competition social services have a hard time winning. Without consensus management social services lose out.

Why? The professionals of medicine outrank those of social services in status and income, and consequently in political power. They are also better organised through the BMA and Royal Colleges, which are easily a match for the advocacy and professional organisations of social services. Client status also affects perceptions of tasks, and social services focus on lower-status populations such as the elderly, teenagers, and the poor. Almost all the medical professions have incentives to side with doctors, both as recipients of medical care resources and as professions whose status is higher than social services, and thus are careful not to appear too closely affiliated with social services. Finally, acute care is very popular. Hospitals as institutions are usually much loved by their users and their communities, and have a high profile in the press. Keeping them in good condition is a point of pride for many. In Northern Ireland, the Troubles strengthened this attachment to hospitals. It is difficult to deny funds to any hospital anywhere; it is harder still in Northern Ireland after the insecurity of life during the Troubles and the stories of the 'angels in white coats' rescuing victims of terrorism.

With the establishment of the internal market after 1989 Northern Ireland simply established broader trusts to handle the range of non-tertiary care. In Northern Ireland the process of establishing the internal market was broadly similar to that in the rest of the UK. High-profile advanced hospitals led the way in shaking off board control and becoming trusts, as did well-resourced urban GPs in becoming fundholders; in both cases the motivation appears to have been the desire for autonomy from boards. Beyond the big trusts and Belfast, the process moved more slowly. In delaying implementation Northern Ireland had the great advantages of direct rule. Pressure from London, whether directly from Downing Street and Whitehall or indirectly through the media and professionals' networks, was refracted through the Secretary of State (preoccupied with security and constitutional affairs – the late 1980s and early 1990s were a bad time for prospects of peace), the junior minister of health (carrying multiple portfolios), and the civil servants (who consulted their counterparts in London, tried to avoid snags, and often therefore filtered ideas). All these actors benefited from the low visibility of Northern Irish public policy (even in Northern Ireland) and the reluctance of policy makers to increase conflict of any kind in Northern Ireland. None of them showed much interest in ramming the policy through, and consulted with their managers and professionals to see what was feasible. The process was much less conflictual, and much slower than the establishment of the internal market in the rest of the UK – the Western Health and Social Services Board was the last part of the UK fully to establish the institutions of the internal market and only did so when obliged by the incoming Labour government.

Summary

The result of the legacies of Stormont and direct rule – undemocratic regimes in a deeply divided society – was that Northern Ireland, a small place, had a small policy community. Policy came from London, with little Northern Irish input. Much of that policy was then filtered by groups in Northern Ireland. In Northern Ireland, institutional elites with staying power and a role in implementation (or groups that could claim to speak for those groups, such as the Royal Colleges) entered into dialogue with the civil servants in order to work out what should be brought in from the British sources of policy ideas, what items were not worth putting on the Minister's agenda, which ones should be resisted even if the Minister did like them, and how Northern Ireland would implement decisions. The small circle of big players and informal interlocutors in Belfast dominated policy. As none of these players relied upon public support, none had much incentive to create or expand conflicts, and the media and visible politicians of Northern Ireland were otherwise engaged. Thus Northern Irish health and social services was more consensual than in other parts of the UK, but the marked characteristics were the lack of pluralism and the contraction of conflict. It was very difficult to participate in policy as an outsider and the society did not allow many contesting policy advocacy coalitions able to try. The comfortable result freed insiders such as trust executives to do much of what they wanted, and ran adequately.

None of this was particularly surprising. The premise of direct rule was, after all, that Northern Ireland was incapable of democratic self-government.

Policies and politics

Neither a civil war in otherwise tranquil North West Europe nor the existence of a strange part of the UK governed without reference to its inhabitants' wishes was acceptable in the long run – not to the bulk of the population of Northern Ireland, nor to decision makers in London. The result was that from the first days of the Troubles there have been efforts to bring the two sides together, with regular efforts to test various formations of actors (Northern Irish parties and the UK state in the 1970s; London and Dublin, without reference to the Northern Irish parties in the 1980s; and finally London, Dublin, the USA, and most of the Northern Irish parties in the 1990s). The Belfast Agreement marked an agreement to end the war by creating a devolved Northern Ireland cocooned in various 'strands' of councils, voting schemes, and inclusive government. The new government came into existence – which was the main thing asked of it – and was faced with issues such as health policy, for which Northern Ireland's politicians had had little preparation.

The policy community

The gravitational pull of the Troubles in Northern Ireland had, via the instruments of Stormont and direct rule, already shaped the Northern Irish health policy community in several unusual ways. First, it was small and insider-dominated. While all policy communities are to some extent organised around the needs of government, this one was more so than usual. The Northern Irish policy community in health was quite closely confined to the NICS and those who could provide the NICS with advice, acquiescence, and approval in the terms that it defined. The devolved Minister did not markedly change this, as she chose for her special adviser a former political prisoner with no known expertise in health. One NICS official, after reflecting on various sources of information and advice, concluded in a 2002 interview that 'you would have to say that we [the NICS] have the only serious policy capacity in Northern Ireland' (2–5). The sources of information tended to be within the health service (in good part due to lack of investment in others in policy) – top managers and chosen clinicians. The policy community also included the hardiest participants – a few academics, representatives of the Royal Colleges, and the BMA. Partly balancing this insider-dominated community, Northern Ireland had a voluntary and community sector of unusual strength and organisation. This was able to invest in thinking out policy proposals and its role in implementation meant that it had substantial advice and acquiescence powers of its own. The community sector, with its closer links into Northern Ireland's society, was less willing or able to develop the policy expertise and resources required to work its way into the policy community.

The Belfast Agreement

The Belfast Agreement is a largely unprecedented experiment in political design. It exercises a powerful pressure for immobility in policy terms, even if its existence is a political achievement. It therefore preserves the policy structures, geared to immobility, that arose under direct rule. This section explains how it shapes the action of other political actors, primarily by constraining the executive, just as Northern Ireland's historic legacies constrain pluralist politics. It thus explains why the much-welcomed arrival of 'local decision makers' proved something of a disappointment.

The Belfast Agreement (also known as the Good Friday Agreement), approved in a 22 May 1998 referendum, was a dramatic moment in efforts to establish a stable, peaceable democracy in Northern Ireland (Ruane and Todd 1999; Cox, Guelke, and Stephen 2000; Wilford 2001). As part of the peace process, the Belfast Agreement was embedded in a complex web of deals and understandings as well as tensions and conflicts. Its main institutional attributes are far more marked by its role as a stage in the peace process than by any conventional sense of what it means to engineer political institutions for good government.

Devolution was 'strand one' of the Belfast Agreement (Bew 2000). The complex document included two more strands: number two established a north–south ministerial council, and strand three, known as 'east–west,' established a British-Irish Council and Intergovernmental Council. The Agreement also included extensive provisions of greater or lesser specificity on security, rights, policing, equality of opportunity, and arms decommissioning by paramilitaries. In June 1998 108 members were elected to the Northern Ireland Assembly (Table 6.1). Originally, the UK government had hoped to start all three devolved bodies at the same time, but the timetable slipped in Northern Ireland over decommissioning. The UUP, led by David Trimble pro-Agreement but internally riven and under siege from the anti-Agreement Democratic Unionist Party (DUP) of Ian Paisley, demanded decommissioning by the IRA before entering government. The DUP and dissidents within the UUP were volubly critical when Trimble accepted some IRA disarmament, but not as much as they wanted, and entered government. The problem of distrust, focused on decommissioning, would not be solved quickly.

Once Trimble and the UUP entered government they were followed by the DUP. The latter adopted a novel interpretation of ministerial obligations; its ministers did not let down its hostility or sit at tables with Sinn Féin, but did take their allotted ministerial posts. That let the devolved assembly come

Table 6.1. Electoral results for the Northern Ireland Assembly, 1998

Party	Members elected to the Legislative Assembly
Social Democratic and Labour Party	24
Ulster Unionist Party	28
Democratic Unionist Party	20
Sinn Féin	18
Alliance Party of Northern Ireland	6
UK Unionist Party	5
Independent Unionists	3
Progressive Unionist Party	2
Northern Ireland Women's Coalition	2

to life in the same Stormont building on 2 December 1999 (see the Constitution Unit 'Monitoring Devolution' reports for the full story; and Wilford and Wilson 2000; Wilson and Wilford 2001). However, the same problem of Unionist distrust, focused on decommissioning, kept recurring. Trimble faced a sceptical and increasingly opposed Unionist population and anti-Agreement forces both in his party and in the well-organised, growing, DUP. His particular method of responding to the pressure from these anti-Agreement forces was to threaten to resign – and thereby force elections – if the IRA did not visibly decommission weapons. He did this three times, and the IRA did not decommission, in part because the IRA is not culturally an organisation that likes to respond to Unionist ultimata. The British government (as well as the Irish and US), looking at the large prospective losses of UUP votes to the DUP and SDLP votes to Sinn Féin, was not prepared to accept the prospect of new elections that could lead to the DUP and Sinn Féin winning majorities in their communities and in all probability ending the peace process. It opted to suspend devolution in February 2000 (after just three months of devolution), July 2001, August 2001, and September 2001, before the most seemingly permanent suspension in October 2002 (Wilford and Wilson 2000, 2003; Wilson and Wilford 2001). Each suspension introduced direct rule while the politicians sought a face-saving way for Trimble to return to office without elections. The first three times it more or less worked, with the IRA budging less than Trimble wanted but enough to allow him to return to office, but the process remained extremely unstable.

Meanwhile, Sinn Féin ministers were uninterested in east–west meetings and Trimble, demonstrating his toughness on Sinn Féin and the IRA, banned Sinn Féin's ministers from North–South meetings. The DUP held two ministerial slots in the Executive, but its ministers would not sit at tables with Sinn Féin and rotated in and out, so symbolically not holding office while actually holding office. Policing reforms went ahead, without Sinn Féin's approval. In the 2001 general and local elections, the DUP rose very close to the UUP in votes, and Sinn Féin surpassed the SDLP, thereby bringing closer the nightmare of London and Dublin (and advocates of the peace process as it stood) that the next elections would lead to victories for the DUP and Sinn Féin, openly hostile to each other but dominating their communities. The logic of Northern Irish electoral politics, with each election a tribal head-count and policy sidelined, certainly threatened that outcome (Ruohomaki 2001).

Devolution finally lost its momentum in October 2002 when precisely that electoral outcome began to close in. Most observers judged it clear that Sinn Féin and the DUP would almost certainly out-poll the SDLP and the UUP in 2003. Given that the two likeliest winners could not sit at a table with each other (due to the DUP's refusal), the overall Unionist dislike of Sinn

Féin, and the DUP's status as an 'anti-Agreement' party, such an electoral outcome would, most Northern Irish observers assumed, mean the end of devolution and possibly the peace process. The DUP appeared unlikely to soften its stance, while Sinn Féin softened quite a lot by its lights – but not enough for much of Unionist political opinion. As well as this, the UUP, always a poorly organised and riven party, began to look especially fragile. Trimble's leadership had for some time been supported by a bare majority in his strangely organised party, and he began to lose support to hard-liners (and even lost MPs and Members of the Legislative Assembly – MLAs). Given that such a secession of Unionists from the leading Unionist party had destroyed the Sunningdale Agreement, it appeared that history was about to repeat itself. Trimble responded by becoming even more intransigent and demanding fuller IRA decommissioning. Trimble's ultimatum meant that full, visible decommissioning and demobilisation would be required and the IRA did not do that. The result was that the Secretary of State for Northern Ireland, John Reid (a Scottish MP, soon to become Secretary of State for Health after a short spell as Leader of the House of Commons) suspended the Northern Ireland Assembly. The government selected a junior ministerial team to take on domestic policy functions, suggesting that it expected suspension to be the situation for some time to come. Northern Ireland did not go to the polls in May 2003 with Scotland and Wales; 'wake us when something happens' was how several interviewees characterised the public mood. The parties fell to arguing about the requirements of the Agreement with the legalism typical of Northern Irish politics, while not making constructive moves to deal with obvious problems such as the presence of several private armies in an ostensible liberal democracy or the increasing degree of hatred in the society.

The problem was relatively simple. Trimble and the UUP would probably lose votes unless they could demonstrate that they were both delivering the benefits of peace and being tough enough on Sinn Féin to reassure potential DUP voters. Under constant attack from within and from the DUP for coddling the IRA, Trimble had little margin for manoeuvre. Breaking the logjam, the conventional logic went, would require some sort of dramatic IRA step toward disarmament, elections called by London, and a visible victory in the negotiations for Trimble (since elections with a weak Trimble would simply make a DUP victory more likely). The effort to do just this, an effort that would rapidly come to be known as 'the fiasco', took place starting with stories appearing in the broadcast media on 20 October, reporting that London had set a date for elections. Then, on 21 October, the IRA made some sort of a disarmament gesture supervised by international observers, and London called elections. The problem was that the international observers' report on disarmament, which carefully respected the IRA's demand for secrecy, was not specific or dramatic enough for Trimble, who stopped the operation before the final step of agreeing to restart government. Trimble halted the dance, various parties issued angry or triumphalist statements, and despite desultory talks the process stopped again.

Elections could not be stopped, though, and they took place on 26 November. The results were not surprising: the DUP became the largest Northern Irish party, followed by the UUP, then Sinn Féin, and then the damaged SDLP. The DUP, despite much excited rumour, stuck to its pledge to avoid talks with Sinn Féin and try to renegotiate the whole Good Friday Agreement. Given that the new Assembly would have to have a DUP leader for First Minister and a Sinn Féin minister for Deputy First Minister, there was no real chance of it meeting. There is currently little chance of devolution resuming; the protagonists have proceeded to a review of the Agreement that had been scheduled anyway and that offered the latest hope for progress.

Politics: institutions

Northern Ireland is a sectarian, low-trust polity with a Unionist majority, and the Belfast Agreement reflects that. The reason London had not been able to re-establish devolution until 1999 was that the nationalists did not trust the Unionist majority with self-rule, for obvious reasons, while many Unionists were, for equally obvious reasons, suspicious that devolution could lead to their being forced into a united Ireland. Both communities contained substantial groups who were opposed to participation in devolved settlements – Unionists often favoured flat integration into the UK as if Northern Ireland were part of England while loyalists viewed Britishness as a contract Britain was breaking, and many Nationalists accorded no legitimacy at all to institutions that did not belong to a united Ireland (Ruane and Todd 1996). Other Unionists opposed the consent principle and concessions to Nationalists, but had no problems with the old Stormont model. Others had no problem with devolution but chose strategies that placed a low value on it. As a result, the Belfast Agreement was designed just to get the parties to participate in government. Part of the price was not obliging them to govern.

The chief problem addressed by strand one was how to design a devolved settlement that on the one hand could be trusted not to increase repression and that on the other hand would have incentives enough to bring all the major parties into the political system. The solution adopted for the problem of intercommunal suspicion was a ready-to-wear consociationalism, based on (hotly debated) academic analyses of plural societies (Lijphart 1969; Lustick 1997; Wilson 2003). It vests the devolved powers of Northern Ireland in a 108-member Assembly (for a technical analysis, see Burrows 2000). Votes for

Assembly seats then dictate the relative strength of the parties, with parties selecting their ministerial posts according to the d'Hondt system. Unlike in other parliamentary, cabinet-government systems, the First Minister (and partner from the opposite community, the Deputy First Minister), do not have any power to appoint, sack, or shuffle ministers other than those of their own parties. Any party that wins more than 10 per cent of the vote gets seats in the Executive with ministerships. The largest party chooses the First Minister and the largest party of the other large community chooses the Deputy First Minister (framers correctly expected this would, at least the first time, mean the UUP led in the first Assembly, with the SDLP providing the Deputy First Minister). The design overcame fears of majority misrule by first enshrining sectarian differences in politics (parties are Unionist, Nationalist, or Other) and then guaranteeing both communities a veto through a cross-community Executive and a requirement that controversial legislation wins a majority of both community's representatives (the design is far less solicitous of the need to protect the Other parties). This crucially means that there is no collective cabinet responsibility. The Assembly is then subjected to the same, low level of formal supervision of its policies that Scotland enjoys; the UK, almost uniquely in the world, does not constrain substantive policy divergence in health. Within its formula-allocated finances, the Assembly has great freedom – even if its finances are still formally allocated at the pleasure of the Westminster government.

The most striking fact about the design of the system is that the structure of the Executive severs the relationship between policy performance, ministerial accountability, and the party office. A party can keep an underperforming minister in office for the whole of Northern Ireland, based on its own internal politics and the percentage of the vote it won in one of the two big electoral competitions (Catholic and Protestant) that take place during each election on issues unrelated to policy. That means 10 per cent of the population can maintain an unsatisfactory minister whose mandate has nothing to do with his or her job.

Interviewees in Northern Ireland often quote US President Lyndon Johnson to the effect that 'it's better to have them inside the tent, pissing out, than outside the tent, pissing in'. The Belfast Agreement did not design a government to make policy or run Northern Ireland well. It designed a government that would induce the Northern Irish parties to emerge from their conflict and participate in any sort of Northern Irish government. It is full of incentives to bring parties into government, giving them the powers of Westminster-system ministers, and often absolves them of the responsibility that comes with government (such as interdepartmental coordination, cabinet unity, or a reasonable chance of being thrown into the opposition). It is therefore also sluggish and cautious by design. The Agreement outlined an elaborate system of checks and balances designed to prevent majority tyranny by guaranteeing representation of both communities and all major groups and by then liberally distributing vetoes.

Politics: the party system

The Northern Irish party system is a reflection of the region's troubled, divided, and highly politicised society and is no small contributor to the preservation of its sectarian divide and low-trust politics. Northern Ireland has its own party system; despite periodic links between the UUP and the Conservatives (the UUP took the Conservative whip at Westminster in the 1960s, to Harold Wilson's irritation) there is no meaningful extension of the UK party system in Northern Ireland. UK parties, fearing contagion, prefer to keep it that way. For all practical purposes, Northern Ireland has two-and-a-half party systems, with more or less infinite complications but some basic outlines. There are two big party systems, one Unionist and one nationalist. Each big party system contains two big parties (SDLP/Sinn Féin and UUP/DUP), with one more moderate party (the SDLP and UUP) and one more extreme (Sinn Féin and the DUP). There are also a number of small Unionist parties, often linked to loyalist paramilitaries, that are also more vehemently Unionist than the UUP and that did poorly in 2003. There are almost no crossover votes, despite permanent hopes that UUP and SDLP voters will support each other's parties (and moderate politics) rather than give their second preferences to the more extreme party in their system. The half-system is the limited area occupied by small nonsectarian, creative parties such as the Women's Coalition (which lost all its seats in 2003) and the Alliance.

This party system interacts with Northern Ireland's zero-sum politics in which a gain for one side is usually seen as a loss for the other. If a voter does not trust any representatives of the other community, then it is logical to vote not for a moderate party that offers to compromise across the divide but instead to support a more vociferous party that can be relied upon to fight hard for community interests, even if that requires damaging intercommunity relations or the peace process. A low-trust sectarian system gives voters ample incentive to seek a champion for a fight rather than negotiators for a settlement. The Belfast Agreement makes this tendency worse by eliminating meaningful opposition and reducing the electoral value of being a moderate compromiser (Horowitz 2001; Wilson 2003). If all four big parties will be in government and get some of the credit for the peace process, then it is rational for an untrusting voter to vote for the more determined, extreme, one rather than the moderate one. By making it hard to cast the competitions as pro versus anti-Agreement, this politics makes it hard for the SDLP and UUP to make a virtue of their moderation and willingness to compromise. Rather, it helps the DUP and Sinn Féin, well-organised and dynamic parties already, to define the issues as being SDLP-UUP weakness and their own strength and effectiveness. As the Agreement founders, then, it becomes more imperative for worried voters to choose an effective champion (DUP/Sinn Féin) rather than throw more support to the parties closely tied to it but constantly accused of being sell-outs (DUP/SDLP). A vote for the more extreme party will deliver strong representation, and a vote for any party that supports the Agreement will, at least in theory, deliver the continued peace process.

The Northern Irish parties are all organisations that developed before the Agreement and which have been hard put to adapt (to the extent that they want to adapt at all). Each party carries a series of entrenched organisational characteristics that make it ill-suited to making public policy. The independence of departments from each other and from the Executive means that it is crucial which party holds a portfolio; the health portfolio, the second-to-last to be selected, was with Sinn Féin. Sinn Féin is a very effective, centralised party, which won with a combination of excellent organisation, youth, uniformity, starring role in the peace process, and deep roots – not so much in historic Irish Republicanism as in the experience of many Catholics in a discriminatory country (McIntyre 2001). However, its Leninism made it almost unlobbyable and its dedication to a greater goal (a united Ireland) meant that it neither developed policy ideas nor allowed its members to develop them. Its poor relations with the existing Northern Irish power structure also meant that it only occasionally built good relations with the civil servants. The result was that the party was remarkably cut off from policy debates. Other parties have their organisational oddities – the SDLP was organisationally the creation of one man, John Hume, and visibly aged with him; the DUP, half an extension of Protestant fundamentalism, was equally a creature of Ian Paisley; and the UUP was ideologically riven and saddled with a constitution that allowed small numbers of malcontents to freeze the party for months and repeatedly threaten the whole Agreement. With the exception of the SDLP, none of the parties tried to address these organisational flaws.

The structure of political recruitment and competition exacerbated these problems when the Assembly began work. The Assembly immediately faced teething problems in its policy work (in addition to the suspensions and political tensions described earlier). Northern Ireland has simply lacked the usual mechanisms of political recruitment found in liberal democracies. The whole system had to be staffed by politicians who at best built their careers as councillors of particularly powerless local governments or as MPs who were almost totally excluded even from policy scrutiny. Government institutions organised various types of short course for them, and local institutions (such as trusts and health and social services boards) began to make contact with their local MLAs in the hope of explaining the problems and opportunities – and complexity – of the system from their point of view. The MLAs were aware of their need to learn; almost none of the committees in the Assembly met in public at first because the members preferred to have their education conducted in private.

For policy purposes there are four salient characteristics of the Northern Irish party system. The first is that the entire focus of politics is the nationalist–Unionist axis. There appears to be a remarkable decree of consensus on socially conservative welfare policies across the board, but that is a sideshow compared to the sectarian divide. The second is that there is no one party system. Politics is dominated by two separate systems with two large parties in each. In a logic of enemies Northern Irish politics has an inbuilt tendency to polarise at extremes – a tendency that has been powerful over the last decade. The third characteristic is that the parties, reflecting their system, de-emphasise policy to focus on constitutional politics, symbolism, and organisation. The fourth is that the Belfast Agreement, by effectively trying to collect nine-tenths of the society into a unified cabinet government, dramatically reduces the likelihood that any party will pay a price for damaging devolution, let alone bad policy.

Policy outcomes

Northern Irish health policy changed remarkably little with the advent of devolution and substantial money. The policy community remained small and stable, with far less personnel turnover than the other systems. Meanwhile, outside the civil service and to a lesser extent the strong voluntary sector, policy advocates were thin on the ground – there were too few groups that had the critical mass to import or develop a policy idea.

Organisational form

When Labour arrived in 1997, it found a relatively stable if unloved administrative system. While in the rest of the UK it proceeded to abolish much of the internal market, in Northern Ireland it avoided making decisions. The salience of health care contributed to the delay in decision making: the consensus on the need for reform was so strong as to make Labour hold off reforming it so that Northern Irish politicians would be able to take on the job and earn the plaudits. Northern Ireland therefore inherited the system of GP fundholding from the internal market because Labour wanted to hand over such obvious opportunities for policy changes. All the Northern Irish parties supported the abolition of fundholding. However, nothing happened until December 2001. Then fundholding was abolished. There was no reorganisation on the scale of England, Scotland, or Wales. The reason for this is twofold and again demonstrates the power of the same groups (the professional organisations, managers, and civil service) who set agendas before and after devolution; and the force some of those groups can have when they lobby. The entire complex story can be read as a struggle between civil servants, with UK-based policy ideas and broad experience in the system, importing an English advocacy coalition's victory, and the BMA, representing GPs and attempting to ensure that they would win, and at least not lose, influence and autonomy as they were subsumed into new primary care groups.

As in other policy areas, the direct rule Minister had put forth a Green Paper on primary care policy, entitled *Fit for the Future* (DHSSNI (Northern Ireland Department of Health and Social Services) 1998). Sinn Féin Health Minister Barbara de Brún, once in office, pointed to the lack of consultation within Northern Ireland of a direct rule policy paper, and began to prepare another one. The Minister presented her consultation paper *Building the Way Forward in Primary Care* in December 2000 (DHSSPS (Northern Ireland Department of Health Social Services and Public Safety) 2000). It outlined options and suggested that primary care be organised around local health and social services groups which would be multi-professional local teams with no budgets but which would contribute to commissioning decisions. They would progressively have the boards' commissioning budgets devolved to them. This was broadly the proposal suggested in the direct rule *Fit for the Future* and strongly resembled the English and Welsh organisational forms, and was the one that the civil servants broadly had advocated for years. Subsequently, as the English system began to look extremely labour-intensive and radical, Scotland's system of triage and resource allocation by professionals began to appeal as the less disruptive and more effective way to run a service.

The paper was badly received, finally meeting its end in the Assembly Health Committee. The explicit reason was that the Committee, while just as committed to abolishing fundholding as the Minister, did not have enough faith in the details of the plan for a replacement and was unwilling to support a proposal that might lead to disorder or something worse. As a consequence, the Health and Personal Social Services Act's clause 39, rather than abolishing fundholding, prorogued it for a year so that the Department could design a superior replacement (Wilford and Wilson 2001).

The origins of the Committee's detailed arguments and preoccupations lay partly in the undoubted hastiness of the Department's decision and in the MLAs' own work (part of the evidence that the SDLP, against the odds, does some serious policy work is that two of three SDLP members defied a whip and voted against the Minister's proposals based on their conclusions). However, the conflict also became important because of a conflict within the health policy community that drew the Minister and Committee in on opposing sides. Broadly, the proposals set the GPs (in the form of the BMA) against civil servants, social services, and professions allied to medicine. From the doctors' point of view the design was worryingly fuzzy and the groups did not provide enough representation to doctors. The BMA decided it could bid for better and lobbied the Committee members to turn down the proposals until a more satisfactory replacement could be devised. The BMA created a rare kind of public political conflict in Northern Ireland, namely between two competing insider groups with a role in advice and acquiescence. The Committee vote followed on the BMA's decision to organise a lobbying campaign arguing against the proposal (crucial in this was not financial or other pressure, but a well-orchestrated information campaign directed at MLAs).

The Minister retreated and held further consultations. In October 2001 the Department published the responses to the consultation papers along with a very similar plan. The circulars emerging from the Department, and even more so the informal advice being given by the Department, stressed that the groups would have their budgets devolved rapidly and that they would have physician majorities on their boards. By avoiding legislation when possible, the Minister was able to avoid an Assembly vote and remain ambiguous about details such as the make-up of boards for months after the announcement.

The BMA (one of the best-organised interest groups in Northern Ireland), and professional organisations again protested, and continued doing so into the fraught spring 2002 implementation work. Their arguments were largely the same, as were their tactics. However, this time they failed. The problem was in large part that the party consensus, one shared across MLAs, demanded an end to fundholding but only the Department was capable of designing such an end (on technical grounds alone) and willing to do so. The Department stuck with the plan it had developed from the English and Welsh plans. The civil service's preferences won, reflecting the weakness of any (BMA) strategy of expanding conflict in a party system that did not cleave along policy debates. In turn, the civil service's attention to broad UK-wide discussions meant that the civil service transmitted English and Welsh ideas straight on to the Northern Irish agenda. As nobody else added new ideas to the agenda, eventually the politicians tired of waiting and adopted the civil service view.

The explanation for such small change in the notoriously change-prone UK lies in the small and managerially dominated policy community. After the 2002 suspension, the focus of activity became the direct rule ministers, the scheduled review of the Agreement (started in January 2004), and a novelty, the Review of Public Administration. The latter was part of the Belfast Agreement and was intended to reform the quango-laden public services, which were generally agreed to be fragmented and bureaucratic as well as illogical. On the one hand, opening a new front for political reform and activity seemed like a desirable strategy after high politics ran into the sand; on the other hand, administrative reform might improve the public services and introduce more democracy, debate, and accountability.

New public health

Northern Ireland, like the other devolved countries, has grim public health statistics. The population has many bad habits, principally smoking, drinking, and eating a poor diet, and these are exacerbated by deprivation and social exclusion. Other public health problems such as accidents are significant. While the Troubles had positive effects on the suicide rate, drug abuse, and many mental problems, peace has led to an explosion of those problems as people deal with problems created by the Troubles that they had repressed during the tension (McKittrick 2002). The full range of public health challenges are to be found in Northern Ireland's wide variety of poor urban and rural areas. The new public health had numerous advocates in the health services and voluntary sector, who had developed advocacy skills and resources over the years during which the government hoped social inclusion would help solve the Troubles. In part the large number of advocates was a result of the strength of the voluntary sector; it was also because of the widespread sense that multiple deprivation helped explain sectarianism (an early victory for new public health). New public health also had the Minister for an ally. She came into office with a focus on improving access to health services and improving public health and well-being. Public health advocates, even those who were deeply critical of her for other reasons, did stress that her verbal support for public health made their work easier by shielding them from pressure.

New public health goals are enshrined into the devolved Executive's plans. The *Programme for Government*, a consensus document agreed by the Executive (with input from the formally absent DUP members), is the basis of policy and is deliberately organised along cross-cutting rather than depart-mental lines. It thus includes many cross-departmental goals in the health section. The focus of these goals on new public health has helped, and is fully in tune with the wider-determinants agenda, but the goals have nevertheless been much more slowly turned into implemented policy than points on which the political and health service agendas join together, such as improving funding for hospitals (Office of the First Minister and the Deputy First Minister 2001).

Health policy in Northern Ireland, perhaps more than in the other devolved countries, has a built-in institutional bias towards classic health ser-vices because of the importance of service providers among the insiders who make policy (where besides hospitals and clinics would direct rule officials look for advisers?). In internal conflicts over spending, acute-care facilities and GPs have the upper hand due to their higher status and visibility. This means that the problems that the system must solve tend to emerge from these groups, and from the civil servants preoccupied with smoothly administering the health services, rather than from outside sources which are more likely to raise health and well-being. Even when these groups are consulted, as they are and were under direct rule, consultation is not the same as agenda-setting influence.

Despite these problems, the combination of the slow change in the health system and the political cover that the rhetoric affords mean that entrepre-neurial new public health advocates in the system can develop their ideas even though they have not reoriented the system. This is the permissive half of per-missive managerialism. The long tenure of many health chief executives allowes them to build up local networks and good degrees of trust. Public health local working means that the health system can interact with Northern Ireland's strong professional voluntary sector and benefit from its support. It produces local new public health work; policies from above, such as Health Action Zones, like most other policies from above, come from 'across the water'.

Quality

New public health and quality are the two main new and advancing policy advocacy coalitions in health care in the advanced industrial countries. In Northern Ireland, despite the efforts of some managers and professional elites, quality remains a very minor part of policy – the case study of quality in Northern Ireland is a case study not of a decision but of a non-decision.

Labour, with its UK-wide perspective, started a debate about quality for Northern Ireland that discussed the case for measures to improve medicine

and different strategies, ranging from a fully devolved Northern Irish standards and technology evaluation infrastructure to full integration into that of
England (i.e. offering the Scottish and Welsh options). Unlike the other
Labour-led debates, Northern Ireland hardly continued the debate, let alone
adopted Labour's conclusions (DHSSPS (Northern Ireland Department of
Health Social Services and Public Safety) 2001a). Quality dropped off the
agenda because the advocates were scarcely represented in the policy community and, secondarily, there was little political interest. The quality agenda in
Scotland, one country where it matters, depends on professionalists, and they
are overwhelmingly academic and professional medical elites. Northern
Ireland has few high-level professionals (the region is small) and not many of
them are interested in Northern Irish public policy. In England, quality is
partly about professional elites, and builds on their arguments and infrastructure, but it is also driven by the need to regulate the quasi-market that governments have been building since 1991. Without a market to regulate,
Northern Ireland again is hostile territory for those advocating quality policies. Meanwhile, politicians pay little attention to these intricate, professionalist issues. Problems tend not to find policies or politicians, so Northern Irish
politics resists policy. The result is that 'we're doing nothing at all. Nothing.
And that's shocking', according to one manager who complained bitterly
about the difficulty of raising new agenda items (2–23).

Public and private

Contrary to the general impression, there is a Northern Irish outcome in the
public–private provision debate. Like the other systems in England, Scotland,
and Wales, Northern Irish politics is subject to enormous pressures to deliver
services; the high profile of waiting lists and images of decrepit hospitals afflict
Northern Ireland as much as the rest of the UK and PFI looks like a solution
to the problem. The result is that, over the objections of unions, the Executive
is continuing to try to operate PFI projects that will allow it rapidly to deliver
new facilities without short-term budgetary consequences it cannot afford.
However, many PFI firms are reluctant to venture into Northern Irish politics, and thus the Executive is finding it hard to find partners (Ward 2001).
The small size of Northern Irish projects reduces the interest of PFI contractors; the largest PFI project, the Royal Courts of Justice in Belfast, is only
around £30 million. Even if Northern Ireland embraces PFI, it is unlikely that
the region's size, amount of business, and exotic risk profile will attract many
contractors. Many leaders of producer groups find PFI objectionable, but it
has been successfully sold by advocates as a modern solution to capacity problems and inefficiency. Thus, given its small incidence, there is little political

conflict (and most of that is made up of unions expressing disquiet at PFI). On the other hand, there is no incentive for politicians to follow the English and experiment with greater public–private integration. PFI was inherited, and has not turned into a problem, but the policies suggested in Northern Ireland today by those with roots in Northern Ireland are almost anything but suggestions for greater experimentation with the private sector.

The civil service imports the PFI agenda along with other English innovations, while politicians, to whom it is not a core belief that the public sector should be publicly run, can use it to increase the numbers of new buildings as part of a solution to public problems of capacity. The new hospital in the South West (serving Tyrone and Fermanagh) will be tendered as a PFI – mainly because the decision to proceed was made by the post-suspension direct rule ministers, whose careers are, as always with direct rule ministers, British.

Acute care restructuring

On the major issues of health policy compared in this study, Northern Ireland tends to non-decisions. Even when the institutions posed no obstacle and devolution was not suspended, Northern Ireland's policy and politics tended to motionlessness. The lack of attention to issues that are widely agreed to be crucial in health systems does not mean there were no health politics, however; it just means that Northern Ireland focused on different issues. Northern Irish policy making under the devolved Executive is well illustrated by the real focus of attention, namely acute care rationalisation. Acute care rationalisation – better, resisting acute care reallocation – is the best opportunity local groups have to mobilise around a policy issue, surmounting both the problems of Northern Irish society and the problems of its political institutions. Nevertheless, its advocates are fighting a slow losing battle. The Royal Colleges (which demand certain staffing and throughput standards) are not devolved and decide the fate of the hospitals along with the EU Working Time Directive (which reduces working hours), and both the Royal Colleges and the EU Directive are constantly requiring more staff in hospitals that cannot necessarily afford or justify it. It is worth tracing out two of the conflicts in some detail; they are among the few big contests about policy in Northern Ireland, and the only one in health where there are truly opposing groups in conflict. Two case studies, one urban and one rural, make this point and provide the clearest instance of policy conflict in devolved Northern Ireland. Every system of the UK has these conflicts; in 2001 a Labour MP lost to a doctor opposed to the closure of a hospital in the Wyre Forest constituency and in 2003 Labour lost an MSP to a similar campaign against closures in Glasgow. The difference is that, despite the passion, these hospital closures were not the centre of health politics. In Northern Ireland, they were, and that means that they are both integral to a study of Northern Irish health politics and an interesting case of Northern Irish politics focused on something other than its divisions.

BELFAST MATERNITY HOSPITALS

The first major decision de Brún took upon entering office was to decide one of the acute care rationalisation issues that had been on the agenda for years. Managers, civil servants, and professional leaders were all broadly agreed that Belfast was ill-served by its numerous maternity units and that it would be better to establish one major unit with new technology and standards. This conviction meant that the decision as to where to locate the new maternity unit, and which ones to close, was on the agenda when de Brún arrived in office. De Brún, who is a West Belfast MLA, opted to locate the new unit with the Royal Group on the Catholic Lower Falls (in her constituency) rather than at the City Hospital, in largely Protestant South Belfast near Queen's University. The decision provoked an uproar, with de Brún accused of favouritism to her constituency, Catholics, or both. The decision was poorly presented and was quickly challenged in the courts (although the eventual decision was made slightly less important by the quick demolition of the City's maternity unit). De Brún was forced to began a review, asking the Royal and the City to submit arguments for the location of the new maternity unit on their grounds. Interviewees suggested that the maternity experience was so disagreeable that the Minister afterward shied away from any decisions, and the decision was cited in many interviews as dramatically worsening her image.

Nevertheless, the decision was constrained by two of the most important institutional factors conditioning Northern Irish politics. First, the decision was conducted on an extremely narrow agenda, an agenda not created by politicians. When de Brún arrived in office, the agenda involved acute care rationalisation; specifically, the rationalisation of maternity units in Belfast; and more specifically, the establishment of a large new maternity unit at either the Royal or City Hospitals, with the closure of both hospitals' older units. Other options – such as altering the roles of small maternity units at the Mater or Ulster Hospitals in greater Belfast – were not on the agenda. What is striking about this agenda is the extent to which it developed in debates among the civil servants, professional organisations, and health service managers. This constriction of the range of alternatives reflects the lack of broad public participation; under direct rule, policy was negotiated by those charged with implementation and based on UK trends. The maternity decision was a case of this constriction; interviewees focused on how the various hospital trusts competed to construct the decision in various ways.

The second institutional factor was the demonstration that the politicians, without alternate sources of policy ideas, slotted directly into the agenda set by the insiders and attempted to fit their political views to a prepackaged option. This reflects the Northern Irish problems of political recruitment and electoral competition and the party system in which they live and die.

CENTRALISING WESTERN HOSPITALS

One of the major reasons that the Department and Minister are at least formally unwilling to make major decisions on primary care organisation is that acute care organisation remained under review for a decade. Years of reviews by policy makers went on as the non-devolved Royal Colleges slowly shut down small hospitals by denying them certification. This process of closure by cumulating decertification had already led to the demise of the South Tyrone Hospital in Dungannon in 1998 and the Bangor Hospital in 1995. In both these cases direct rule ministers made the decision, pointing to the inability of the hospitals to offer a full range of services, to do it well, and to the availability of superior services within driving range. Nevertheless, both were polemical decisions that led to much public complaint against the direct rule administration and were remembered years later. However, the western part of the province posed a more difficult problem. It had two small acute-care hospitals, the Erne in Enniskillen (capital of County Fermanagh) and the Tyrone County Hospital in Omagh (capital of County Tyrone). Both were important facilities in their towns, and both had particularly strong local associations as their staffs treated the victims of the traumatic Remembrance Day Enniskillen bombing and the Omagh car bomb.

Debates about provision in this area had gone on throughout the 1990s. Solutions had mostly included closure of the two hospitals and creation of a new hospital at a greenfield site somewhere accessible to people from across the two counties. After devolution, de Brún announced that she would restart consultations on a different basis. Rather than the sole issue of acute care planning in Tyrone and Fermanagh, the siting and type of new hospitals would have to at a minimum involve rethinking Northern Ireland's health care needs and the relationships of health bodies on both sides of the border. To begin this debate, she commissioned former civil servant Maurice Hayes (a former Permanent Secretary of the Northern Ireland Department of Health and Social Services, and also at the time a Senator in the Republic of Ireland) to lead an Acute Hospitals Review Group. Hayes and the Group took the terms of reference to think anew to include proposals to integrate health care not only across Northern Ireland and the northern parts of the Republic, but also to include a lucid discussion of the future of health care.

The Acute Hospitals Review Group concluded that there should be a new, greenfield acute care hospital that would replace both the Erne and South Tyrone Hospitals along with small hospitals lacking accident and emergency (A&E) departments in both Enniskillen and Fermanagh. The new hospital would take over maternity, A&E, and other difficult tasks for the region. The decision was largely uncontested, reflecting the power of professionalism as enunciated by the experts Hayes consulted. What was contested was the location the report proposed for the new hospital, which was a site near Enniskillen. The justification was that a site in Omagh would leave people in south-western Fermanagh more than an hour's ride by ambulance from A&E facilities (DHSSPS (Northern Ireland Department of Health Social Services and Public Safety) 2001b).

Omagh erupted. A council officer was instrumental in designing a campaign that the local council endorsed (across party and community lines) which created a multi-sectoral steering committee and a three-strand plan of action. The campaign, one that would be instantly recognisable to activists in most of the democratic world, raised funds, commissioned a report from outside consultants evaluating the Hayes Report conclusions, and organised a series of events culminating in a very large demonstration in Omagh. Omagh's campaign was one of the largest non-sectarian political campaigns in recent Northern Irish history. Meanwhile, Enniskillen had two campaigns, one run by UNISON representing the Erne staff and the other a low-key lobbying-oriented one.

Omagh's campaign resembled well-organised campaigns outside Northern Ireland, whether in Britain, the Republic, or elsewhere, while Fermanagh's focus was more reminiscent of direct rule campaigning in that it relied on insiders and ended with a public fireworks display – 'to thank the people for their support' (2–16). Omagh's campaign tried to win what seemed like a lost cause by expanding the conflict intellectually (with the consultants) and in support (by bringing in many previously apolitical groups such as small business, and its large demonstration). Intellectually, both campaigns entered a detailed debate about cross-border working (i.e. if the people in south-western Fermanagh could go to Sligo or Cavan in the Republic for emergencies, then Omagh would be the more accessible location for the rest). Oliver Gibson MLA, of the DUP, campaigned for residents on the far side of Lough Fermanagh to go to the Republic of Ireland in emergencies, noting that he thought they would find the NHS better value than the South's system. This crossed party lines; Northern Ireland had finally found a way to introduce 'normal', or at least distributional, politics into its sectarian polity. 'If Northern Ireland changes' remarked one interviewee in Omagh, 'it will because of things like this campaign' (2–9).

The Minister, as the two towns' campaigns went on, faced a new problem, one of party management. In the 2001 general elections, Sinn Féin, which already held Tyrone West (Omagh), took Fermanagh and South Tyrone (Enniskillen) from the UUP. Now, any decision would redistribute between two Sinn Féin constituencies. The Minister's response was to declare, after the closure of the Hayes Report consultation period, that the Report's consultation had actually been a 'pre-consultation' and that the Department would issue a consultation paper, for consultation, on favoured options. Coming close on the heels of her being forced to restart consultations on the Belfast maternity hospitals, it did her standing little good. In many ways, this tarrying might be the victory of the Omagh campaign, in that it demonstrated the political costs of trying to pursue the Acute Hospitals Review Group recommendations, and the Minister declined to pay costs not associated with party strategy. As the consultation period lengthened, the Department increasingly mentioned the virtues of tying the South West hospitals, decision to the broader Review of Public Administration, which would have the virtue of reporting after Sinn Féin was free from the health portfolio, due to either suspension or elections.

In a crystallisation of much that is wrong with Northern Ireland, suspension cut off the ability of the DHSSPS to review the issue. A junior minister in the newly enlarged NIO team made the decision. The new greenfield hospital was to be put on a site closer to Enniskillen. Northern Ireland would retain its integrity as a unit for public provision with public emergency services accessible from any corner without crossing the border. The debates and campaigns, whether the insider-toned campaign of Enniskillen or the mobilisation of Omagh, did not change what was in some senses a foreordained solution. They did demonstrate the ability of the Northern Irish party system to deflect interest in policy.

Conclusion

Why did Northern Ireland do so little with devolution when so much could be asked? The answer is that the Northern Irish party system is very poorly adapted to produce public accountability for and political debate around public policy, and Northern Irish society lacks the numerous advocates of other parts of the UK. Its structure of politics is built on and perpetuates sectarianism; its devolved formal institutions, an office-seeker's dream, create ministerial fiefdoms and limit public accountability; its informal institutions are parties and a civil service that are best adapted to the days when the civil service administered and the parties fought (sometimes literally) in sectarian and constitutional battles. The result is that the policy debates and practices, although disrupted, hardly changed; being an insider with advice and acquiescence still matters in Northern Ireland, while the outlines of policy changes still travel from Britain to Belfast via the civil service. To relate it back to the three tests, policy does reflect the relative influence of different advocates and shows their influence or lack of it, and does resemble pre-devolution policy.

It is important to keep the importance of policy in Northern Ireland in perspective. Public policies touch the people from cradle to grave, but politics in Northern Ireland is organised around other issues that also follow people from cradle to grave. The justification for the strange polity established under the Belfast Agreement was its role in the peace process, and the justification for its reinstatement or modification will be the service that devolution can do for the peace process. This means that Northern Ireland will always run the risk of creating a system of government that almost eliminates the need to govern (or compromise), since office, rather than responsibility or even power, is what appeals to the untrusting and often extraparliamentary forces that devolution tries to tame. Running Northern Ireland well is a secondary concern for even those politicians who believe in stewardship but must bow to its politics.

That said, it is easy to critique the Belfast Agreement on the grounds of its poor policy performance. But the evidence of the policy case studies here suggest that the institutions are not primarily to blame for the failure to govern. The self-reinforcing sectarian division cuts off the incentive for politicians to do something as risky as govern. Unlike in England, Scotland, and Wales, failure to perform in policy terms has probably never destroyed a political career in Northern Ireland. The lack of demand for policy, the focus of the political stream on communities and constitutions, and the lack of supply of policies from a policy community virtually restricted to administrators explain why Northern Ireland's policy debates so often end in a non-decision. There are admirable efforts to create a broader and more pluralistic policy community in civil society, in the voluntary sector, the SDLP and small non-sectarian parties (Women's Coalition, which lost all its seats in 2003, and Alliance), the press, and Northern Ireland's few think-tanks and academic institutions. The policy community faces a drought of demand. Until the society and the party systems change, it is probably asking too much of political institutions or policy thinkers that they produce government. Although campaigns around local hospitals are intensely appealing intrusions of 'normal' politics into Northern Irish society, they might not be enough.

Northern Ireland's politics are centripetal, drawing every issue into constitutional and national politics, and centrifugal, driving people apart on those issues, and are unlikely to change quickly.

Notes

1 Good analyses of the broader issues are in Rose (1971), Whyte (1990), O'Leary and McGarry (1993), Ruane and Todd (1996), Hennessy (1997), Arthur (2000), and Bew, Gibbon and Patterson (2002).
2 Northern Irish Prime Minister Craigavon explained in 1934: 'in the South they boasted of a Catholic State. They still boast of Southern Ireland being a Catholic State. All I boast of is that we are a Protestant Parliament and a Protestant State' (Fitzpatrick 1998:224).

7
Creating divergent policy in the UK

The autonomy of regional governments such as the devolved administrations of the UK is limited not just by practicality and desirability but also by concrete limits of institutions and finance. Institutions in politics and their effects on policy outcomes have been one of the main topics in comparative politics for years, and there is an abundant literature on the subject (for reviews, March and Olsen 1989; Powell and DiMaggio 1991; Thelen and Steinmo 1992; Hall and Taylor 1996; Immergut 1998; Thelen 1999). The previous chapters show that with the exception of electoral rules (which sustain small parties and hurt larger ones), the institutional variation between UK systems does not explain much of the variation. Either UK governments are still essentially powerful, autonomous parliamentary governments with few veto points, or, in the case of Northern Ireland, there is not much political forward motion.

The institutional framework of intergovernmental relations, however, matters, and the way that it matters is most clearly visible with a comparative glance sideways. The structure of devolution in the UK is the necessary condition for the degree of divergence presently being seen. By giving great spending policy autonomy to the devolved countries and sealing them off from most central government interference and market forces, propitious conditions are created for divergence and innovation in health policy. There is less pressure for a race to the bottom because policy is decoupled from taxes. The overall structure of intergovernmental relations is, however, vulnerable. It entails financial limits that soon will matter in the development of health policy in the devolved UK, and threatens a potential crisis if the variation in citizenship rights – the extent of Britain's 'postcode lottery' in health policy – becomes a political issue anywhere (Simeon, Rachel 2003:216–17). Given the tendency of polities to diverge, the UK's intergovernmental finance and regulations effectively create a fragile but powerful divergence machine.

The loosely coupled Union

In organisational sociology the term 'loosely coupled' refers to organisations where there is significant looseness and play in the connection between one function and another (Hagan 1994). The UK since devolution is loosely coupled. Its existing devolution settlement effectively insulates the different components of the Union from each other. The chief attributes of the UK devolution settlement are its lack of central government regulation of the activities of the devolved bodies and its financial foundation on a block grant set by a formula. There are good analyses available of both aspects of devolution (Hazell 2000b, 2003c; Trench 2001b, 2004; Heald and McLeod 2002; House of Lords Select Committee on the Constitution 2002a). The crucial point is that the devolution settlement created very few shared policy areas where there is genuine space for competition or cooperation between governments.

The devolved UK has unusually clearly demarcated competencies and intergovernmental frontiers. Its workings resemble old analyses of 'dual federalism', in which competencies are clearly marked out and particular governments are clearly accountable for particular policies. Under the pressure of credit seeking, blame avoiding, and problem solving, politicians in most countries have made government mixed and interpenetrated. Federal and decentralised countries of the world have under the pressure of policy making and politics been replacing 'layer cake' with 'marble cake', that is, cooperative and interpenetrated, federalism (Grodzins 1984:8). The newly devolved UK, by contrast, is cleanly divided between governments that come close to being sealed vessels. This is particularly true of health, where Scotland is particularly autonomous, Northern Ireland is particularly autonomous when governing itself, and even Wales has substantial freedom.

Banting and Corbett (2002) identify the two key forms of constraint on policy divergence within states. One constraint is normative and regulatory, namely the extent to which the central state or institutional framework can oblige or prevent a policy decision. The other is financial, namely the extent to which the financial system constrains regional governments. This includes the extent to which it creates autonomy through the trade-off between transfers and taxes as well as the ability of the central state to intervene via finance. The UK has an autonomy-promoting settlement in both respects, above all in Scotland.

Normative legal frameworks

In regulation and shared competencies, the UK (especially highly devolved Scotland) is something of an international outlier because of its lack of frameworks constraining the regional governments. The various mechanisms by which the central government constrains decentralised jurisdictions by law in other countries are simply missing in the UK's formal institutions. Poirier (2001:147–52) identifies the mechanisms that allow central governments to set frameworks. The first mechanism is the constitutional norm that guarantees certain rights or competencies. The second is framework legislation, which in Switzerland, Spain, and Germany creates general norms but leaves the regional governments to set means and some ends. The third is policy, in which the central government adopts legislation and the execution is carried out by the regional government. The final mechanism is intergovernmental accords and agreements, which can be politically or legally binding. The UK lacks all of the above. It has no constitution. It has no framework legislation (although the Welsh arrangement vaguely resembles such an idea). It does not give devolved governments legislation to execute without rights to legislate on it. Its intergovernmental agreements ('concordats') are abstract to a fault. The overarching legal framework that constrains UK governments is to be found in EU and international law, and that is limited in its impact so far.

Northern Ireland should be unconstrained and gaining competencies with time, but its road is rocky since the Westminster government has opted several times to suspend it – and currently it is not clear when, if ever, it will be restored. Wales, meanwhile, has 'secondary legislative' powers. Secondary legislation is the legislative power spelled out in primary (Westminster) legislation; the power to make secondary legislation is invariably delegated, whether to a Secretary of State or to the National Assembly for Wales. The scope of secondary legislation is therefore never fixed; it varies with each Westminster law. Some such laws are very broad and leave great scope for secondary legislation, and some are tightly prescriptive. The decision as to how to write the law lies with the UK government and not Wales. That means that Wales cannot pass important constitutive legislation; rather, its powers lie in the development of lesser instruments within legal frameworks set by Westminster. This is not regulation, since Westminster is not well equipped to set out standards for Wales to follow and cannot oblige Wales to do so, but can legislate in almost any area of Welsh politics. In health, under current primary legislation, Wales has extensive autonomy and has used it.

Finance

The financial structure cements autonomy. Finance is as crucial as the formal distribution of powers in understanding the real autonomy of different levels of government. US states, for example, deliver most services on their own or through their local governments. In constitutional law they are immensely important. This division of powers, entrenched in a written and venerated constitution, is undermined by the dependence of most states on federal grants, which both shape incentives and give the federal government oversight over the programmes that spend the grants (Sparer 1996; Weissert and Weissert 1996:188–95; Conlan 1998). That story is repeated in many other countries where the use of the central government 'spending power' gives it the ability to intervene in policy areas allocated to other governments, create important incentives to change the activities of other governments, or both (Watts 2000). If the UK government had such a carrot, it could intervene quite a lot in devolved politics, despite its lack of a stick.

The Barnett formula for allocating spending, which is the keystone of devolution finance, prevents such detailed intervention. Barnett is a formula-based block transfer (Bell and Christie 2002; Heald and McLeod 2002; House of Lords Select Committee on the Constitution 2002a). It is becoming less shadowy and more rigid over time as questioning and political visibility turn it from a Treasury convenience into a sort of institution. Being formula-based means that it is relatively predictable and transparent, and therefore difficult to manipulate. Being a block transfer means that funds may not be earmarked or ring-fenced for particular programmes that the central government favours. The formula, unique in the world (Bell and Christie 2002:139), works by allocating spending to Northern Ireland, Scotland, and Wales in a fixed ratio to *changes* in spending in England. For every new pound of expenditure in England by the central government, a sum of money is automatically added to the block grants for Scotland and Wales, and for every new pound of Great Britain spending a sum of money is then allocated to equivalent tasks in Northern Ireland. This sum of money is allocated on a per-capita basis; each person in Britain, effectively, receives an equal share of the new pound of public spending, so Wales, for example, receives a budget increase equal to the total made up of each Welsh resident's share of the pound.

Thus from 2001 onwards the UK government substantially increased spending each year on the NHS in England (Department of Health 2003a:31). This created a significant upward change in the whole England budget, and therefore created significant upward 'Barnett consequentials', or flows of new money, to the three devolved countries. This Barnett consequential, despite ensuing from a decision about English health spending by the UK government, flowed into the budgets of the three devolved countries to be used anywhere. Hypothetically, Scotland could have abolished its NHS and spent the consequential and the existing NHS budget on something else. The UK government, too, could abolish England's NHS – with disastrous consequences for Northern Ireland, Scotland, and Wales. The Treasury has stated in so many words that Barnett could work in reverse. If the UK government were to abolish its NHS and thereby lower English government spending, the Barnett consequential, at least according to Treasury officials, would be a sharp drop in devolved budgets (House of Lords Select Committee on the Constitution 2002b:357).

The formula's general effects are agreed. As it works over time, it drives the whole UK toward equal per-capita spending. In 1979, when it was established, it was intended to deal with a legacy of higher per-capita funding in Northern Ireland, Scotland, and Wales relative to England. It does this because the new spending will eventually drown the old spending levels, and the new spending will be governed by Barnett. The UK will approach, and might be fairly rapidly approaching, a point when there is equal per-capita spending in each area (Bell and Christie 2002:143–7).

One of the virtues of Barnett is, despite its reputation, simplicity. The UK government has all the money and power and most of the information but very little trust. An essentially simple, albeit intricate, formula such as Barnett that can be calculated from public documents helps reduce the asymmetry between governments. The block transfer, meanwhile, means that the devolved countries are free to establish their own spending and policy priorities without central government oversight. Assuming that the formula is applied and spending continues a general upward trend, the formula provides a degree of transparency that might otherwise not exist.

Barnett also shields the devolved countries from potential consequences of the cost of their programmes. We cannot truly know what would be the consequences for Scotland or Wales if they had to tax to fund all or most of their expenditure, but we know that the logic of 'Tiebout traps' could apply (Tiebout 1956; Peterson 1981, 1994; see also Oates 1999). This is the dynamic whereby mobile people, businesses, and investors select locations based on their combination of tax costs and amenities, and governments act like firms trying to appeal to customers by offering desirable combinations of services and taxes. Under these conditions it is possible to charge high taxes, offer good services, and thrive. It is also likely that for many areas, though, an increase in 'fiscal freedom' would start some sort of race to the bottom. The UK historically has had small tolerance for such jurisdictional competition (in local government the central government tries hard to equalise services). Outside England, there is really no working connection between taxes and spending. Voters, of course, are likely to want economic growth and punish governments that do not seem to produce it, but there is no direct mechanism that connects economic failure to the ability of the devolved governments to provide services. The impact of this race to the bottom is weaker than the clarity of the argument suggests; there are many factors behind locational decisions in addition to taxes (Simeon forthcoming), but the UK funding system allows for no real effects. Voters should reward and punish them by their record in public services; the governments are insulated from the effects of their policies on the economy.

The paradox of small changes

Seen in comparative perspective the UK has an unusually low degree of intergovernmental constraint on the natural tendency of political systems to diverge with their policy communities and party systems. Westminster might have the ultimate trumps of control over the devolution legislation and the financial formula, but it has no good day-to-day levers over much devolved policy. The UK should therefore see more divergence in policy and social citizenship as its polities mark out different trajectories with their different decisions and its intergovernmental relations do little to constrain policy divergence within their delineated competencies.

The reason for this policy divergence lies in the paradox of small changes. The fact that devolution began with the smallest possible institutional disruption is likely to magnify its consequences for citizenship rights and national identity over the long term. Devolution essentially meant changing the governance of three departments. It replaced most tasks of the Secretaries of State for Northern Ireland, Scotland, and Wales with the Northern Ireland Assembly, the Scottish Parliament, and the National Assembly for Wales. The simple transfer of power and responsibility from a UK Cabinet minister to a new elected body allowed a momentous change in the history of the UK and its nations to take place with remarkably little administrative disruption. Existing departmental borders provided a structure of competencies that was well established in administrative practice, while the presence of a unified and highly disciplined UK civil service ensured a smooth transition and minimised intergovernmental conflict (Hazell 2000a; Trench 2001a). The UK avoided the brutal disputes over competencies that marred the early years of the Spanish autonomous communities, the powerlessness of the French regions' early years, and the eternal intergovernmental disputes that amuse Canadians and Australians.

The price of this short-term ease was that the UK transplanted a set of institutions designed for unified Cabinet government into a new regime based on divided political power. The three territorial offices, until devolution, were departments like the Home Office or Department of Health. This reduced their overlap, since in the context of UK government it is rare to find two Whitehall departments sharing their core competencies. The Department of Education and Department of Health have well worked-out frontiers. There might be clashes around shared areas like medical education, but it remains clear that one runs health services and one runs schools and neither ran hospitals or schools in the territory governed by the Scottish Office. The political culture of the UK restrained the departments and their ministers from full-scale invasions of each others' territory, since that would breed conflict, overlap, and bad administration. It was the unified UK government that ensured their overall consistency. Aside from that, the Whitehall departments have vast formal autonomy and control over their core competencies.

It was this formal autonomy that the devolved bodies acquired overnight, but without the Cabinet unity. The various departments in a single government will usually respect each other because to do otherwise would damage the whole government. That means there is no real point to putting tight formal limits on what the departments can do to each other. Once some of these departments have their own governments with their own mandates, however, the incentive to unity is greatly weakened. The old Secretary of State for Scotland had good reason to resolve and hide disputes with colleagues over powers and responsibilities: British politics expects unified government. The Scottish Executive and UK government, by contrast, might have no incentive at all to resolve disputes politely and behind the scenes. If there is gain to be had from shifting blame on to the other, or invading the other's powers, then there is no reason to expect they will not do it.

If there is no longer a unified government to hold all the parts of the UK state in check, then what stands out is how much power a department (which is what the Scottish Parliament inherited from the Scottish Office) actually has. The informal consultations that resolve disputes between parts of the same government are nothing like the machinery of intergovernmental relations, and provide very little constraint on a determined government anywhere. To this attractively unfettered collection of powers can be added the formula-based funding system, which gives the central government comparatively few effective levers with which to intervene in devolved policy. In this system of virtual dual federalism, there is no regulation from above (as in Spain) and no room for the UK and devolved governments to argue about finance (as in Canada). In major competencies such as health and education on the one hand or pensions and taxation on the other, there is almost no room for intergovernmental conflict, whether productive or otherwise. Even Wales, in health care, has extensive powers, since its 'secondary legislative' powers are the raw material of much health policy (barring the presence of a Westminster government bent on damaging Welsh devolution by writing intrusive primary legislation on health).

The small size of Scotland relative to the rest of the UK (let alone Northern Ireland or Wales) and the widespread acceptance of the regions' differences also abetted the decision not to establish (or, better, the non-decision) a UK-wide framework for social policy. The English tolerance for political autonomy elsewhere in the UK seems to be quite high (Curtice 2001:230–1). What Heald writes of politics before devolution remains substantially true: 'Even taken together, the three territories account for only 16% of the UK population, and what happened there was something of a mystery, and of little interest, in London. The territorial departments were able to exploit the situation to their own advantage, profiting from being unimportant' (Heald 2003:8). It is hard to imagine a UK entirely divided into units with the autonomy of Scotland; there would be almost no centre. In terms Spaniards use, the debate over decentralisation was between champagne for the few (extensive powers for stateless nations' governments) or coffee for all (weak powers for every region). Spain opted for coffee for all, with perhaps some liqueur for stateless nations. The UK has chosen good champagne for the Scots, a rather inferior vintage for the Welsh and Northern Irish, and not much for the English (Agranoff 1999).

Since devolution, the centre has clearly identified reasons to highlight the extent of devolution and disengage publicly. The Prime Minister has limited real tools with which to deliver health outcomes in Wales, and his officials and advisers recognise the very serious problems in Welsh health services. They accordingly go out of their way to avoid creating any public impression that they are responsible for Welsh health policy. Meanwhile, in Scotland the Scottish Executive, uninterested in England's policy directions and always criticised by the SNP for supposed subservience to London, rarely seeks visible public connections with the Department of Health. It is not likely that the different governments would be so willing to hold their tongues about each others' perceived inadequacies after a change in the colour of government such as the arrival of a Conservative government in England or an SNP one in Scotland.

This loose control and central disengagement is highly desirable from the point of view of countries that seek to be autonomous. Catalan nationalists fought for two decades to achieve only a part of what Scotland immediately inherited. As a model for other countries, this suggests that the UK has found an effective way to establish policy autonomy for the component unit, showing it with the example of Scotland. Scotland is a clean transfer of competencies and staff, with a block budget set by a formula and no power to set a normative framework or broad device for permitting central government involvement in policy making. This structure gives great play to the inbuilt tendency of political systems to policy divergence through the cumulation of small decisions influenced by territorial policy communities and separate party systems. Within the formal structure of the devolution settlement, the government in London has few effective tools to intervene in policy. Its desire to make devolution as small and smooth a process as possible has paved the way for more policy divergence than it probably expected.

Prospect

The lack of a central normative framework is as yet uncontested, and the political price of trying to roll back or regulate the autonomy of Scotland and Wales would almost certainly be too high to attract sensible politicians. It is possible to imagine ways around the devolution settlement, but the essential control over the activities of the organisations involved in health services will remain with the devolved governments. Most of the pressure is actually in the other direction: in the direction of primary legislative powers for Wales, for various kinds of greater autonomy for Scotland, and for English regionalism (Hazell 2003a, 2003b).

The Barnett formula might be politically vulnerable. The problem is that it starts from a very asymmetric base (with much higher funding for Northern Ireland, Scotland, and Wales, measured on a per-capita basis) and that it drives expenditure towards convergence on an even per-capita spending basis. This means that it could irritate everywhere in the UK. On the one hand, for the short term it entrenches greater per-capita funding levels in Northern Ireland, Scotland, and Wales. This can offend people living in England. On the other hand, over the medium and long term it erodes the greater per-capital expenditure in neighbouring Northern Ireland, Scotland, and Wales. This 'Barnett squeeze' has already been taken up as a cause by nationalist parties in the devolved countries. Their argument for greater expenditure is not necessarily spurious (Wales quite possibly 'needed' more even in 1979, before the formula had done anything to reduce its per-capita funding; McLean 2003) and neither is their argument for greater taxing power ('full fiscal freedom' in the words of the SNP) objectionable on grounds of democratic autonomy and responsibility. The squeeze has particularly animated the Northern Irish and Welsh political elites; Scotland is still doing well and is accordingly usually very quiet about Barnett.

Given that neither the present level of funding nor the eventual equal per-capita funding reflects any sort of needs analysis or even serious political discussion, it is inevitable that politicians (especially in Northern England, Northern Ireland, and Wales) see value in attacking it. One way or another, the Barnett formula can be said to hurt their constituents (even, in the long, term, Scots). Unpopularity matters more because of institutional impermanence. The Barnett formula is getting more formal with public exposure but is still essentially a Treasury device adopted in-house, and within living memory substantially modified by strict or lax application. As a result, authoritative accounts can stress equally that it makes the devolved countries highly autonomous – and that it makes them powerless to control their own budgets (Bell and Christie 2002).

The UK government could object to divergent policy on the grounds of cross-border effects or it could attempt legal challenges, but above all it could alter the Barnett formula. Given that Barnett is simply a procedure adopted by the Treasury (each year), and that it has in the past been unilaterally tightened or loosened, it could be replaced with something else by a simple decision of the UK government. Such a decision could be justified in a variety of ways. If attached to a suitably designed needs analysis, it could even promise an increase in projected funding to the devolved government. Or it could be presented as a redress for English grievances. Regardless of its possible modes of execution, the funding system is important, potentially unpopular, and formally little more than a Treasury convenience. That makes it vulnerable. As citizenship rights and party governments across the UK diverge, along with performance, Barnett will be put under increasing pressure.

Without goodwill, governments (especially the UK government) could start to exercise their ingenuity in the search for ways to compete for credit and block each others' plans. Once there is alternation in government in some part of Great Britain, the different administrations will lose much of their partisan incentive to coordinate and bury differences between each other and instead will acquire many of the incentives seen in other systems to use intergovernmental relations to embarrass each other. It is possible, for example, to imagine a leftist Scottish government embarrassing a rightist UK (English) government by trumpeting its social welfare, and the UK (English) government retaliating with a review of the funding formula that sustains the different benefits. Equally, if a nationalist government wins office in Scotland or Wales, a UK government might emulate the Canadian federal government and experiment with programmes in the devolved countries that would allow it to impress the public with the good it does, even if it irritates the devolved government. Universities, for example, are devolved, but Research Councils – research and student funding agencies with great influence over quality issues – are UK-wide. They could be the basis for a repeat of the Millennium Scholarships that the Canadian federal government enacted over provincial politicians' heads (see below). Health is devolved, but professional regulation through the General Medical Council is UK-wide. Both research funding and medical quality control could be turned by an enterprising UK government into tools to intervene in devolved university education or health, as the Spanish central state is doing. If Wales keeps its present structure, there is scope for even more conflict. A UK government could simply refuse to enact primary legislation requested by Wales or enact legislation undesired by the

National Assembly. This would create a serious crisis born of Welsh voters' dual representation as UK and Welsh electors, and there is no fixed mechanism to solve it amicably (Westminster's victory is built into the formal structures).

It is not difficult to imagine the ways intergovernmental relations could change. Nevertheless, the last UK experience with Westminster intervention in devolved affairs mostly shows how difficult it might be to breach frontiers of devolution. Even during the early 1970s the dying Stormont government, buried under deserved criticism and disintegrating into civil war, enjoyed remarkable protection behind the walls of convention. An account of central government policy at the start of the Troubles testifies to how difficult it is for UK governments to make the leap to using their financial or regulatory powers to intervene in even very troubled devolved politics (Rose 2000). If devolution becomes settled, and the devolved governments do not disintegrate in such a spectacular manner, then the conventions protecting them might become very firm.

Finally, the EU contains potential threats to the structure of devolution in the UK (Greer 2005). The EU might seem to be a federal entity, a confederal entity, or an international organisation, but at its heart is a decision-making body made up of states. Neither Spain nor the UK permits its regional governments a fixed position in the Council, which is the organisation that eventually adopts legislation. This means that the EU redistributes competencies. Areas handed over to regional governments become the subject of directly effective European legislation decided by a Council that includes the central state. Madrid and London have pooled their sovereignty and use it, among other things, to regulate Barcelona and Belfast (Brugué, Gomà, and Subirats 1997). Health is still relatively well defended against direct EU regulation, although the draft constitution for the EU suggested a competency in public health. More significantly, single market and labour legislation shape the regulatory environment within which the NHS works. Increasingly, the Northern Irish, Scottish, and Welsh health services must work within regulations on labour, credentials, and purchasing that are set by a qualified majority vote of states in which they have no independent, or even audible, voice.

In short, the UK settlement maximises the odds of policy divergence because its informality and the considerable autonomy of the devolved governments (in health, even in Wales) mean that there are few stable limitations. The sustainability of this model, as with any other, may be questioned. In one direction, it might produce such policy divergence that public opinion or a UK government reacts with an effort to impose limits. If there is no broad agreement on the balance between diversity and social citizenship, and there does not appear to be one in the UK at present (Jeffery forthcoming), then the divergence produced by devolution might produce a backlash that would lead to the imposition of some sort of UK-wide framework or financial regime. The price in terms of autonomy and the stability of the UK state might be very high. In the other direction, there might be progressive erosion of the power of devolved governments via the EU, primary legislation (in Wales), UK use of its remaining powers, and possibly veiled threats by the centre to funding. So long as the different party systems give governments incentive to differ, there is little reason for it to happen by accident and it would become highly controversial if it happened as part of a campaign by one government to undermine another.

Different limits

It is always possible to have debates about whether autonomy is enough – whether the glass is half full or half empty. This section adds some perspective to the debates about whether the devolved countries have too little, too much, or just enough autonomy by looking at two similar cases. Both Canada and Spain have done more to establish institutionalised intergovernmental relations and central involvement in regional policy, and both therefore make Scotland look highly autonomous. Should the design of devolution prove politically unsustainable, the Spanish route of central government intervention and the Canadian route of shared cost financing are both possible replacements, with distinct costs and benefits or warnings of what can go wrong if intergovernmental relations are left unattended.

Canada is a longstanding federal democracy closely linked in form and institutions to the UK. Spain has a very different state tradition and history but has since 1975 faced the same questions of asymmetric devolution as the UK. These are not fully fledged comparative case studies. Rather, they are illustrations of other ways in which intergovernmental politics can shape political systems' tendency to diverge. Both incorporate, in different forms, a degree of intergovernmental relations in health. Unlike the Scottish settlement, they do give the central government a right to participate in the region's affairs, and, unlike the Welsh settlement, they do it in a defined manner with rules of the game that channel intergovernmental negotiation in certain ways and for the identifiable end of guaranteeing Canadian or Spanish citizenship rights across the autonomous communities and provinces. The Spanish system values consistent citizenship rights and Spanish national unity, embodied in the central government, and pays the price in its crude mechanisms for limiting divergence. The Canadian system gives the federal government's health policy makers carrots but no sticks and therefore produces constant negotiations in which the federal government tries to 'buy' services from provinces. Both, by combining different governments in the same policy areas on the same territory, guarantee constant intergovernmental wrangling even when there are no conflicts of nationality and separation. Both have far more institutionalised systems of intergovernmental relations. This suggests that the extremely informal UK system, in which networks among Labour politicians and civil service bear much of the weight, will not be adequate as policy and political divergence increases (House of Lords Select Committee on the Constitution 2002a:5).

Different limits: Spain

Spain shares key attributes with the UK. Both states enjoy a recent history of asymmetric decentralisation in a formerly unitary state as well as similar health service models. The contemporary Spanish model of decentralised health services builds on a model of shared competencies with great (and increasing) central government regulation and steadily decreasing central government financial control. Its basic financial system resembles a more stable version of the UK system (block transfers determined by formula) but introduces framework legislation that shifts the balance in favour of uniformity rather than diversity, and tutelage by the central state rather than regional autonomy. It also shows what intergovernmental relations can be in such a situation of entrenched conflict.

The Spanish system of policy regulation and fiscal decentralisation has been in constant evolution since the democratic transition and establishment of its 'devolved governments' (autonomous communities) in 1980 (Aja 1999, 2001). Spain faced the problems not only of creating stability in a multinational state but also the difficulties of democratic transition and the legacy of a violently centralist authoritarian government that had oppressed the smaller Basque, Catalan, and Galician nations (Díez Medrano 1995; Conversi 1997, 2000; Greer 2003). Unlike the UK, most of the regional governments established in Spain were not built on any pre-existing administrative structure (a few are simply built on old provinces). Central government had traditionally and against Catalan opposition divided Catalonia into four provinces. Under Franco, they were further split between two larger administrative regions for tasks such as social security administration. As a result, the leaders of the new, democratic autonomous communities had to hew a new administration and polity out of an existing, highly centralised, authoritarian state. There was nothing like a Catalan or Basque administration to take over and the constitution forbade the elimination of any of the other pre-existing levels (Solé Tura 1986). Given that there were often very bad relations between the leading autonomous communities (the Basque Country and Catalonia) and the central government, the creation of the separate policies and administrations often required hard political combat and many lawsuits between governments.

The Spanish state has been a classic case of an asymmetrically devolved state because of the compromise that its constitutional framers developed in order to cope with the tension between state nationalists, other nationalists, some of them separatist, in the three historic nations of Catalonia, Galicia, and the Basque Country and rest of Spain, which proved quite able to summon localist sentiments in unequivocally Spanish regions. The constitution compromised between the pressures for autonomy from non-state nationalists and the pressure from state nationalists for a consistent form of government that did not accord any area different treatment: the constitution created a template of regions across Spain but gave them different initial powers and different mechanisms for acquiring powers. The result was that through the 1980s Spain was extremely asymmetric, with some governments such as the Basque Country and Catalonia responsible for a large and increasing number of policy areas and others only slowly acquiring policies or political institutionalisation (Subirats forthcoming). This meant, for example, that some autonomous communities established their own health systems and of them some opted for very substantially different policies, while others remained part of a state-run system called INSALUD. In 1992 the Socialist government concluded 'autonomous pacts' with the various autonomous communities, which brought them up to a largely equal list of competencies. This included the transfer of INSALUD's operations to the autonomous communities that had not developed health policies. This transfer was being planned in the 1990s and was essentially complete by 2003.

The Spanish system, like most, operates relatively well in areas where the basic partisan dynamics are similar – where the large Spanish Socialist Workers Party (PSOE) faced off with a small leftist party and the right (in the form of the small 1980s Alianza Popular and later the successful Partido Popular). The presence of the large parties 'vertebrated' the system, creating nexuses of common interest between central and regional politicians that muted or at least hid disputes. The benefits of unity, for public consumption and for internal negotiation, generally exceeded the benefits of conflict within parties (Grau i Creus 2000). There are good arguments that the result is mild and positive competition in which, for example, Socialist Andalucia embarrasses Popular governments in Madrid into matching its superior drug benefits (Moreno 2001, 2002). The problems arose in the areas with different party systems, above all in the Basque Country and Catalonia. These autonomous communities did not just have distinctive regional organisational ecologies and party systems that, like the Scottish and Welsh systems, encouraged differentiation. They have also been governed by nationalists since their recreation in 1980. They have no analogues in the rest of the country, no consistent interest in helping a Spanish party, and every incentive to try to use their deputies in the Spanish Parliament to extract better powers and financing, while their goals are poorly regarded in Madrid and subject to constant attack from the right-nationalist Spanish press and the Partido Popular as part of its electoral strategy. As nationalist parties they also generally seek further autonomy and are almost viscerally offensive to the partisans of the centralist Spanish political tradition. While there is no tradition of centralist passion in Britain it is not at all difficult to imagine such a situation emerging in the UK, given that all four party systems have it in them to create nationalist governments unshackled by shared Labour party loyalty (and, further, to make the Labour party itself a very loosely coupled organisation over time).

FINANCE AND REGULATION

As everywhere else, including the UK, the Spanish regions got what they fought for. Thus the autonomous communities that won health responsibilities early were the ones that had intense preferences for control of the health systems, usually because they had strong complexes of regional organisations and policy advocates frustrated with Madrid (Greer 2003). These intense preferences for control came with strong views about what should be done in health policy and almost certainly meant that the health policies were better and better thought out (Rico Gómez 1998). Their intense preferences then were born of the same social forces that gave these communities ready-made, sophisticated policy goals in a process akin to that which took place in Scotland.

The essential logic of the autonomous regime in Spain, like that of the Spanish territorial settlement overall, is that the 'nationalities and regions' collectively embody an otherwise intangible Spanish unity (Rodríguez–Zapata 1996:74–5). Their governments, the autonomous communities, have a right to substantial autonomy, but the central state has the right, or obligation, to ensure a basic level of citizenship rights. This means that responsibility for organising services and administering them, along with the necessary staff, budget, and plant is in the hands of the autonomous community. The central government then regulates them through a technique called the 'framework law' (Alvarez Conde 1993). There is one such law for each of the policy areas where there are shared competencies, including large and expensive areas such as health, education, and universities (Aja 1999:108).

The framework laws can be defended from the assumption that the various components of Spain have an obligation to ensure a basic standard of provision of key social services, and that individual Spaniards have a right to the same standards regardless of where in the country they live. The problem lies in the implementation. The constitution does not specify what the framework laws do, but the central government's ability to regulate provision in order to guarantee equality of citizenship rights permits substantial interventions in the activities run by autonomous communities (Viver i Pi-Sunyer 1990). Thus, for example, the central government has acted on the medical quality agenda by creating a statewide council, despite the fact that this irritates autonomous communities such as Catalonia that were far ahead of the rest of Spain in work on technology assessment and other quality issues. Establishing quality control potentially gives the new organ of the central state substantial ability to intervene in rationing, investment, and policy decisions of the autonomous communities. The Constitutional Tribunal's jurisprudence is the only check on this dynamic, and it is not necessarily as much of a check as decentralisers would like.

The financial regime, meanwhile, has been moving in the opposite direction, with questionable equity (Omnium Cultural 1998) but increasing degrees of freedom (Castells 2001). The Spanish financial regime has changed over time and is regularly renegotiated. It started with an obviously provisional model that funded autonomous communities according to the total of the spending of the Spanish state on the competencies transferred. Then the system moved in the mid-1980s to a set of formulas intended to equalise standards and progressively reduce the extent to which funding was tied to individual programmes (a key demand of the autonomous communities). When the Catalan nationalist government held the balance of the Spanish Parliament in the 1990s, one of its chief achievements was a decisive shift to a block funding formula under which almost all funding was collapsed into a single transfer based on a fixed percentage of specified revenue (mostly income tax). As a result, most autonomous communities are now mostly funded according to a relatively transparent block grant formula entrenched in law. The Basque Country and Navarre operate under conditions of much greater fiscal independence, in which they collect their own taxes and negotiate their payments to the central state.

The main system is redistributive, since richer autonomous communities such as Catalonia pay higher income taxes per capita but are reimbursed from income tax revenue across Spain according to a negotiated formula that essentially mirrors population. The system shifts considerable funds from Catalonia (with its income only around the EU regional average) to Spain's poorer areas. Catalan politicians and civil servants in the late 1990s were apt to argue that the block transfer is an achievement since it reduces central government constraints on their ability to innovate in social policy. Only in 2003, since elections that put a left-nationalist government in office, has Catalonia began to seek a better settlement, including its own taxing agency (*El País,* 14 December 2003). Health was one of the last policy areas to be shifted into the block grant. Previously much of the health budget was a subsection of the social security budget, given to the autonomous communities to provide health services, and accordingly was difficult to spend outside health services (López-Casanovas 2003:124–31). At any rate, the Spanish autonomous communities now enjoy a system of finance based on relatively transparent formulas and block transfers that do not tie funds to specific programmes.

POLITICS

The essential political logic of this system of constraint reflects the basic bargain in the constitution's allocation of shared powers, with the central state exercising a degree of tutelage over the autonomous communities. This bargain has three implications. First, the Spanish state began as an ideologically and organisationally unitary entity, modelled on republican France, without any equivalent for the territorial offices (and therefore without any overall acceptance of the concept of distinct, autonomous, territorial governments). Second, the actual system as it works in Spain today emerged from decades of political conflict between autonomous community politicians and the central state over the degree of political autonomy and therefore divergence that Spain could tolerate. The constitution smoothed over the conflict between partisans of a strong Spanish unity led by the central state and partisans of political autonomy for subunits (especially 'nationalities') by displacing conflict into the legislative arena via framework laws. It is up to the representatives of different tendencies to win in the Spanish central legislature and not have their victory annulled by the Constitutional Tribunal. Third, it is a system often biased against the most determined autonomous communities. Catalans and Basques will never form a majority in Spain: they must develop various techniques for preserving their autonomy in the complex and shifting environment of the central legislature, lobbying opportunities, and the party systems of the country. In practice, this means that finance is often easier to negotiate than regulation. An autonomous community can only influence regulation if it has coalitions with elites in the policy sector, so allowing information and support in the Spanish policy community, and, ideally, if it has a role as a 'hinge' (centre) party in the lower house of the Spanish Parliament during a minority government. It demands both a great deal of information and political strength greater than that of a supplicant in negotiations with Madrid. By contrast, financial negotiations are conducted at regular intervals and can be a focus of real political and research effort.

One way around the problems of unilateral framework setting, regularly canvassed in contemporary Spanish (and Catalan and Basque) political thought, is reform of relations with the central state, tied to century-old debates about federalism (Prats i Català 1988; Caminal Badia 1998). The central government has transferred powers, resources, and actions to the autonomous communities, but can still intervene in their activities in these policy areas as a superior level of government and has no formal obligation to listen to these implicitly junior governments. If it has no interests in common with an autonomous community, whether due to partisan differences, conflicts over nationalism, or policy disagreement, the central government can unilaterally create serious policy problems. There are optimistic arguments that the problem will sort itself out as governments learn – that the pressure of EU policy making and the policy problems that result from poor coordination are slowly obliging them to develop more cooperative styles and share more information (Börzel 2002). However, in the complex problems that policy makers face even goodwill (often sorely lacking in contemporary Spanish intergovernmental relations) and appropriate mechanisms may be unlikely to tackle the problems of complexity and short time-frames exacerbated by EU negotiating. If anything, the EU's state-run decision making process disenfranchises autonomous communities whose competencies are subjected to EU regulations decided by the states. In the last analysis the only necessary cost of the present arrangements to the central government is a greater likelihood of policy problems that are often borne by the regions. If the central or a regional government chooses to polarise politics around state versus stateless nationalisms – around Spanish nationalism versus Basque and Catalan nationalisms – then provoking conflict could benefit both sides while undermining policy and the state's coherence. That is exactly what has happened in Spain, where the clash between Basque (and now Catalan) nationalists and the state nationalists of the governing Partido Popular has become destructive, bitter, and electorally useful at times to both.

The absence of autonomous community representation in the decisions of the central government exacerbates the conflict and policy problems. The only mechanism intended to provide a territorial form of representation in the legislature is the territorial upper house, the *Senado* (Russell 2000). The *Senado* effectively represents nothing, however, since it is mostly elected by provincial circumscriptions rather than the much more important autonomous communities. Reform either to elect members by regional constituencies, or to give the autonomous communities a direct role in choosing members of the senate, would give autonomous community concerns a role in central state decision making. There are many problems with plans for upper house reform, and it is not clear what combination of intergovernmental pressure and party politics would produce such changes (Russell and Sandford 2002).

EFFECTS

The state of the Spanish autonomies has created substantial divergence in health policy, down to basic questions such as the public–private mix in health services. Spanish welfare state regimes show considerable divergence, with the dissimilarities most marked between Valencia, the Basque Country, and Catalonia, and on the other end the block of provinces with the least historic identities (and membership in INSALUD) (Subirats and Gallego 2002; Gallego, Gomà, and Subirats 2003:164). Both INSALUD and the Catalan system have their parallels in the UK. The Catalan system is a contract-based system with mixed private and public provision contracted by the regional government out of its general funds; Catalan policy makers refer to the kinship with the internal market, or England's 'diversity' agenda (Gallego 1998, 2001). INSALUD, by contrast, is modelled on the original NHS model of direct government ownership and a great deal of professional autonomy (de Miguel and Guillén 1989; Guillén and Cabiedes 1998). The divergence reflects history and the different strategies of the governing parties. The central state, deciding on a form of universal health services, opted for the NHS after a lively debate between advocates of it or the French insurance-based system. The choice was made because of NHS's proven record of cost control and possible linkages with other public services compared to an insurance model. At first this looked to doctors like simple nationalisation and the state found itself plunged into conflicts with the medical profession over doctors' entrepreneurial autonomy (such conflicts erupt almost anywhere when governments consider national health plans). Once it had finished bargaining with the doctors over the same issues as the UK government bargained (contracting, private work), the state established a system built on rationing through professions that was good value for money (Rodríguez and de Miguel 1990:98–217). Catalonia preferred to build on its existing independent hospitals and contract with them, in pragmatism that could later be advertised as an example of an internal market similar to the UK internal market.

The essence of the Spanish system of intergovernmental relations, then, is the combination of formula-based block finance and tight regulation by the central state in the name of national unity and citizenship rights. Framework legislation allows the central government to control the degree of variation

between regions. Given that there is no direct representation for the autonomous communities in the central state's decision-making process, the result
is less divergence but an extreme degree of legalisation and serious policy
problems that can emerge from efforts to combine the different policies
found in central government regulation and in autonomous communities'
policy regimes. To the extent that the autonomous communities do diverge,
it is because of accidents of timing (such as the late arrival of a framework law
regulating health care across Spain) and of their own political activities and
determination. The Spanish central state has been able to use its framework
legislation to edge into important areas of autonomous community competency and specify policies in considerable details. The only formal limit, the
jurisprudence of the Constitutional Tribunal, and the informal limits of party
politics have not prevented this often intrusive oversight.

The particular Spanish mechanism for structuring shared competencies –
an effort to combine citizenship rights with diversity – has the advantage of
preserving standards across the country as well as separate organisational
forms. It has three disadvantages. It creates an open invitation to the central
state to expand its regulation into core competencies of the autonomous communities. It creates constant pressure for legal conflicts. And it displaces the
question of national identity and citizenship into dysfunctional policy debates.

Different limits: Canada

Canada is a territorially and socially diverse country whose nature and politics
are fundamentally federal and where federalism is much discussed (Simeon
2002). Not only is life different in each province, but the vicissitudes of
Canadian politics means that the 'horizontal' connection between regional
social, political, and economic variation is tied to an enunciated sense of
regional rights and identification with the provincial governments that is long
gone in the USA. The diversity shows in, and is exacerbated by, its lack of
an integrating party system. The broad-based, regionally representative
'omnibus' of federal political parties stalled some time ago (Meisel 1992). The
party system makes Canadian politics look exotic to outsiders. Federal
Liberals and Liberals in the provinces are not usually the same party and do
not occupy the same position on left–right or Unionist–separatist spectra (the
Liberal leader of Quebec elected in 2003, Jean Charest, parachuted in from
the federal Progressive Conservative party that was defeated by the federal
Liberals); some parties exist on the federal or provincial level but not both (so
the Alliance had no provincial candidates and the Saskatchewan Party no
federal ones); the federation is at present dominated by Liberals based in
Ontario, even though the federal and provincial Liberals have basically been

extinct west of Ontario for decades (Smith 1981); in the 1990s the opposition could scarcely be found east of Manitoba, until the (Western) Alliance merged with the (Eastern) Progressive Conservatives; Quebec has a strong separatist party; and most provinces, or at least groups of provinces, have their own, very distinct party systems with dynamics like no others and some parties like no others. At best, this means that parties do not integrate the country in the way that the PSOE or Labour claim to. At worst it gives different orders of government incentives to compete in ways that create conflictual intergovernmental relations.

Unlike Spain or the UK, where a centralised state gave way to a decentralised one, in Canada a group of British colonies came together to form the core of the federation (under Westminster legislation) in 1867. Until the growth of the federal welfare state from the Second World War until the 1970s, the provinces were the dominant actors in health policy, and federal government involvement was marginal. In this period, a time of increasing central government activity in most countries, the expansion and change in the role of the state 'was achieved not by the dominance of the central government but by the collaboration of both orders of government, federal and provincial' (Simeon and Robinson 1990:120). For example, in health care, it was the federal government that generalised a system of state-funded provision begun in a few provinces. It did it by promising joint funding for services provided by the provinces and thereby assuaged the fears of the provinces of the costs associated with a popular programme (Maioni 1998; Tuohy 1999).

This era of increasingly interpenetrated governments and expanding state activity had been for some time compatible with the preservation of a well-organised and conservative Quebec. The 1960s and 1970s ended that period as a 'quiet revolution' dethroned the old conservative elites and mores of the province, replacing the elites with new and often nationalist politicians amidst substantial social change. Canada became embroiled in intense debates about its identity, the place of Quebec, and its constitution (Simeon and Robinson 1990; Russell 1993). The debates changed the federation. The federal government actively promoted a new, binational identity in an effort to make the case for unity and symmetry (which probably backfired; McRoberts 1997). The provinces gained power, and asymmetry became a major issue anyway. State building, something discussed around the world, in Canada competed with province building (Black and Cairns 1966). While there had always been a degree of Quebecois resistance to incorporation in the Canadian federal welfare state, its nature changed. Once, the resistance had focused on the preservation of (generally Catholic) voluntary social institutions and the accompanying conservative society; now Quebecois resistance focused on Quebec's right to build its own welfare state. The broad provincial autonomy won partly as a consequence of constitutional debates meant that large swathes of public policy diverged a great deal (there is really no pan-Canadian medical quality or professional standards regime). The result is that Canada is practised in both the operation of diverse welfare states and in the politics of diversity within common grounds of social citizenship. Its argumentative intergovernmental relations, explained by Trench (2003), guarantee an articulate debate with real policy consequences between standards of provincial autonomy (represented in the provinces) and Canadian social citizenship (represented by the federal government) – a debate that is missing in the UK and Spain.

FINANCE AND REGULATION

The Canadian federal settlement in health policy is in its essentials quite simple. In constitutional terms, there is no significant federal power or responsibility in health policy areas that touch most Canadians. Federal responsibilities are small (such as Native American health and quarantine) and as institutions and jurisprudence develop they have become even smaller (the federation provides little direct health care even to Native Americans). The federation has, however, a considerable spending power, authorised largely by a 'POGG' clause that permits it to enact policies for the capacious ends of peace, order, and good government. Federal government power in health comes from this spending power, and it is not difficult to find serious thinkers who propose that the federal government should give up its largely voluntary involvement in health and abandon health spending, standards, and politics altogether.

Reliance on the spending power comes from the fact that the Canadian federal government lacks detailed framework powers over provincial health policy. What it has, it buys. In the core of health policy, there is no Spanish-style mandate for the federal government to give provinces orders, deal directly with their citizens, or oversee their policy decisions. Unlike the UK, however, the Canadian federal government does use its ability to make conditional transfers to provinces to exercise what influence it can. Thus, for example, the Canada Health Act of 1984 sets out basic requirements for a Canadian federal health system (Medicare), namely universality, portability, accessibility, comprehensiveness, and public administration. These are actually important and by global standards restrictive, but have little impact on day-to-day policy (Maioni 2002:88–9). Enforcement, however, is entirely through withdrawal of federal health finance from the offending province. A province can flout the Canada Health Act if it is willing to bear the loss and if its government is willing to pay the political price for being thought to have violated the basis of a programme of which Canadians are proud. Given that

Canadian provinces are substantial fiscal entities in their own right, with a large share of tax income and the ability to set their own taxes and user fees, they are theoretically all capable of opting out of any Canadian health system. It is the political cost that would probably weigh more heavily on a rich province.

There is considerable evidence for a breakdown in trust between the federal government and the provinces since the late 1970s, driven not so much by the high constitutional politics of those years as by the way the intergovernmental relations and finance of Canada dealt with the end of welfare state expansion. The end of the thirty years of welfare state growth were painful in most countries, but in Canada it repeatedly took the form of the federal government coping with its financial difficulties by offloading pain on to provinces in ways that (often unilaterally) redefined the nature of bargains between the federation and provinces (for useful discussions see Bernier and Irwin 1995; Hobson and St-Hilaire 2000). The first chapter of this was the 1977 end of cofinancing for health. Cofinancing had created Medicare, but it looked to a straitened federal government like a blank cheque to the provinces and to the provinces like a straitjacket of regulations. The federal government replaced cofinancing with Established Programs Financing (EPF), which was a simple block transfer. Along with the creation of EPF, the deal combined an important reduction in federal taxes with an equivalent tax increase in provincial taxes, an operation called 'transfer of tax points'. The result was that medical provision ceased to be a joint federal-provincial activity and instead became an earmarked transfer from the federal government to the provinces. In 1984 the federal government then unilaterally limited its growth at the same time that the Canada Health Act imposed new regulations on provinces. After reducing the growth of contributions twice more, the federal government froze EPF entirely in 1989–90. Adding insult to injury, the federal government then unilaterally capped the rate of growth of its Canada Assistance Plan (CAP, social security) transfers to richer provinces in 1991. The 'cap on CAP' still rankled in 2003 interviews with Ontario officials. The federal government then repeated the exercise of simultaneously merging and damming funding streams in 1995. As part of major budget cuts that year it merged EPF and CAP to create the Canada Social Transfer, later renamed the Canada Health and Social Transfer. This was again cut over the next years and from 1996 moved towards equal per-capita distribution (different equalisation funds respond to poverty and wealth differences).

There are arguments for and against retrenchment, federal policy, and the particular decisions, but the overall effect reshaped control of health policy. As Keith Banting puts it, 'no government can defend disputed territory effectively unless it is prepared to occupy it' (Banting 1987:173). The federal government had a balanced budget but it achieved it at the expense of its ability to influence directly provincial health decisions. The two-decade shift to block funding removed the federal government from real health spending decisions. The cuts and unilateral decisions reduced federal-provincial trust and federal ability to change provincial policy. The result was that the provinces and federation turned the intergovernmental aspect of health policy into high-level arguments about very large budget headings. When the federal government in 2000 began to spend money on health again, in its effort to demonstrate the benefits of federation, it met with considerable irritation from provincial governments who saw it as trying to gain credit for re-entering an area from which it had withdrawn in an antisocial manner. The block transfers had indeed got the federal government out of its spending commitments (and the autonomy had purchased provincial acquiescence), but now it had few good levers with which to affect provincial policy.

POLITICS

Constraints on divergence in Canadian federalism come from the federal spending power. The Canada Health Act, which passes for regulation, is a small set of provisions fortified entirely by the threat that the federal government will cut off funds and embarrass the province (Boase 2001). The leverage that the federal government does have stems from its ability to offer new funds to provinces in return for their agreement to certain policy goals.

After decades of constitutional turmoil Canadians have debated most of their institutions, and Canada's vestigial, appointed upper house is no exception. As in Spain, Senate reform would be a way to inject regional concerns into federal government activity and thereby produce a more consensual, or at least integrated, policy. Reform did not work in Canada either; it was driven largely by Western provinces irritated by asymmetry, perceived favoritism by Ontario in favour of Quebec, and a sense of disenfranchisement. Senate reform turned out to be too abstruse a demand to maintain for long. A second option was to strengthen intergovernmental accords, principally through a device called the Social Union Framework Agreement (SUFA). SUFA is the subject of much discussion, although its real impact on policy is hard to gauge. The idea, essentially, is to codify cooperation to avoid surprises and permit a more constructive relationship between orders of government; it went wrong at its inception when Quebec dropped out after being, as it saw it, sold out by the other provinces. A provincial official dismissed SUFA as 'about nothing' in April 2003, while a federal official, faced with that remark, responded that it created a strong 'challenge function' within the federal government that ensured Ottawa thought about the acceptability of policy ideas to provinces before announcing them.

SUFA grew out of an era when high-level change such as Senate reform or secession was unpopular. There is a broad federal strategy to back down from the 'mega-constitutional politics' that exhausted Canada (Russell 1993) and instead demonstrate that federalism is flexible and can be made to work (Lazar 1997). Such politics include a maple leaf branding campaign wherever possible; federal interventions that touch Canadians directly such as Millennium Scholarships for college students; and social policy activity, including the new health spending. The intent is to demonstrate that the federal government makes a valuable contribution to domestic concerns and that all the different orders of government can usefully cooperate. Such a strategy is built on what the federal government does have, namely money and flexibility and some ability to speak in the name of the whole country.

The story of the Romanow Commission is instructive in the mechanisms that combine argument, oratory, and money to change policy. Roy Romanow, a successful former New Democratic Party (NDP) premier of Saskatchewan, carried the legacy of the Saskatchewan NDP's leadership in public health care with provincial credibility. The report commissioned an imposing amount of research, including papers from a wide cross-section of Canadian researchers, and public listening efforts (Commission on the Future of Health Care in Canada (2002). The process and the eventual report called for an increase in federal spending and new commitments intended to sustain Medicare, such as investment in public diagnostic service and a council that would benchmark quality (so that the public, and the federal government, might know what the money had purchased). Between public pressure and the preparatory work put in, as well as determined federal politicking, the provincial premiers accepted the report shortly after its publication. However, squabbles soon resumed; for example, provinces were suspicious of a quality council that might embarrass them in front of their electorates, and with some reason thought that the federal government was reneging on its financial obligations. Nevertheless, there was now a council and greater financing as well as a firmer consensus.

Effects

The virtue of Canadian federalism can be summarised in the dictum that 'two heads are better than one'. The provinces are responsible for health services and raise much of the funds. The federal government, however, is also involved because of its spending power. This tension between the two levels of government helped create the Medicare programme. Federal cofinancing provided the incentive for poor or recalcitrant provinces to provide public health care and funded a substantial increase in health spending. Now the spending power ensures that both levels of government are involved in health policy. It thereby produces arguments, which can be constructive, but also minimises the opportunity for policy conflict by confining the federal government to the role of funder and does not permit it to try and run its own services in some areas (a recipe for poor integration and cost shifting; Wilkins and Greer 2003). Ottawa is free to propose, suggest, embarrass, heckle, and otherwise try to use its funds and megaphone to try to affect provinces, but in the last resort it has no other levers it can use to change their policies. Most health policy is not Ottawa's to change, but most provinces find federal finance a constraint on radical change. The federal government's confinement to finance and absence of framework capacity, meanwhile, ensure that it cannot be the brusque and often counterproductive presence that is the Spanish central state. Provinces might not appreciate the federal government, but it is structurally better positioned to help and hector than to hurt.

The vices lie in the blame-shifting, cost-shifting, and elitist tone of 'executive federalism' and intergovernmental relations. Tension between two orders of government might be productive overall but can be petty in the moment. Intergovernmental relations can often be the story of good policy ideas that degenerate into intergovernmental spats, closed negotiating sessions, and blame-shifting. This hardly impresses the public and lacks much justification as a form of political deliberation. Intergovernmental relations looked more like interstate diplomacy than democratic decision making in 1972 (Simeon 1972:5, 279–80) and accordingly centralised power in the negotiating teams around premiers. The political scientist Donald Smiley later dubbed this 'executive federalism' (Simeon and Cameron 2002). This process of sorting out intergovernmental relations necessarily distorts the democratic choice of the electorate. After electing two governments, the federal and the provincial, the Canadian voter might be presented with a policy outcome desired by neither of them and possibly explained by the preferences of a different province entirely. The combination of Westminster-style parliamentary government with intergovernmental negotiations then leads to a closed, combative decision-making process dominated by the executive and closed to public scrutiny. The result is to inch government further away from its electors. At the same time, the process of intergovernmental negotiations and point-scoring can damage the coordination needed to develop and implement good policy. These dynamics seem to occur whenever parliamentary governments must negotiate policy outcomes: it is certainly taking place in the UK, where important meetings go unreported, high-level Joint Ministerial

Council meetings between the four ministers are explained only by anodyne press releases, and coordination in areas of shared powers can be quite poor.

Conclusion

The drawback of strong parliaments in unified systems, such as those found in Westminster, Cardiff, and Edinburgh, is neatly stated by Heclo and Wildavsky (1974:12):

> The danger in Britain is . . . [that] the government may agree all too quickly, before the major implications of the policy are understood or the affected interests realise what is about to happen to them, leaving all concerned agape and aghast as the machine implements the policy with its usual splendid impartiality. If the time for the American to worry is before his policy is approved, the day of reckoning for the Briton is after.

A government in such a political system will use its autonomy to the fullest, whether it intends to do so or not, and the British devolved systems create strong governments. Intergovernmental relations can constrain strong governments, but if there must be constraint the logical consequence is that the Canadian system of argument will be more productive than the Spanish system, which merely translates unilateralism to a different level. At present, the UK has multiplied the number of governments with the propensity to speedy action, but done little to make them check and balance each other.

The divergence creation machine contained in devolution means that there is a strong likelihood that the divergence we have already seen will continue. It is powered by the natural functioning of politics, in which day-to-day efforts to identify problems, policies, and political opportunities are conditioned by local forces and therefore slowly pick out their own trajectories. The powerful secular trends towards divergence present in any political system and discussed throughout this study are nurtured and enabled by the structure of the UK. The high degree of autonomy in devolved systems over their own activities (as against power over the central state or responsibility for itself) permits the different policy communities and party systems to have their maximal effects, relatively untrammelled by interaction with a different level of government or by the consequences of self-financing. Removing most ways to put pressure on them suggests that they will continue to diverge in policies, making decisions such as those catalogued in this volume that cumulate into markedly different health systems. Whether the political systems of the UK can and will stand such divergence is open to question. The divergence machine is powerful but might prove fragile.

8
Conclusion: international debates, local conclusions

The National Health Service is one of the most popular and most visible institutions across the UK, but the nation in the name is changing. What was once a British National Health Service and a totem of British unity – even in Northern Ireland, where the health service was always technically separate – is now NHS Scotland, NHS Wales, the Northern Ireland Health and Social Services, and 'the' NHS, only an English service. These institutions are a four-fold testimony to the autonomy of different parts of a multinational state. They do and will continue to use that autonomy. The UK is likely to see considerable policy experimentation in the future, and increasing variation in the real meaning of citizenship rights across its component parts.

That is because there is no right answer to most problems in health politics, political economy, and policy, and it is rare that there is a right question either. The case studies of the past chapters illuminated the extent to which the day-to-day decision making in different political systems relies on local mechanisms to identify problems and decide on solutions. Different polities become concerned with issues at different times, in different ways, and with different results. Policy ideas and decisions have autonomy from external pressure but are closely tied to existing social institutions. This is because the processes that generate problems, policies, and politics are fundamentally based in social institutions that are proper to England, Northern Ireland, Scotland, and Wales. The likelihood that any given policy decision will be an answer not seen elsewhere to a question not asked elsewhere is high enough to mean that over time the decisions can cumulate into distinctive welfare states. In other words, political systems have a natural tendency to scatter across the landscape.

This chapter reviews the trajectories and then turns to the questions posed and answered by the experience of the UK. Its policy divergence also carries international lessons. First, health policy and politics since devolution in the UK carry lessons for the analysis of globalisation and other structures that arch above and influence political systems. There are many who expect greater convergence as travel and communications deepen and broaden international networks. The experience of health, a precociously global policy area with well-networked, professional employees, suggests that divergence will remain alive and well, since local balances of power and influence will never be quite the same in two places. Second, it contains a lesson for the study of decentralising institutions in the world. The UK's institutional framework presently combines considerable autonomy for the devolved governments (above all Scotland) with considerable fragility, or even powerlessness. Third, it carries lessons for the study of mature welfare states. The decisions analysed here are the kinds of decisions that dominate the study of welfare politics. The days of major expansion are mostly over in the rich countries, and retrenchment of the welfare state has proven difficult. 'Small' decisions about how to allocate resources, respond to new problems, and interpret issues are now the tenor of welfare politics, and the British experience suggests that in such small decisions local institutions, interpretations, and politics predominate. And fourth, how far can divergence go? We need not fear, nor prepare to welcome, convergence; rather, we should ask what constrains the propensity to diverge.

The policy trajectories reviewed

Scotland's health politics are increasingly built around the professional structure of medicine rather than around the use of management. Reflecting the strength and policy skills of its medical elites, Scottish policy builds on their analyses of how medicine does and will work. Professionalist policy suggestions carry the possibility of Scottish distinctiveness and a distinctive approach to the welfare state, and therefore appeal to Scottish parties competing well to the left of English Labour and on terrain that puts a premium on Scottish distinctiveness. The resulting policy solutions to different problems entail greater reliance on professionals, efforts to align formal structures with professional ways of working, decreased reliance on managers to operate the system, a focus on quality improvement led from within the professions, and the elimination of the quasi-autonomous trusts that form one of Thatcher's most important legacies and the building blocks of any contract-based system.

In 1997, when the incoming Labour government delivered the first separate English, Scottish, and Welsh health White Papers, the Scottish White Paper visibly rolled back the internal market and placed more emphasis on partnership. It was still a document from a unified UK Cabinet, though, and commissioning remained (Scottish Office 1997). Abolishing trusts is a daunting financial and legislative challenge that no government likes, which gave trusts a short reprieve from the consequences of their unpopularity with professionals and Scottish Labour. In the Scottish health plan of 2000 (Scottish Executive Health Department 2000) trusts remained but policies shifted towards their integration into the boards. These fifteen boards increasingly came to be the key management units for the whole of the Scottish health service. Finally the 2003 White Paper (Scottish Executive Health Department 2003) announced the abolition of the trusts.

Such changes, at face value, look like a simple centralisation of the system and reduction in the autonomy of the component units. Where there had been multiple trusts, primary care organisations and boards, now there will be fifteen boards and their subunits. It is not, however just a recentralisation of management. It is also a reduction in the role of management. Scottish health policy, reflecting the ability of its medical elites to formulate cogent policy proposals, is increasingly based on aligning the formal structure of health policy with the structure of the professions. Backing up the transition to this professionalist model in organisation, the Scottish NHS is taking quality improvement more seriously than most jurisdictions around the world. It is doing this not just because of a respect for the professions but also with leadership from within the professions. Improving medical quality has for decades been a chief campaign of medical elites around the world, and the success of Scotland in establishing quality improvement mechanisms before the rest of the UK is an indicator of their influence in the Scottish policy community, as is the focus of the organisation on professional improvement rather than external regulation.

Finally, Scotland takes public health and the wider determinants of health relatively seriously. This is an unexpected consequence of a system in which medical leaders dominate much policy debate. For particular historic reasons the leaders of Scottish public health medicine are as strong and well-organised as other medical elites in Scotland and are as entrenched in the universities as any other group. They are able to influence the agenda in favour of attention to public health concerns and population health. The result has been marginal in the overall context of the health services, but there is a steady drumbeat of interest from ministers (and their challengers on the left) in local-area public health initiatives, as well as lively debates around issues such as providing free fruit in schools.

If Scotland has bet on professionalism to give it good value and extract its politicians from 'running' the health services, *England* has bet on its ability to construct an efficient, properly regulated market-like structure that will rescue the government from responsibility for every detail of health services while providing high-quality, responsive care. English policy combines a variety of measures that have in common the effort to make health services work better by using organisation and techniques borrowed from the private sector.

In organisation, there are three broad and interrelated English policies. These have been visible from before the arrival of Labour and in the 1998 White Paper (Department of Health 1998b), but were for some time hidden by an initial rush to demand performance via targets, allocate substantial new funds and a great deal of pragmatism; *The NHS Plan*, which makes no mention of most of the policies that dominate government activity, uses rather a line that New Labour used a great deal in its early years, namely 'what counts is what works'. Now, policymakers say, the initial drive to clean up the worst quality and efficiency problems is over and the system can be steered on to a new, self-regulating, market-based course, and can move on to priorities such as care for the elderly and even public health.

The first aspect of the English reliance on markets is in NHS services organisation. A market, minimally, requires buyers, sellers, and some form of regulation. The English NHS has been reconstituted into such a creature. At the centre are primary care trusts (PCTs), which are responsible for providing the population with a health service either by doing it directly or by contracting with sellers. The sellers are in other trusts, predominantly acute, mental health, and community trusts, which supply services to PCTs. The highest-rated acute trusts are now able to apply to become foundation hospitals, which are not as autonomous as proponents or opponents say, but which will not be subject to the same degree of central control; they will rather be driven by the demands of PCTs, patients, and regulators. A large and changing regulatory apparatus is expected to prevent failure – there are, in total, around 30 organisations in the English NHS that are intended to ensue quality. In theory, these organisations will guarantee good and improving quality, probity, and efficiency, while the demands of the market will produce innovation, responsiveness, and local flexibility. In practice, centralism is just as likely.

The second thread, of unknown but possibly great importance, is the effort to improve the patient's ability to be a consumer with a degree of choice. This 'choice' agenda is based on the view that patients are increasingly consumerist, decreasingly deferential, and increasingly willing to choose a hospital with a shorter waiting time or, in theory, nicer accommodation or a better location. The third thread, confused and hotly debated, is the direct import of the private sector to enhance capacity and improve management (or at least stimulate it to do better). This 'diversity' agenda is of a piece with New Labour thought (and ingrained English affection for new public management), which argues the ends, not the means, are what matter. If the government's goal is to provide high-quality primary care at a good price, there is no principled reason why it should not be provided by Boots the Chemists rather than by a traditional GP, and there is no reason why capacity increases should be through traditional capital investment rather than contracting private-sector, or French, facilities. The diversity agenda includes efforts to stimulate NHS management, and PFI. England has embraced PFI in a way no other part of the UK has done, and has been able to develop a PFI sector in a way that smaller Northern Ireland, Scotland, and Wales cannot.

The shift to commissioning, choice, and diversity are more than enough to keep any manager, minister, or official fully occupied. It certainly has had that effect on public health, which despite high hopes has found itself almost as marginal under the Labour government as under the Conservatives. The simplest indicator is organisational form. Scottish public health officers are in the same jobs, and strong in the increasingly powerful boards. Welsh public health officers are in a unified, Wales-wide corps and central to government plans. England's public health teams are partly in government offices for the regions, partly in PCTs (where public health is effectively an optional extra), and partly in a series of quangos that are being reorganised around health protection issues rather than health promotion (Department of Health 2002). Quality, in stark contrast to Scotland, is a regulatory function that might be friendly and helpful but is nevertheless regulatory rather than carried out from within the professions. The various organisations are there to make sure that the pseudo-market produces the desired outcomes rather than to help the professions fulfil their ambitions. This regulatory tone has become increasingly marked.

Scotland and England have taken opposing sides in an old and well-entrenched NHS debate between managers and professionals. England opted for managers and markets, reflecting the prominence of their advocates and arguments in the English policy community. Scotland, reflecting its weaker market reformers and its proportionately stronger medical institutions, opted for professionalism. The *Welsh* policy community has neither of these traditionally dominant groups in the same strength as in England or Scotland, and has accordingly offered opportunities to groups that are typically excluded and have a different agenda.

That means that when the Welsh party system, which is structurally similar to Scotland's, seeks distinctively Welsh solutions that are likely to be to the left of England's (reflecting the main party cleavage to the left of England's), it hears very different suggestions. There are principled leftist arguments for both professionalism and localism; the party systems predispose Scottish and Welsh politicians to seek professionalist and localist solutions and the policy communities shape the likelihood that the ideas they find will be one or another. The result has been a health policy in Wales with real input from public health and local government, reflecting their shared interest in the development of local solutions to problems of population health. Wales has placed its bet on localism.

The localist logic is well-known but rarely implemented. Its essential argument is based on two uncontroversial statements. The first is that the health services are often provided in quantities and ways that do not reflect or involve the local community. There are few channels by which the local community could be brought into an essentially technocratic health policy community, and the result is a missed opportunity for local involvement that might lead to better planning and joint working. The second is that the NHS as it exists is misnamed. The NHS, for all practical purposes, is a national sickness service that treats people once they are ill. This is expensive and unpleasant. It would be cheaper and more agreeable to reduce the causes of ill health and thereby improve the population's quality of life, the economy (which is hurt by sick days and large populations incapable of working), and the budget of the health service itself.

The promise of local joint working for population health promises to kill two birds with one stone. Moving responsibility for key parts of the health system to the local level promises both to increase local participation and integration and shift the emphasis of the health services away from service provision towards population health. This is the organising idea of Welsh health policy since devolution. There are two main threads to it. The first, in health services itself, has been an important reorganisation designed to shift the centre of gravity of the health service downwards and better integrate local government and social services (National Assembly of Wales 2001b). The essential technique was to make local health boards, the analogues of PCTs, into the chief commissioning bodies of the system, make them conterminous with Wales' twenty-two local government areas, and create both local government representation on the boards and an obligation to the LHBs and local authorities to work together.

The second thread is increased investment in and regard for the public health function overall. The Welsh health plan of 2000 was a strikingly original document that focused on health rather than the provision of health services and treated NHS Wales as one more tool available to add quality and length to life, alongside education, police, transport, and economic development. Inequalities reduction and social inclusion have both received substantial budget increases, while the public health corps in Wales is now unified and in a key position to influence policy in a fragmented, information-poor system (and the subject of an occasional envious glance from English public health; Griffiths 2003).

The costs, at least, have started to show. To some extent, the Welsh health policy agenda has already moved from the localist agenda to the problems of the acute services sector, crystallised in the review advised by Derek Wanless (Review of Health and Social Care in Wales 2003).

Northern Ireland differs from the three British systems in that it is not always self-governing, not necessarily capable of self-government, and not well structured to produce government when it is self-governing. The essential problem of Northern Irish politics is that the gravitational pull of constitutional and sectarian politics overpowers anything else, including policy debates. Elections are largely a contest about who can most vociferously represent two large groups (Unionists and nationalists) rather than a policy debate. This tendency of Northern Ireland's sectarian society is exacerbated by decades without real policy debate. What Northern Ireland's governors wanted was stability and functioning services in a troubled environment. The insider-dominated policy community that emerged was geared to this need. The insiders, though, were not the already strong, organised, and relatively ideological elites of Scottish medicine but rather the key managers operating the Northern Irish boards and, later, trusts.

The resulting policy trajectory has two faces. One is, to many frustrated Northern Irish observers, anachronism and immobility. Northern Ireland took years longer than the rest of the UK to establish the internal market and longer to get rid of it. Acute care allocation has been painfully slow. The result is that on any given agenda item – organisation, public health, quality, or the use of the private sector – Northern Ireland has simply not moved much or at all. There is little pressure from a stability-oriented policy community and almost none at all from politicians preoccupied with the fate of nations and unschooled in policy making.

The other face is less visible. Northern Irish institutions have more room to diverge from each other because they and their leadership are subjected to less top-down pressure than in other systems. The result is that the internal operations of the different organisations can vary a great deal, as can their priorities. There was an exception under devolution, when the Department of Health, Social Services, and Public Safety became involved in extremely detailed questions, going so far as to allocate new electric wheelchairs to different trusts. The likely effect of such centralism, given the lack of an overall policy agenda, would probably be to stifle valuable local efforts without improving the performance of the system overall.

Northern Ireland, then, has placed no great new bets in the manner of England, Scotland, and Wales. Rather, it has persisted with what is perforce incremental change. It is not difficult to find critics of this politics. It reflects a party system that sidelines policy and a policy community that generally lacks respect for politicians. It is offensive to believers in democratic self-government (although not necessarily to the many who do not believe in the existence of Northern Ireland). Perhaps Northern Ireland is storing up trouble and passing up opportunities. Perhaps, worse, it is thereby becoming a dangerous anachronism. But if local variation, organisational stability, and coherent identities are worth having, and the other three systems claim to think so, then Northern Ireland's situation is not all bad.

The four trajectories, then, are each coherent despite the multiplicity of policy decisions that go into making them. Their broad coherence stems from the repetition of political conjunctures (such as Welsh Labour's interest in 'clear red water' separating it from England) and policy ideas from the different policy communities. Even if there are ideas adopted across borders or from minority positions, they have strong systemic regularities because some arguments are more persistently and effectively made. The result is that the UK has created a natural experiment in the governance of health systems. It is too early to look for major population outcomes, or even system efficiency outcomes, and it would require another book to do so, but in the future the difference of these four trajectories should provide ample scope for comparative outcomes research.

Lessons

Visible effects of these policies on overall health outcomes might be some way off, but the political lessons from the first years of devolution can contribute to larger debates about health, territorial politics, and the role of politics in today's world. In particular, there are lessons for the study of globalisation and transnationalism; for the study of decentralisation and autonomy; and for the study of mature welfare states.

Globalisation and global professions

Divergence in health policy is particularly interesting because health is such a likely sector for internationalisation and convergence, and because health, in its global intellectual integration, is a harbinger of developments in many other policy areas. If health, long international, sees such divergence then we can expect policy divergence and political complexity to have a long and healthy future even in a more closely connected world.

This history of Western medicine has always been transnational, with ideas, influences, and prominent physicians crossing borders since time immemorial; Galenic medicine or the germ theory of disease spread far beyond the countries of their progenitors. It is nothing more than a doctor's professional responsibility to be aware of medical advances in order to be able to use them on their patients' behalf. Today, journals such as *The Lancet* and the *New England Journal of Medicine* are read throughout the world, and literacy in

English – the language of medicine today – is very desirable. Collaborations between scientists span continents and innovations travel rapidly between medical centres. Movements such as quality advocacy are global. They are created by policy advocates and elites around the world who both work to change policies in their own jurisdictions and to create a movement successful everywhere, while their goal is to bring research from around the world to bear on any new issue of medical innovation. The increasing ease of communication speeds this dynamic and welds different advocates together into increasingly global coalitions.

This means that the health politics and policies of the UK are arenas for increasingly global battles. We should not so much look for England, Northern Ireland, Scotland, and Wales to develop radical new policies as for them to take their places amidst other international experiments, all strung together by international policy debates and trends but conducted for reasons particular to the experimenters. Advances might happen there, or as elsewhere, but radical new departures are unlikely because international policy communities are too tightly bound together. The political systems might not learn from each other but the substructure of health systems – the practice of Western medicine – has always been global and changes in response to global debates, communications, and networks. Policy makers in a given country, no matter how parochially minded they might be, are both adopting ideas from around the world that are consciously championed by consciously global policy advocates, and are dealing with health systems that respond to global movements as simple as the publication of new findings in a widely read medical journal.

Health politics and policy should also be leading the way in an increasingly common phenomenon, namely the increasing degree of interaction between organisations across frontiers. Medicine, to some extent, has always been there. As other professions and sectors become the preserves of international professions and quasi-professions, the experience of health policy – and the lesson of its divergence and its common arguments and vocabularies – should be a harbinger for other policy fields where international conferences and journals have not been quite so long established. Given that health policy has diverged and continues to diverge even in the UK, we can expect that the mere presence of tightly woven global networks of ideas, people, and challenges will do little to change the way politics and policy actually work, nor create convergence. Global debates will arrive at local conclusions.

Institutions

The UK, building its devolution settlement out of the old territorial Whitehall departments and pushed forward by powerful coalitions in (especially

Scottish) civil society, has created very autonomous (in health) regional governments that are to a high degree protected against the most brutal forces of interjurisdictional competition. The fixed-sum Barnett formula, combined with no or nugatory tax-raising powers, means that Northern Ireland, Scotland, and Wales are unable to either start a race to the bottom or experiment with charging higher taxes for a better quality of service. It also means that they have a great deal of autonomy, since the link with taxes is severed but the block grant limits the ability of the UK government to meddle in policy and budgeting. Lack of tax-raising powers is a constraint on the autonomy of the devolved administrations; it also buffers them against the competition that so constrains governments that must raise their own revenue. Even Wales, which is constrained by its lack of primary legislative powers, has unlimited autonomy with its secondary powers (and it would be very difficult for Westminster to write primary legislation so detailed as to truly control a recalcitrant Wales). At the same time as the lack of framework legislation and earmarked finance enhances the devolved administrations' room to innovate and diverge, their structure preserves the autonomy and decisiveness of a parliamentary government; electoral rules that virtually guarantee coalitions and a measure of partisan fragmentation do not eliminate the ability of a coherent Scottish Executive to stake out a policy and drive it through. In short, the UK settlement takes governments with substantial presumptive legitimacy, gives them substantial room to work with their own budgets and policy decisions, and then endows them with governments that need not labour too long to build coalitions and can instead take decisive, rapid action. This is a formula for maximal policy divergence – something that should shape the UK in the future.

There are other ways to structure devolution settlements that do not place such a premium on permitting difference. Their attributes and those of the UK are clearer for comparison. There are other values which could be balanced against innovation and divergence in constructing a devolution settlement (and it is an open question how many architects of the UK devolution settlement intended to create such autonomous governments as Scotland). For example, there is the Spanish model, in which the central state has a constitutional responsibility to guarantee citizenship rights, which can be extended to include a great deal of central government interference. There is the Canadian model, which allocates many carrots (and few if any sticks) to a federal government but lets provinces run and largely fund the health service. Two orders of government in Canada argue and seek credit amidst constant friction and possible productive tension. Both of these orders of government, and other countries, must live with constant intergovernmental wrangling over funds, competencies, and framework legislation, wrangling that can become envenomed when there are two nations involved (as with Quebec, Catalonia, and the Basque Country). Such systems do, however, come up with mechanisms for providing services such as health care in ways that place more implicit value on state-wide standards and citizenship rights than the UK, which creates the conditions not for equality or equity but for maximal divergence by the 15 per cent of the population living in Northern Ireland, Scotland, and Wales. This UK model might both be advisable for states coping with demands for strong autonomy from a particular region, and might pose serious problems if extended across parts of England or into other states.

There is little public or professional interest in discussing the potential consequences of tinkering with the devolution settlement. Nor is there much appreciation of how easy it would be to make unintentionally large changes. Chapter 7 argued that the Barnett formula is vulnerable. More autonomy, such as 'fiscal freedom' (important tax-raising powers) would reduce dependence on Westminster decisions but would expose the devolved governments to the different pressures that come with the need to nurture a tax base and an economy. Wales or Northern Ireland, freed from UK fiscal formulae, might decide that they cannot develop a high-productivity, high-amenity economy, but could improve their jobs base by winning a race to the bottom in taxation and public services. Other jurisdictions faced with the same problems have certainly adopted that strategy. Without Barnett or a good equalising formula, a 'fiscally free' Northern Ireland or Wales that retained a commitment to the welfare state might price itself straight out of the European economy. Formula-based funding has permitted Welsh experiments of potentially global value; it is not clear that more Treasury intervention in finance or more pressure for tax cuts would allow such innovation.

Big welfare states and 'little' decisions

Many discussions of the politics of the welfare state operate on the level of major forces – classes, wars, modernity, and states – and discuss historic policy decisions such as the establishment of universal health care or state pensions rather than the operation of health systems or other policy areas (for influential examples, Flora and Heidenheimer 1981; Weir, Orloff, and Skocpol 1988; Esping-Andersen 1990; Huber, Ragin, and Stephens 1993; O'Connor and Olsen 1998; Huber and Stephens 2001). Analyses with such big inputs and outcomes are suited to the era of expansion, rather than today's time of limited welfare state growth and extensive recalibration. In this era of mature welfare states (Pierson 2001), great decisions such as the creation of the NHS are largely past. The essence of social politics now is in 'small' decisions about administration, organisation, provision, and the margins of services that can cumulate into important shifts in policy direction and institutions.[1] These decisions only look small compared to those made during the 'heroic age' of welfare states – it is next to the creation of the NHS that a decision to reorganise it seems small. But there is a broad consensus developing that the politics of mature welfare states are not like those of expanding ones, simply because decisions about policy are not the same as decisions to establish welfare states.

This means that the comparative politics of the welfare state must now more than ever be the study of comparative public policies and must look at the political processes and arguments behind them. The tenor of welfare state politics since at least the 1980s has been the making of small decisions about organisation and marginal benefits, albeit often at large political cost (Pierson 2001) Even the most radical change in the welfare state in this study, the decisions by England's government slowly to unpick the NHS model of direct state provision, are actually a sequence of small and hotly contested battles that can cumulatively have dramatic effects.

The politics of mature welfare states demands a new look at many variables, and decentralisation is one of them. Decentralisation largely had inconsistent, interactive effects on the growth of the welfare state (Pierson 1995; Banting and Corbett 2002). Comparative politics has been broadly sceptical of decentralisation, possibly more sceptical than findings merit; multistate statistical studies tended to drop decentralisation into some larger category of 'institutional fragmentation' (i.e. more veto points) and find that fragmentation has a mild negative effect on welfare state expansion (Swank 2001:211 is typical; but see Simeon forthcoming). Case studies certainly find much more complex mechanisms and interactions than any simple 'fragmentation' (Banting 1987:172–80; Maioni 1998; Tuohy 1999).

Decentralisation might now come into its own as the setting of the decisions that now matter (Greer, S. L. forthcoming-b). While federalism does not consistently shape the growth and extent of major programmes such as social security, it does shape the scope of programmes, the balance of interests, and their redistributive impact – all that makes up contemporary welfare politics (Banting 1987:172). Now, when neither the establishment nor the removal of programmes on the scale of the NHS is on the agenda, these decisions are the essence of policy. That means that methods and theories appropriate to such issues will begin to explain big issues such as the shape and size of the public sector and the role of the market in the advanced industrial societies.

In the comparative study of the welfare state, a major item in the debates about the impact of globalisation on democracy and social democracy, there is a strong case that we will continue to see a great deal of political autonomy and policy divergence. 'Small' decisions above all are made by the interaction of policy, politician, and politics, and these are all highly variable and contingent on territory. Nevertheless, the process of responding to such influences, if it produces convergence, will either be over a long period of learning as each country adopts, for all practical purposes, a strategy of trial and error, or will reflect not so much an objective constraint as a potent set of policy prescriptions (such as neoliberalism) that lodge firmly in the policy communities of many states and international organisations.

If the politics of the welfare state is the politics of public policy, then there is a good case for studies that start with the explanation of policy outcomes and build upwards from there. They would look for the systematic regularities of political outcomes and the mechanisms that translate them into outcomes. This is both a perspective that focuses on real political activity and one that emphasises the importance of chance and political debate. From a great distance, the relationship between big trends and outcomes might be visible. From closer up we can see a multitude of decisions at work, which over time shape distinctive welfare states, and a multitude of pressures, which shape agendas, interpretations, and decisions.

Looking forward: uniformity and diversity in the devolved UK

Compared to its peers around the world, the UK has great potential for policy divergence and different policy solutions in different places. Its system of intergovernmental relations and finance, with its combination of formula funding and very limited normative legal frameworks, permits extensive divergence, particularly between Scotland and England. This strengthens the workings of day-to-day politics, which drives divergence – and which particularly drives divergence in a complex multinational state such as the UK. All political systems should have a tendency to diverge, but the greater the divergence in party systems and policy communities the greater the differences in policy outcomes should be. The UK's polities have markedly divergent policy communities and divergent party systems, which means that the policies and politics at work in a decision differ from each other.

Divergence, then, is likely, and particularly likely in the UK and similar multinational states. What constrains divergence, overall? What in the analysis of the politics of England, Northern Ireland, Scotland, and Wales might limit divergence over time?

This book has canvassed the three largest and most immediate factors. The first is the extent of divergence in the politics – the party system. English regional party systems, assuming they remain a Conservative-Labour-Liberal Democrat oligopoly, should produce less policy divergence between regional and local governments than between English governments as a group and the governments of Northern Ireland, Scotland, and Wales. The second is the extent of divergence in the policy communities. England, Northern Ireland, Scotland, and Wales are not just different societies with very different endowments of managers, think-tanks, teaching hospitals, and suchlike; they are also inheritors of four established administrative decisions whose needs and fortunes created particular policy communities over time. Given that policy communities are built on institutions, institutional trajectories will change policy communities over time and the four policy communities should grow apart from their fairly similar baseline. It is unlikely that a whole health system can fail, and smaller failures can be identified and made problems in a common feedback loop. The third reason for constraint on divergence is the system of intergovernmental relations. Scotland is least constrained, Wales is second least constrained, and Northern Ireland would be almost as free as Scotland but for suspension. Financial formulas and normative frameworks as well as the distribution of competencies can all shape the ability of regional governments to develop divergent policy. They also increase or decrease the strength of regional governments' negotiating positions in the intergovernmental negotiations that are inevitably required to coordinate and develop policies that cut across competencies.

These three factors do much to explain divergence and should be adequate predictors of divergence in decentralised states or English governments. Still, though, there are surrounding facts that constrain divergence. The three likeliest restraints on divergence are path dependency, common citizenship rights discourses in the broad public, and changes in intergovernmental relations within the UK or on the European level.

Path dependency

Outside those three large factors limiting divergence, the first potential constraint is simply the shared legacies of the NHS. The logic of path dependency is the economist's tool to explain why organisations do not converge on 'optimal' outcomes: The costs of changing direction on to a new path – metaphorically, going back to the fork in the road and taking a different path – are greater than the potential benefits. This is the case for the welfare states and health politics of any rich country (Thelen 1999; Myles and Pierson 2001). The costs of changing the bases of these huge economic sectors would be enormous. Despite the abolition or reorganisation of almost every organisation in the UK health services since 1997, there are common institutional factors that are likely to be prohibitively expensive to change. The existence of the NHS and its essential basis in tax finance and state ownership would be difficult to change. Introducing greater reliance on private insurance, for example, would require some kind of impressive subsidy to create private providers (out of a limited labour market) or would simply increase the costs charged to the NHS, thereby creating a highly manipulated market and an expensive residual system (Australian experiences with federal efforts to increase private insurance suggest as much). So long as there is meaningful political and public support for any national health service, the damage to the system (or the increase in spending) required to shift it to a different basic financing mechanism would be likely to prevent change.

Legacies can change, of course; today's decisions are tomorrow's legacies. The changes in the English NHS can be construed as laying the foundations for an essentially private or not-for-profit system funded by the state. The speed of the changes made in the UK since devolution, reflecting the power and autonomy of parliamentary governments, are because the costs of change in UK systems are relatively low compared to other systems. The health systems of the UK are more likely to change paths than most others because of their health service model and parliamentary governments, but they still would face substantial bills were they to try to change the financial, political, and perhaps moral bases of the systems.

These costs are defined and processed by policy communities in each country, which add another layer of path dependency of their own. The inherited policy communities of the four UK systems are all shaped by their experiences of 'the' NHS to 1998 and by their experiences of working in a system with its blend of tax financing (and consequent competition as a public priority with roads or schools), close political contact and professional autonomy over work if not finance, and tangible commitment to equity and equality. They have institutional bases, and change more or less with them, and institutions change slowly. Cultural change also comes slowly, and even more slowly if it fails to build its own organisational bases. It took twenty years of intense effort, with a strong ideological headwind, to implant managers and corporate rationalisers as dominant parts of the system and the policy community in England, yet their power in the wards remains contested by professionals and patients. The institutional positions of the different groups in the health system are strong and mean that the costs and benefits and policy ideas are shaped not just by outsiders' notions of practicality but also by the inherited policy communities themselves. The result is that real change is hampered both by underlying problems of rapid change and perceptions among those who define questions and answers.

Citizenship discourses

This book has focused on the likelihood that territorial decentralisation will lead to variation in citizenship rights. There is abundant evidence that it does do that, internationally. Yet there is also an intriguing and little-studied vein of evidence that suggests there are limits to divergence contained in the democratic public itself. As Keith Banting asks, why is it that the pressure for consistent citizenship rights trumps pressure for divergence (Banting forthcoming)? With a few marked exceptions such as the USA, whose citizens tolerate extraordinary degrees of territorial inequality, the similarity of welfare provision across intrastate borders is as noteworthy as the divergence. There are multiple explanations for this phenomenon, but one under-researched one is the impact of public opinion. What are the basic understandings of citizenship rights in public, policy, and media debates, and what constraints do they place on policy divergence? And how?

The meaning and significance of citizenship discourses is remarkably little explored and only now being investigated. Public opinion data on the subject is relatively scarce but suggests that there is limited public tolerance for substantive citizenship rights divergence in other decentralised countries such as Germany and Spain (Jeffery forthcoming). For all that different governments focus on their own problems and politics, their publics help set the limits that constrain their perceptions of feasibility and desirability. That could very well be the case in the UK, where the media is relatively well integrated and dramatic differences could start to become an important issue for the press.

The likely presence and power of citizenship rights discourses in the public also make the divergence machine of UK intergovernmental relations more fragile. An enterprising politician might see a solution to some problem in using expectations of common citizenship rights to attack the freedom contained in the Barnett formula or the lack of normative frameworks in the Scottish settlement. If the structure of intergovernmental relations produces divergence in citizenship rights that politicians think the public finds intolerable, then the result could be sudden and important changes in the structure of devolution. Or the extent of common citizenship discourses could merely pull governments away from adopting policies that would create too much of a gap and towards a measure of equality across the country (vocal interest groups certainly leapt to recommend free personal long-term care for the rest of the UK after Scotland made its decision). In that way, the ideology and strategy of governing politicians across the country might lead them to avoid policies that create real divergence in citizenship rights for fear of public backlash.

Power

Finally, divergence can be limited by the simple exercise of intergovernmental power. There are two actors in the UK against whom Northern Ireland, Scotland, Wales, and English subnational governments are defenceless save in extreme situations. One is Westminster, and the other is the EU.

Westminster, as the word devolution suggests, remains essentially sovereign in the UK. Parliament, and no other part of the state, is intrinsic to the continuity of the state, and neither international law nor its own decisions bind Westminster. We see this power clearly in the repeated suspensions of the Belfast Agreement. The Agreement has components (related to cross-border strands) that are embedded in international law, and involved a referendum vote to change part of the Irish Republic's written constitution, and the Agreement has no provision for suspensions by Westminster, but Westminster was perfectly capable under UK law of deciding to suspend the Assembly (Hazell 1999:233).

Outside the invariably exceptional case of Northern Ireland, Westminster has not used its power. The Barnett formula, despite a process of formalisation that has elevated it from an accounting tool to a high-profile part of the UK state, remains essentially a convenience that HM Treasury adopts. Autonomy for Wales is a function of the division between primary and secondary legislation in Westminster, and tightly written primary legislation could cause Wales real problems. And, in constitutional law and in reality, there is nothing to stop the revocation of the Scotland and Wales Acts altogether.

But it was hard to suspend Stormont in the 1970s when it was rightly known as 'John Bull's Political Slum' (Rose 2000:53). The political price of actually abolishing a healthy devolved polity like Scotland would almost certainly be staggering, since it would be the most effective way to prompt secession and the break-up of the UK. Political reality buttresses the existence of devolution along with many other rights and institutions created over years of political struggle; Westminster could also in theory restrict the franchise to men, but it is unlikely to do so for the same reasons. What the power and distinctiveness of Scottish or Welsh (or English regional) civil society might *not* be able to do is defend 'their' governments from little encroachments by Westminster over time. The histories of Spanish regions certainly testify to the difficulty.

The EU, meanwhile, has largely been absent from health, but in health as in other policy areas the EU is a threat to regional autonomy across Europe. Essentially, the EU is a group of states. Unless regional governments can successfully band together and win the right to vote on behalf of the state, it will be the central state that decides EU policy regardless of whether or not the issue is an EU competency. Europeanisation lets central governments into regional competencies by a sort of back door. Health has largely escaped Europeanisation to date, but the EU is slowly changing the environment of health services, with policies as diverse as harmonisation of professional qualifications, establishing the right of Europeans to be treated wherever in the EU they wish, the Working Time Directive that threatens to close services across the continent by restricting historically very long professional hours, medical research funding, and purchasing regulations that could potentially create serious problems for commissioning-based systems such as England's (Greer 2005).

There have been efforts by regional governments to 'get around' their states by approaching Brussels directly or through the EU's largely powerless Committee of the Regions (Morata 1995; Jeffery 1997). These have been relatively unsatisfactory because they did not change the fundamental imbalance between states and others in the EU. The abundance of lobbyists in Brussels and Strasbourg means that their direct access to the EU institutions is likely to be limited and often fruitless, while the ubiquity of EU legislation taxes their ability to identify issues and lobby appropriately. The solution in comparable European countries has been some form of regional participation in central state decisions on topics allocated to regions (such as education in Germany), but the UK's devolution settlement and state traditions so far appear to offer unpromising territory for formalising any such solution (Jeffery forthcoming). While the theory behind Westminster's legal, if not political ability, to reshape devolution as it likes is a reminder of hierarchy, it is in the Westminster government's ability to shape EU policy that hierarchy is likely to matter.

The four nations' health services

Arguments about policy convergence driven by large-scale forces have their allure. Appealing to globalisation, the EU, consumerism, demographic change, or neoliberalism to explain decisions brings the observer analytic clarity and seemingly testable propositions about inexorable forces. Skilfully used in political debate, they put policy advocates on the right side of history and turn conditions into problems or vice versa. The problem with such arguments is often that while they identify large-scale constraints on policy autonomy they have difficulty in reliably specifying the policy consequences. Politics, policy debate, interpretation, and their chancy interactions fill in a crucial part of the gap between the fact of an ageing population or free trade and the actual policies. In the policy making of mature welfare states, hemmed in by existing institutions, extensive commitments, and limited new resources, such different interpretations and policy decisions matter greatly. In health, a complex arena particularly gifted with articulate policy advocates and global debates, the likelihood that policy agendas and interpretations will be the same in different jurisdictions is slim. Fine differences between the ideas put forth and their bearers can then produce substantial differences in the health services ordinary people encounter. The result is that for every new challenge to the welfare state we can expect multiple responses, driven as much by interpretation, local debate, chance, and history as by the challenges themselves.

The degree of divergence in the UK also points to the limitations of an analysis based on the constraints facing the devolved governments. There is always room for debate about whether a jurisdiction has 'enough' powers; such debate is the mainstay of territorial politics. What the experience of the UK in comparative perspective shows is that Northern Ireland (when devolved), Scotland, and even Wales have considerable policy autonomy and can adopt markedly different policy trajectories little distorted by central financial or normative control. This might not be the case in other policy areas or in the future, and indeed the degree of social policy autonomy in the UK model might prove its undoing, but at present the UK has created good conditions to show the extent to which the policy communities and politics of its four components are different and drive divergence.

The four health services of the UK each has an opportunity to demonstrate the relevance, feasibility, and desirability of a democratic, public health system that treats patients with equity, respect, and honour. They have placed high-stakes bets on health service strategies. The burden of this book has been to explain why they marked out distinct strategies as each puzzles collectively and half-listens to important international debates while trying to solve its problems of rationing and provision. The answers lie in the spirit, organisation, presence, and persistence of different policy advocates and their interaction with politicians' need to make a mark and hold on to office – and therefore constitute at least a qualified tribute to the workings of public debate and democratic responsiveness in the devolved UK. If the essence of politics is about being in the right place at the right time with a convincing policy idea that survives the policy community and seems to solve a problem, then participating in policy debates is worthwhile and admirable. Policy arguments in democratic polities shape interpretations of and responses to even the most seemingly obvious pressures, and that means there is little excuse for quiescence but rather a genuine incentive to act.

But does any UK health policy 'work?' There have not been many studies comparing health outcomes in different parts of the UK (two, one by the *parti pris*, Conservative-leaning think-tank Civitas and one by respected analysts were sceptical about Scotland's pre-devolution use of extra funds; Dixon,

Inglis, and Klein 1999). It is very difficult to make comparisons. Policy changes take time, sometimes decades, to show their effects. No system will score highly on the full range of indicators. Mutually contradictory indicators of health service success include patient satisfaction, throughput, local employment and community development, costs per patient episode, advanced medical research, length of waiting lists, quality chronic care, treatment of 'Cinderella' services such as speech therapy or mental illness, and the scientific quality of medicine. UK debates, inflected as ever with accountancy, tend to focus on throughput, cost per unit, and waiting lists for discrete treatments. A healthy newspaper reader in the UK, bombarded by stories about surgical capacity, would probably be unaware of the existence (let alone the prevalence) of chronic disease.

We could logically try to seek out the impact of health services on population morbidity and mortality, but as advocates of the new public health point out, far more than health services go into creating a healthy or an unhealthy population. Glasgow has some excellent hospitals and an unhealthy population, and it is far from clear whether it is the Mediterranean diet or a great deal of unsuspected high-quality medical provision that explains good health in parts of Southern Europe.

So obviously desirable indicators such as population health are too far from our policies to be worthwhile in a discussion of health services, and more or less achievable indicators are essentially political decisions. The result, for example, is that England is indeed building the capacity it requires to dispose of waiting lists for particular acute treatments, but chronic care is little better than it was years ago, and by all indicators (including the rebellions by doctors in contract negotiations) professional and staff morale in the English NHS is low even by English NHS standards.

What this means is that the ends as well as the means must be debated. The goals of a health service cannot be taken for granted. They should not be taken for granted because they play such a large role in society and because they are necessarily set by the kinds of political processes studied in this book. All the UK systems, for example, value research and advanced techniques more highly than some Continental systems that seemingly produce better patient satisfaction, and all the UK systems incorporate a belief in equity that is missing in the often-admired US or German systems. So when we find a comparison that makes one system look particularly good in some way, we cannot simply praise it overall. We must look for the costs that come with that benefit before admiring the system as a whole. Only after examining the difference facets of health systems, their costs and benefits, and the aims set for them, would we be able to reliably say a health system is failing compared to others. A system might be mostly cost and not much benefit, but that is hardly

a conclusion we can draw from either society-level statistics or tabloid headlines about waiting lists. We do not know what we really want from health services, and the only way we can decide is through democratic politics as we
know it today.

In turn that means we must study the politics of health as much as the
policies. The different policy communities and party systems of the four UK
systems have driven divergence in ends and means. This is to be expected and
is one of the strongest justifications for devolution and for the UK model of
autonomy. In every part of the UK there are policy advocates who are pas-
sionately unhappy about their trajectories and wish their polity were not
making the decisions it is making. Their complaints are just as much participation in health politics as the explanations given for policy decisions, and the
losses of these advocates reflect not just luck but also, over time, the weakness
of the advocates. And if the purpose of devolution is to give fuller expression
to the different societies of the UK, then it is entirely appropriate that it leads
to their health systems developing different missions, cultures, organisation,
and relationships with society.

A health system is good for many different things, if not for all of them
at the same time, and if the UK is a diverse enough country to require multiple regional and national governments then it is diverse enough to have health
systems with different values and organisation. The countervailing tendency
certainly has been pernicious when we see it in the history of local government. It assumes common ends (generally 'efficiency') and looks at the policies of different elected governments as so many experiments in or abdications
of the responsibility to provide just those ends. It has suffocated local democracy and policy innovation in Britain. It is thankfully unlikely that Scotland or
Wales will fall into being seen in the same way, as just two more arenas in
which small variations in service delivery may be piloted before the centre rolls
them out. Scotland and Wales's self-confidence and distinctive politics and
policy debates presumably insulate them from that.

One thing that all the cultures of the UK share is that they are often far
too critical of themselves, and critical with their usual elegantly effective artic-
ulacy. Complaining in the UK is usually done to a very high standard. That
makes it all the more important to remember the achievements of all four
systems. The thought, care, and determination that legislated to create public
health services in the UK and that went into building the National Health
Service in each country has created four systems that despite their distinct
costs and benefits are probably as good as any others in the world. The legacies may be squandered, but they also live on in assumptions few policy
makers in the world are lucky enough to make. The NHS systems of the UK
can focus attention on specific problems such as cancer care, develop service

integration with others such as local authorities, build primary care's effective and efficient role, shift funds in and out of health services, and maintain a balance of high-technology medical research and grassroots equity with an efficiency that most of the world can only envy. The disparate policy advocates of the UK show this in their ambitions for their systems, high by international standards, and in an ethic of equity absent in the many other countries that formally entrench status and economic inequalities or corporatism in their health services. Such an ethic, and the achievements we see in every GP surgery or cathedral of health technology, are a formidable legacy that informs the policy debates of the whole UK.

Where the four systems go from here, though, is up to them. The autonomy and difference of England, Northern Ireland, Scotland, and Wales reflects the problems and pressures facing politicians and the researched, well-intentioned efforts to policy advocates that surround them. Struggling with uncertainty and chance in the difficult careers politics offer, the policy advocates compete to interpret, recommend, and decide. Their struggles, victories, and losses are local, set in local institutions, policy communities, and electoral competition and tossed about by luck. Their problems and strategies have always been at the heart of politics and the experience of the devolved UK shows just how much they can do. For all that the world is changing and impinging on the slightest decision and for all that the institutions of devolution and international organisations shape what can be done, the US politician Tip O'Neill had a point: all politics is, indeed, local.

Note

1 I owe this point to Margitta Mätzke.

Appendix: interviewee profiles

This list covers formal, transcribed interviews with as much information about each interviewee as is compatible with the agreed level of anonymity. It does not include re-interviews, short fact checks, participant observation of health events, or 'Chatham House rules' seminars in all four jurisdictions.

Northern Ireland

2–31 Manager, Belfast, 3 November 2003

2–30 Civil servant, Belfast, 2 November 2003

2–29 Manager, Belfast, 31 October 2003

2–28 MLA, Member, Northern Ireland Executive, Belfast 18 January 2002

2–27 Manager (acute care), Belfast, 18 January 2002

2–26 Manager (primary care), Belfast, 18 January 2002

2–24 Senior civil servant, Belfast, 17 January 2002

2–23 Senior doctor (public health function), Belfast, 16 January 2002

2–22 MLA, Member, Northern Ireland Executive, 16 January 2002

2–21 Officer, Northern Ireland Voluntary Trust, Belfast, 7 December 2001

2–20 MLA, Health and Personal Social Services (HPSS) Committee member (SDLP), Belfast, 7 December 2001

2–19 MLA, HPSS Committee member (UUP), Belfast, 6 December 2001

2–18 Voluntary sector manager, Belfast, 5 December 2001

2–17 Enniskillen hospital campaigner, Enniskillen, 23 November 2001

2–16 Enniskillen hospital campaigner, Enniskillen, 23 November 2001

2–15 Four managers, Derry, 21 November 2001

2–14 Manager, Derry, 21 November 2001

2–13 MLA (Sinn Féin), 20 November 2001

2–12 Local councillor, Omagh, 20 November 2001

2–11 MLA (DUP), Omagh, 20 November 2001

2–10 Local government officer, Omagh, 19 November 2001

2–9 Omagh hospital campaigner, Omagh, 19 November 2001
2–8 Manager (public health function), Belfast, 16 November 2001
2–7 Senior civil Servant (retired), Belfast, 16 November 2001
2–6 Manager (social services function), Belfast, 15 November 2001
2–5 Community activist, Belfast, 15 November 2001
2–4 Hayes Report Committee member, Belfast, 1 October 2001
2–3 anonymous
2–2 Two managers, Belfast, 28 September 2001
2–1 Manager, Belfast, 27 September 2001

Scotland

3–30 MSP (former minister), Edinburgh, 12 February 2003
3–29 Manager, Highlands, telephone, 21 May 2002
3–28 Manager (primary care), Paisley, 21 May 2002
3–27 Doctor (primary care), Argyll, 20 May 2002
3–26 A Doctor and a manager (primary care), Argyll, 20 May 2002
3–25 Doctor (acute care), Paisley, 20 May 2002
3–24 Manager (acute care), Glasgow, 9 May 2002
3–23 UNISON officer, Glasgow, 8 May 2002
3–22 Manager, Paisley, 8 May 2002
3–21 anonymous
3–20 Senior civil servant (retired), Glasgow, 7 May 2002
3–19 Former Scottish Executive adviser, Edinburgh, 6 May 2002
3–18 Representative of a management organisation, 3 May 2002
3–17 Manager (acute care), Glasgow, 3 May 2002
3–16 Doctor (public health function), Glasgow, 2 May 2002
3–15 Senior official, Scottish Executive, Edinburgh, 2 May 2002
3–14 Manager, Glasgow, 30 April 2002
3–13 Manager-doctor, Glasgow, 30 April
3–12 BMA officer, 29 April 2002
3–11 Official, Scottish Executive, Edinburgh, 29 April 2002
3–10 Doctor (public health function), Paisley, 29 April 2002
3–9   BMA officer, Edinburgh, 19 April 2002
3–8   Manager, Highlands, 19 April 2002
3–7   Manager, Glasgow, 18 April 2002
3–6   Chair, Local Health Council, 18 April 2002
3–5   RCN officer, Edinburgh, 17 April 2002
3–4   Former Labour minister, Glasgow, 17 April 2002
3–3   MSP (Conservative), Edinburgh, 25 September 2001

3–2 MSP (Health Committee member, Labour), Edinburgh, 24 July 2001
3–1 MSP (Health Committee member, SNP), Edinburgh, 24 July 2001

Wales

4–26 Doctor-manager (Glamorgan), Cardiff, 14 November 2003
4–25 Doctor (public health function), Cardiff, 13 November 2003
4–24 Manager (acute), North Wales, 4 November 2002
4–23 anonymous
4–22 Manager (acute), Glamorgan, Cardiff, 15 February 2003
4–21 MP (Labour, former Welsh Office), London, 5 December 2002
4–20 Manager (primary care), Glamorgan, 3 December 2002
4–19 Manager (primary care), Glamorgan, 3 December 2002
4–18 AM (Labour, deputy minister), constituency office, 2 December 2002
4–17 John Redwood MP, London, 19 November 2002
4–16 Academic, former NHS manager, Glamorgan, 18 November 2002
4–15 Former NAW staffer, Cardiff, 13 November 2002
4–14 Doctor (public health function), Cardiff, 13 November 2002
4–13 AM (Labour, former MP), Cardiff, 13 November 2002
4–12 Doctor (public health function), Glamorgan, 12 November 2002
4–11 NAW official, Cardiff, 11 November 2002
4–10 AM (Conservative, Health Committee member), Cardiff, 11 November 2002
4–9 NAW official, Cardiff, 6 November 2002
4–8 Academic, Cardiff, 6 November 2002
4–7 Academic, Cardiff, 5 November 2002
4–6 NAW adviser, Cardiff, 5 November 2002
4–5 Academic, former manager, Glamorgan, 18 July 2002
4–4 Two academics, Cardiff, 17 July 2002
4–3 Manager (public health function), North Wales, 16 July 2002
4–2 Academic, North Wales, 16 July 2002
4–1 Former Manager, North Wales, 15 July 2002

England: East Midlands and Trent

5–8 Regeneration specialist, Nottingham, 27 July 2001
5–7 East Midlands Regional Assembly officer, Melton Mowbray, 19 July 2001
5–6 Two East Midlands Development Agency officers, Nottingham, 27 July 2001

5–5 Official, Nottingham, 19 July 2001

5–4 Manager, Doncaster, 10 July 2001

5–3 Two managers, NHS Executive Trent region, Sheffield, 10 July 2001

5–2 Manager, NHS Executive Trent region, Derby, 14 June 2001

5–1 Doctor-manager (public health function), NHS Executive Trent region, Derby, 14 June 2001

England: London

(Not including interviews by M. Sandford with results reported in Greer and Sandford 2001)

6–5 Officer, London Health Commission, 17 October 2001

6–4 Voluntary sector representative, 16 October 2001

6–3 Social enterprise representative, 18 September 2001

6–2 NHS manager, 18 September 2001

6–1 Officer, King's Fund, 21 May 2001

England: other (primarily central government)

0–12 anonymous

0–11 anonymous

0–10 anonymous

0–9 Department of Health official/doctor (retired), London, January 2003

0–8 Manager (primary care), London, August 2003

0–7 Former Department of Health minister (Labour), Birmingham, June 2003

0–6 anonymous

0–5 anonymous

0–4 anonymous

0–3 anonymous

0–2 CHI officer, May 4, 2001

0–1 anonymous

References

Books, articles, and papers

Abbott, A. 1994. *The System of Professions: An Essay on the Division of Expert Labor.* Chicago: University of Chicago Press.

Adams, J., and P. Robinson, eds. 2002. *Devolution in Practice: Public Policy Differences within the UK.* London: Institute for Public Policy Research.

Agranoff, R. 1999. Intergovernmental Relations and the Management of Asymmetry in Spain. In *Accommodating Diversity: Asymmetry in Federal States,* ed. R. Agranoff, 94–117. Baden-Baden: Nomos.

Aja, E. 1999. *El Estado Autónomico: Federalismo y Hechos Diferenciales.* Madrid: Alianza Editorial.

——, 2001. Spain: Nation, Nationalities, and Regions. In *Subnational Democracy in the European Union,* ed. J. Loughlin, 229–54. Oxford: Oxford University Press.

Alford, R. 1975. *Health Care Politics: Ideological and Interest Group Barriers to Reform.* Chicago: University of Chicago Press.

Alvarez Conde, E. 1993. *Curso de Derecho Constitucional: Los órganos constitucionales, el estado autonómico.* Madrid: Tecnos.

Anderson, O.W. 1972. *Health Care: Can there be Equity?* New York: Wiley.

Anderson, P. 1997. *Safety First: The Making of New Labour.* London: Granta.

Andrews, L. 1999. *Wales Says Yes: The Inside Story of the Yes for Wales Referendum Campaign.* Bridgend: Seren.

Appleby, J., A. Harrison, and N. Devlin. 2003. *What is the Real Cost of More Patient Choice?* London: King's Fund.

Arthur, P. 2000. *Special Relationships: Britain, Ireland, and the Northern Ireland Problem.* Belfast: Blackstaff.

Ashton, J., and H. Seymour. 1988. *The New Public Health: The Liverpool Experience.* Milton Keynes: Open University Press.

Atkinson, M., and L. Elliott. 1999. Brown's Mechanics behind the Machinations of Government. *The Guardian* (9 November).

Bachrach, P., and M.S. Baratz. 1962. The Two Faces of Power. *American Political Science Review* 56:947–52.

Baggott, R. 2000. *Public Health: Policy and Politics.* Basingstoke: Macmillan.

Balsom, D. 2000. The Referendum Result. In *The Road to the National Assembly for Wales,* ed. J.B. Jones and D. Balsom, 151–60. Cardiff: University of Wales Press.

Banting, K.G. 1987. *The Welfare State and Canadian Federalism*. 2nd edn. Kingston/Montreal: McGill-Queens University Press.

——, Forthcoming. Social Citizenship and Federalism: Is the Federal Welfare State a Contradiction in Terms? In *Territory, Justice and Democracy*, ed. S.L. Greer. London: The Constitution Unit.

Banting, K.G., and S. Corbett. 2002. Health Policy and Federalism: An Introduction. In *Health Policy and Federalism: A Comparative Perspective on Multi-Level Governance*, ed. K.G. Banting and S. Corbett, 1–37. Kingston/Montreal: McGill-Queens University Press.

Bardon, J., and D. Burnett. 1996. *Belfast: A Pocket History*. Belfast: Blackstaff.

Barzelay, M. 2000. *The New Public Management: Improving Research and Policy Dialogue*. Berkeley: University of California Press.

Baumgartner, F.R., and B.D. Jones. 1993. *Agendas and Instability in American Politics*. Chicago: University of Chicago Press.

Becker, H. S., B. Geer, E. C. Hughes, and A. L. Strauss. 2002 [1961]. *Boys in White: Student Culture in Medical School*. New Brunswick, New Jersey: Transaction.

Beecham, L. 2003. NHS Should be Removed from Government Control. *British Medical Journal* 325 (13 July):66.

Beer, S. H. 1982. *Modern British Politics: Parties and Pressure Groups in the Collectivist Age*. 2nd edn. London: Faber and Faber.

——. 1993. *To Make a Nation: The Rediscovery of American Federalism*. Cambridge, MA: Belknap/Harvard University Press.

Bell, D., and A. Christie. 2002. Finance— The Barnett Formula: Nobody's Child? In *The State of the Nations 2001: The Second Year of Devolution*, ed. A. Trench, 135–52. Thorverton: Imprint Academic.

Bell, P. N. 1987. Direct Rule in Northern Ireland. In *Ministers and Ministries: A Functional Analysis*, ed. R. Rose, 189–225. Oxford: Clarendon.

Bennie, L., J. Brand, and J. Mitchell. 1997. *How Scotland Votes*. Manchester: Manchester University Press.

Berg, M. 1997. *Rationalizing Medical Work: Decision-Support Techniques and Medical Practices*. Cambridge, MA: MIT Press.

Bernier, G., and D. Irwin. 1995. Fiscal Federalism: The Politics of Intergovernmental Transfers. In *New Trends in Canadian Federalism*, ed. M. Smith, 270–87. Peterborough, Ontario: Broadview.

Best, G. 1979. *Mid-Victorian Britain*. London: Fontana.

Bew, P. 2000. The Belfast Agreement of 1998: from Ethnic Democracy to a Multicultural, Consociational Settlement? In *A Farewell to Arms? From 'Long War' to Long Peace in Northern Ireland*, ed. M. Cox, A. Guelke, and F. Stephen, 40–8. Manchester: Manchester University Press.

Bew, P., P. Gibbon, and H. Patterson. 2002. *Northern Ireland 1921/2001: Political Forces and Social Classes*. London: Serif.

Birrell, D., and A. Murie. 1980. *Policy and Government in Northern Ireland: Lessons of Devolution*. Dublin: Gill and Macmillan/Barnes and Noble.

Black, E. R., and A. Cairns. 1966. A Different Perspective on Canadian Federalism. *Canadian Public Administration* 9:27–44.

Blair, T. 2002. *The Courage of Our Convictions: Why Reform of the Public Services is the Route to Social Justice*. Vol. 603. London: The Fabian Society (Fabian Ideas).

Blane, C. 2002. The RSSPCC as an Agency of Child Welfare, 1960–1990. Paper presented at 'Crossing the Divide', Glasgow Caledonian University, 18 May 2002.

Bloom, S. W. 2002. *The Word as Scalpel: A History of Medical Sociology*. Oxford: Oxford University Press.

Boase, J. P. 2001. Federalism and the Health Facility Fees Challenge. In *Federalism, Democracy, and Health Policy in Canada*, ed. D. Adams, 179–206. Kingston, Ontario: Queens University Institute of Intergovernmental Relations.

Bogdanor, V. 1999. *Devolution in the United Kingdom*. Oxford: Oxford University Press.

——.2001. Constitutional Reform. In *The Blair Effect: The Blair Government 1997–2001*, ed. A. Seldon, 139–58. London: Little, Brown.

Börzel, T. 2002. *States and Regions in the European Union: Institutional Adaptation in Germany and Spain*. Cambridge: Cambridge University Press.

Breeze, C., and R. Hall. 2002. *Health Impact Assessment in Government Policy-Making: Developments in Wales*. Brussels/Copenhagen: European Centre for Health Policy/WHO.

Bridgeman, J. 2002. Learning from Bristol: Healthcare in the 21st Century. *Modern Law Review* 65 (2):241–55.

Briggs, A. 1993 [1968]. *Victorian Cities*. Berkeley: University of California Press.

Brogan, B. 2001. Cancer Victim's Friend Savages PM over Health Service. *Daily Telegraph* (17 May).

Brown, A., D. McCrone, L. Paterson, and P. Surridge. 1999. *The Scottish Electorate: The 1997 General Election and Beyond*. London: Macmillan.

Bruce, A., and T. Forbes. 2001. From Competition to Collaboration in the Delivery of Health Care: Implementing Change in Scotland. *Scottish Affairs* 34 (Winter):107–24.

Brugué, Q., R. Gomà, and J. Subirats. 1997. Multilevel Governance and Europeanization: The Case of Catalonia. In *Europeanization and the Southern Periphery*, ed. K. Featherstone and G. Kazamias, 95–118. Portland, OR: Frank Cass.

Bulpitt, J. 1983. *Territory and Power in the United Kingdom: An Interpretation*. Manchester: Manchester University Press.

Burrows, N. 2000. *Devolution*. London: Sweet and Maxwell.

Butler, D., A. Adonis, and T. Travers. 1994. *Failure in British Government: The Politics of the Poll Tax*. Oxford: Oxford University Press.

Butler, D., and G. Butler. 1994. *British Political Facts*. 7th edn. London: Macmillan.

Butler, D., and D. Kavanagh. 1997. *The British General Election of 1997*. Basingstoke: Macmillan.

Calvert, H. 1968. *Constitutional Law in Northern Ireland: A Study in Regional Government*. London: Stevens and Sons/Northern Ireland Legal Quarterly.

Caminal Badia, M. 1998. *Nacionalisme i Partits Nacionals a Catalunya*. Barcelona: Empúries.

Campbell, C., and G. K. Wilson. 1995. *The End of Whitehall: Death of a Paradigm?* Oxford: Blackwell.

Carmichael, P. 2001. The Northern Ireland Civil Service. *Public Money and Management* 21 (2):33–8.

——.2002. The Northern Ireland Civil Service: Characteristics and Trends since 1970. *Public Administration* 80 (1):23–49.

Carson, K., and H. Idzikowska. 1989. The Social Production of Scottish Policing 1795–1900. In *Policing and Prosecution in Britain 1750–1850*, ed. D. Hay and F. Snyder, 267–97. Oxford: Clarendon.

Castells, A. 2001. Models i polítiques de finançament de la Generalitat: pautes d'estabilitat, canvi i conflicte. In *Govern i polítiques a Catalunya (1980–2000)*, ed. R. Gomà and J. Subirats, 49–68. Barcelona: Universitat de Barcelona/Universitat Autònoma de Barcelona.

Cochrane, A. L. 1972. *Effectiveness and Efficiency: Random Reflections on Health Services*. London: Nuffield Provincial Hospitals Trust (Rock Carling Fellowship Lecture 1971).

Cohen, M., J. G. March, and J. P. Olsen. 1972. A Garbage Can Model of Rational Choice. *Administrative Science Quarterly* 1:1–25.

Colley, L. 1992. *Britons: Forging the Nation 1707–1837*. London: Pimlico.

Conlan, T. J. 1998. *From New Federalism to Devolution? Twenty-five Years of Intergovernmental Reform*. Washington, DC: Brookings Institution.

Connolly, M. 1990. *Politics and Policy Making in Northern Ireland*. London: Philip Allan.

Connolly, M., and J. Loughlin, eds. 1990. *Public Policy in Northern Ireland: Adoptation or Adaption?* Belfast: Queens University Belfast/University of Ulster.

Constitution Unit and Institute of Welsh Affairs. 2003. *Nations and Regions: The Dynamics of Devolution: Wales Quarterly Report, February 2003*. London/Cardiff: Constitution Unit and Institute of Welsh Affairs.

Conversi, D. 1997. *The Basques, the Catalans, and Spain: Alternative Routes to Nationalist Mobilization*. London: Hurst.

———. 2000. Autonomous Communities and the Ethnic Settlement in Spain. In *Autonomy and Ethnicity: Negotiating Competing Claims in Multi-Ethnic States*, ed. Y. Ghai, 122–44. Cambridge: Cambridge University Press.

Corry, D. 2003. *The Regulatory State: Labour and the Utilities 1997–2002*. London: Institute for Public Policy Research.

Coulter, A. 2003. *The European Patient of the Future*. Milton Keynes: Open University Press.

Cowley, P., and M. Stuart. 2003. When Sheep Bark: The Parliamentary Labour Party, 2001–2003. Manuscript.

Cox, D. 1991. Health Service Management: A Sociological View: Griffiths and the Non-Negotiated Order of the Hospital. In *The Sociology of the Health Service*, ed. J. Gabe, M. Calnan, and M. Bury, 89–114. London: Routledge.

Cox, M., A. Guelke, and F. Stephen. 2000. *A Farewell to Arms? From 'Long War' to Long Peace in Northern Ireland*. Manchester: Manchester University Press.

Crossman, R. 1975. *The Diaries of a Cabinet Minister: Minister of Housing 1964–66*. Vol. 1. London: Hamish Hamilton and Jonathan Cape.

Cunningham, M. J. 2001. *British Government Policy in Northern Ireland, 1969–2000*. Manchester: Manchester University Press.

Curtice, J. 2001. Hopes Dashed and Fears Assuaged? What the Public Makes of It. In *The State of the Nations 2001: The Second Year of Devolution in the United Kingdom*, ed. A. Trench, 225–54. Thorverton: Imprint Academic.

———. 2003. Devolution Meets the Voters: The Prospects for 2003. In *The State of the Nations 2003: The Third Year of Devolution in the United Kingdom*, ed. R. Hazell, 263–84. Exeter: Imprint Academic.

Dahl, R. A. 1967. The City in the Future of Democracy. *American Political Science Review* 61 (4):953–70.

Dartmouth Center for Evaluative Clinical Sciences. 1998. *Dartmouth Atlas of Health Care.* Chicago: Dartmouth Medical School and American Hospital Publishing.

Davies, J. 1993. *A History of Wales.* London: Penguin.

Day, P., and R. Klein. 1983. The Mobilisation of Consent versus the Management of Conflict: Decoding the Griffiths Report. *British Medical Journal* 287:1813–16.

Deacon, R. M. 1997. Identifying the Origins of Welsh Local Government Reform. *Journal of Legislative Studies* 3 (3):104–12.

——.2002. *The Governance of Wales: The Welsh Office and the Policy Process, 1964–1999.* Cardiff: Welsh Academic Press.

Devine, T. M. 1999. *The Scottish Nation: 1700–2000.* London: Allan Lane/Penguin.

Díez Medrano, J. 1995. *Divided Nations: Class, Politics, and Nationalism in the Basque Country and Catalonia.* Ithaca: Cornell University Press.

DiMaggio, P. J., and W. W. Powell. 1991. The Iron Cage Revisited: Institutional Isomorphism and Collective Rationality in Organization Fields. In *The New Institutionalism in Organizational Analysis,* ed. W. W. Powell and P. J. DiMaggio, 63–82. Chicago: University of Chicago Press.

Dixon, J., S. Inglis, and R. Klein. 1999. Is the English NHS Underfunded? *British Medical Journal* 318 (20 February):522–6.

Downs, A. M. 1957. *An Economic Theory of Democracy.* New York: Harper and Row.

Drakeford, M., I. Butler, and A. Pithouse. 1998. Social Services. In *The National Assembly Agenda,* ed. J. Osmond, 266–80. Cardiff: Institute of Welsh Affairs.

Eaglesham, J. 2003. Blair Finds Words to Explain Core Belief. *Financial Times* (1 October):5.

Eckstein, H. 1959. *The English Health Service: Its Origins, Structure, and Achievements.* Oxford: Oxford University Press.

——.1960. *Pressure Group Politics: The Case of the British Medical Association.* London: Allen and Unwin.

Elston, M. A. 1991. The Politics of Professional Power: Medicine in a Changing Health Service. In *The Sociology of the Health Service,* ed. J. Gabe, M. Calnan, and M. Bury, 58–88. London: Routledge.

Enthoven, A. C. 1979. Consumer-Centred vs. Job-Centred Health Insurance. *Harvard Business Review* 57:141–52.

——.1989. What Europeans Can Learn from Americans. *Health Care Financing Review Annual Supplement* ex. series:49–77.

Esping-Andersen, G. 1990. *The Three Worlds of Welfare Capitalism.* Princeton, NJ: Princeton University Press.

Evans, D. G. 2000. *A History of Wales 1906–2000.* Cardiff: University of Wales Press.

Exworthy, M. 2001. Primary Care in the UK: Understanding the Dynamics of Devolution. *Health and Social Care in the Community* 9 (5):266–78.

Exworthy, M., M. Powell, and J. Mohan. 1999. The NHS: Quasi-market, Quasi-hierarchy and Quasi-network? *Public Money and Management* (October-December):15–22.

Feachem, R. G. A., N. K. Sekhri, and K. L. White. 2002. Getting More for their Dollar: a comparison of the NHS with California's Kaiser Permanente. *British Medical Journal* 324 (19 January):135–43.

Field, W. H. 1997. *Regional Dynamics: The Basis of Electoral Support in Britain.* Portland, OR: Frank Cass.

Fitzpatrick, D. 1998. *The Two Irelands 1912–1939.* Oxford: Oxford University Press.

Flora, P., and A. Heidenheimer, eds. 1981. *The Development of Welfare States in Europe and America.* New Brunswick, NJ: Transaction.

Flora, P., S. Kuhnle, and D. Urwin, eds. 1999. *State Formation, Nation-Building and Mass Politics in Europe: The Theory of Stein Rokkan.* Oxford: Oxford University Press.

Flynn, P. 1999. *Dragons Led by Poodles: The Inside Story of a New Labour Stitch-Up.* London: Politico's Publishing.

Foot, M. 1975 [1973]. *Aneurin Bevan.* Vol. 2. London: Granada and Davis-Poynter.

Foulkes, D., J. B. Jones, and R. A. Wilford. 1983. Wales: A Separate Administrative Unit. In *The Welsh Veto: The Wales Act 1978 and the Referendum,* ed. D. Foulkes, J. B. Jones, and R. A. Wilford, 1–18. Cardiff: University of Wales Press.

Fox, D. M. 1986. *Health Politics, Health Policies: The British and American Experience, 1911–1965.* Princeton, NJ: Princeton University Press.

Fox, D. M., and J. K. Iglehart, eds. 1994. *Five States that Could Not Wait: Lessons for Health Reform from Florida, Hawaii, Minnesota, Oregon and Vermont.* Oxford: Blackwell.

Freeman, R. 2000. *The Politics of Health in Europe.* Manchester: Manchester University Press.

Funkenstein, D. H. 1971. Medical Students, Medical Schools, and Society During Three Eras. In *Psychosocial Aspects of Medical Training,* ed. R. H. Coombs and C. E. Vincent, 229–84. Springfield, IL: Thomas.

Futures Group. 2002. *The Future of the NHS: A Framework for Debate.* London: King's Fund.

Gallego, R. 1998. New Public Management Reforms in the Catalan Public Health Sector, 1985–1995: Institutional Choices, Transactions Costs, and Policy Change. Ph.D. dissertation, London School of Economics and Political Science.

——. 2001. La política sanitària catalana: la construcció d'un sistema universal de provisió pluralista. In *Govern i polítiques públiques a Catalunya (1980–2000): Autonomia i benestar,* ed. R. Gomà and J. Subirats, 137–58. Vol. 2. Bellaterra: Universitat Autonoma de Barcelona.

Gallego, R., R. Gomà, and J. Subirats, eds. 2003. *Estado de bienestar i Comunidades Autonomás.* Madrid: Tecnos.

Giaimo, S., and P. Manow. 1999. Adapting the Welfare State: The Case of Health Reform in Britain, Germany, and the United States. *Comparative Political Studies* 32 (8):967–1000.

Givan, R. 2003. Seeing Stars? Performance Management and Human Resources in the National Health Service. Manuscript, London School of Economics.

Gourevitch, P. 1986. *Politics in Hard Times: Comparative Responses to International Economic Crises.* Ithaca: Cornell University Press.

Grau i Creus, M. 2000. The Effects of Institutions and Political Parties Upon Federalism: The Channeling and Integration of the Comunidades Autónomas within the Central-level Policy Process in Spain (1983–1996). Ph.D. dissertation, European University Institute, Florence.

Greer, A. L. 1987. Rationing Medical Technology: Hospital Decision Making in the United States and England. *International Journal of Technology Assessment in Health Care* 3:198–222.

———. 1988. The State of the Art vs. the State of the Science. *International Journal of Technology Assessment in Health Care* 4:5–26.

Greer, S. L. 2001a. *The Real Regional Health Agenda: Networks, Soft Money, and the Wider Determinants of Health in the East Midlands.* London: The Constitution Unit.

———. 2001b. *Divergence and Devolution.* London: Nuffield Trust.

———. 2003. Self-Government: The Politics of Regional Autonomy in Scotland and Catalonia. Ph.D. dissertation, Northwestern University, Evanston, Illinois.

———. 2004a. *Four Way Bet: How Devolution Has Led to Four Different Models for the NHS.* London: The Constitution Unit.

———. 2004b. Why Do Good Health Politics Make Bad Health Policy? In *UK Policy Futures*, ed. S. Dawson and C. Sausman. Basingstoke: Palgrave.

———. 2005. Europe, Whitehall, and Devolution: Multi-level politics and Health Policy in the Devolved UK. In *The State of the Nations 2005*, ed. A. Trench. Exeter: Imprint Academic.

———. Forthcoming-a. The Fragile Divergence Machine: Citizenship, Policy Divergence, and Intergovernmental Relations. In *Devolution and Power in the United Kingdom*, ed. A. Trench. Manchester: Manchester University Press.

———, ed. Forthcoming-b. *Territory, Justice and Democracy.* London: The Constitution Unit.

———. Forthcoming-c. An English Institution: Territory in the NHS. In *The English Question*, ed. R. Hazell. Manchester: Manchester University Press.

Greer, S. L., and M. Sandford. 2001. *Regions and Public Health.* London: The Constitution Unit.

———. 2003. *Fixing London.* London: The Constitution Unit.

Griffiths, D. 1996. *Thatcherism and Territorial Politics.* Aldershot: Avebury.

Griffiths, S. 2003. Doctoring the Evidence. *Health Services Journal* 113 (18 December):23.

Grodzins, M. 1984 [1966]. *The American System: A New View of Government in the United States.* 2nd edn. New Brunswick, NJ: Transaction.

Grogan, C. M. 1995. Hope in Federalism? What Can the States Do and What Are They Likely To Do? *Journal of Health Politics, Policy and Law* 20 (2):477–84.

Guillén, A., and L. Cabiedes. 1998. La política sanitaria: análisis y perspectivas del Sistema Nacional de Salud. In *Políticas Públicas en España: Contenidos, redes de actores y niveles de gobierno*, ed. R. Gomà and J. Subirats, 176–99. Barcelona: Ariel.

Hacker, J. S. 1998. The Historical Logic of National Health Insurance: Structure and Sequence in the Development of British, Canadian, and U.S. Medical Policy. *Studies in American Political Development* 12 (Spring):57–130.

Hackey, R. B. 1998. *Rethinking Health Care Policy: The New Politics of State Regulation.* Washington, DC: Georgetown University Press.

Hadfield, B. 1989. *The Constitution of Northern Ireland.* Belfast: SLS Legal Publications/Queens University Belfast.

Hagan, J. 1994. *Crime and Disrepute.* Beverly Hills: Pine Forge.

Hall, P. 1986. *Governing the Economy: The Politics of State Intervention in Britain and France.* Oxford: Oxford University Press.

Hall, P. A., and R. C. R. Taylor. 1996. Political Science and the Three New Institutionalisms. *Political Studies* 44:936–57.

Ham, C. 1999. *Health Policy in Britain*. 4th edn. Basingstoke: Macmillan.

———. 2000. *The Politics of NHS Reform 1988–97: Metaphor or Reality?* London: King's Fund.

Hamlin, C. 1998. *Public Health and Social Justice in the Age of Chadwick: Britain, 1800–1854*. Cambridge: Cambridge University Press.

Hands, D. 2000. *Evidence-based Organisational Design in Health Care: The Contribution of the Health Services Organisation Research Unit at Brunel University*. London: Nuffield Trust (Maureen Dixon Essay Series).

Hanham, H. J. 1965. The Creation of the Scottish Office, 1881–7. *Juridical Review*: 205–44.

Harbinson, J. F. 1973. *The Ulster Unionist Party, 1882–1973: Its Development and Organisation*. Belfast: Blackstaff.

Harris, J. 1983. The Transition to High Politics in English Social Policy 1880–1914. In *High and Low Politics in Modern Britain*, ed. M. Bentley and J. Stevenson, 58–79. Oxford: Oxford University Press.

Harrison, S. 1995. Clinical Autonomy and Planned Markets: The British Case. In *Implementing Planned Markets in Health Care*, ed. R. B. Saltman and C. van Otter, 156–77. Milton Keynes: Open University Press.

Harrison, S., and J. Dixon. 2000. *The NHS: Facing the Future*. London: King's Fund.

Harrison, S., and C. Pollitt. 1994. *Controlling Health Professionals: The Future of Work and Organization in the NHS*. Milton Keynes: Open University Press.

Harrison, S., and R. Schulz. 1989. Clinical Autonomy in the United Kingdom and the United States: Contrasts and Convergence. In *Controlling Medical Professionals: The Comparative Politics of Health Governance*, ed. G. Freddi and J. W. Björkman, 198–209. London: Sage.

Harvie, C., and P. Jones. 2000. *The Road to Home Rule: Images of Scotland's Cause*. Edinburgh: Polygon.

Hazell, R. 1999. The New Constitutional Settlement. In *Constitutional Futures: A History of the Next Ten Years*, ed. R. Hazell, 230–47. Oxford: Oxford University Press.

———. 2000a. Intergovernmental Relations: Whitehall Rules OK? In *The State and the Nations: The First Year of Devolution in the United Kingdom*, ed. R. Hazell, 149–82. Thorverton: Imprint Academic.

———, ed. 2000b. *The State and the Nations: The First Year of Devolution in the United Kingdom*. Thorverton: Imprint Academic.

———. 2003a. Conclusion: The Devolution Scorecard as the Devolved Assemblies Head for the Polls. In *The State of the Nations 2003: The Third Year of Devolution in the United Kingdom*, ed. R. Hazell, 285–302. Exeter: Imprint Academic.

———. 2003b. If Ivor Richards says Yes, will London say No? In *Second Term Challenge: Can the Welsh Assembly Government Hold its Course?*, ed. J. Osmond, 99–109. Cardiff: Institute of Welsh Affairs.

———, ed. 2003c. *The State of the Nations 2003: The Third Year of Devolution in the United Kingdom*. Exeter: Imprint Academic.

———, ed. Forthcoming. *The English Question*. Manchester: Manchester University Press.

Hazell, R., and P. Jervis. 1998. *Devolution and Health*. London: Nuffield Trust.

Heald, D. 2003. *Funding the Northern Ireland Assembly: Assessing the Options*. Belfast: Northern Ireland Economic Council.

Heald, D., and A. McLeod. 2002. Beyond Barnett? Financing Devolution. In

Devolution in Practice: Public Policy Differences Within the UK, ed. J. Adams and P. Robinson, 147–75. London: Institute for Public Policy Research.

Healy, J., and M. McKee. 2002. The Role and Function of Hospitals. In *Hospitals in a Changing Europe*, ed. M. McKee and J. Healy, 59–80. Milton Keynes: Open University Press/European Observatory on Health Care Systems.

Heclo, H. 1974. *Modern Social Politics in Britain and Sweden: From Relief to Income Maintenance*. New Haven: Yale University Press.

——.1975. Social Politics and Policy Impacts. In *What Government Does*, ed. M. Holden Jr. and D. L. Dresang, 151–76. Beverly Hills, CA: Sage.

——.1978. Issue Networks and the Executive Establishment. In *The New American Political System*, ed. A. King, 87–124. Washington, DC: American Enterprise Institute.

Heclo, H., and A. Wildavsky. 1974. *The Private Government of Public Money: Community and Policy Inside British Politics*. Berkeley and Los Angeles: University of California Press.

Heinz, J. P., E. O. Laumann, R. L. Nelson, and R. H. Salisbury. 1993. *The Hollow Core: Private Interests in National Policy Making*. Cambridge, MA: Harvard University Press.

Hennessy, P. 1989. *Whitehall*. London: Fontana.

——.1992. *Never Again: Britain 1945–51*. London: Cape.

——.2000. *The Prime Minister: The Office and Its Holders Since 1945*. London: Penguin.

Hennessy, T. 1997. *A History of Northern Ireland 1920–1996*. Dublin: Gill and Macmillan.

Hobson, P. A. R., and F. St-Hilaire. 2000. The Evolution of Federal-Provincial Fiscal Arrangements: Putting Humpty Together Again. In *Toward a New Mission Statement for Canadian Fiscal Federalism: Canada: State of the Federation 1999/2000*, ed. H. Lazar, 189–212. Kingston, Ontario: Queens University Institute of Intergovernmental Relations.

Holliday, I. 1992. Scottish Limits to Thatcherism. *Political Quarterly* 63 (4):448–59.

Hollingsworth, J. R. 1986. *A Political Economy of Medicine: Great Britain and the United States*. Baltimore: Johns Hopkins University Press.

Hopkin, D. 2000. Labour's Roots in Wales, 1880–1900. In *The Labour Party in Wales, 1900–2000*, ed. D. Tanner, C. Williams, and D. Hopkin, 40–60. Cardiff: University of Wales Press.

Horowitz, D. 2001. The Northern Ireland Agreement: Clear, Consociational, and Risky. In *Northern Ireland and the Divided World: The Northern Ireland Conflict and the Good Friday Agreement in Comparative Perspective*, ed. J. McGarry, 89–108. Oxford: Oxford University Press.

Hough, D., and C. Jeffery. 2003. Elections in Multi-Level Systems: Lessons for the UK from Abroad. In *The State of the Nations 2003: The Third Year of Devolution in the United Kingdom*, ed. R. Hazell, 239–62. Exeter: Imprint Academic.

Huber, E., C. Ragin, and J. D. Stephens. 1993. Social Democracy, Christian Democracy, Constitutional Structure, and the Welfare State. *American Journal of Sociology* 99 (3):711–49.

Huber, E., and J. D. Stephens. 2001. *Development and Crisis of the Welfare State: Parties and Policies in Global Markets*. Chicago: University of Chicago Press.

Hunter, D. J. 1994. From Tribalism to Corporatism: the Managerial Challenge to

Medical Dominance. In *Challenging Medicine*, ed. J. Gabe, D. Kelleher, and G. Williams, 1–22. London: Routledge.

———. 2003. *Public Health Policy*. Cambridge: Polity.

Hunter, D., and G. Wistow. 1987. The Paradox of Policy Diversity in a Unitary State: Community Care in Britain. *Public Administration* 65 (Spring):3–24.

Hutchison, I. G. C. 1986. *A Political History of Scotland, 1832–1924*. Edinburgh: John Donald.

———. 2000. Legislative and Executive Autonomy in Modern Scotland. In *The Challenge to Westminster: Sovereignty, Devolution and Independence*, ed. H. T. Dickinson and M. Lynch, 133–42. Edinburgh: John Donald.

———. 2001. *Scottish Politics in the Twentieth Century*. Basingstoke: Palgrave.

Immergut, E. M. 1998. The Theoretical Core of the New Institutionalism. *Politics and Society* 26 (1):5–34.

Jaques, E. 1976. *A General Theory of Bureaucracy*. London: Heinemann.

———. 1978. *Health Services: Their Nature and Organization and the Role of Patients, Doctors, Nurses, and the Complementary Professions*. London: Heinemann.

Jeffery, C. 1997. Conclusions: Sub-National Authorities and 'European Domestic Policy'. In *The Regional Dimension of the European Union: Towards a Third Level in Europe?*, ed. C. Jeffery, 204–19. Portland, OR: Frank Cass.

———. 2003. Equity and Diversity: Devolution, Social Citizenship, and Territorial Culture in the UK. *Territory Justice and Power*, ed. S. L. Greer. London: The Constitution Unit.

———. Forthcoming. Continental Affairs: Bringing the EU Back In. In *Devolution and Power in the United Kingdom*, ed. A. Trench. Manchester: Manchester University Press.

Jenkins-Smith, H. C., and P. Sabatier. 1994. Evaluating the Advocacy Coalition Framework. *Journal of Public Policy* 14:175–203.

Jones, G., J. Wyn Owen, J. Williams, M. Ponton, and C. Hawker. 1998. Health and Social Policy. In *The National Assembly Agenda*, ed. J. Osmond, 257–65. Cardiff: Institute of Welsh Affairs.

Jones, J. B. 1983. The Development of the Devolution Debate. In *The Welsh Veto: The Wales Act 1978 and the Referendum*, ed. D. Foulkes, J. B. Jones, and R. A. Wilford, 19–33. Cardiff: University of Wales Press.

Jones, J. B., and D. Balsom, eds. 2000. *The Road to the National Assembly for Wales*. Cardiff: University of Wales Press.

Jones, J. B., and R. A. Wilford. 1983. The Referendum Campaign: 8 February–1 March 1979. In *The Welsh Veto: The Wales Act 1978 and the Referendum*, ed. D. Foulkes, J. B. Jones, and R. A. Wilford, 118–51. Cardiff: University of Wales Press.

Kandiah, M. D., and A. Seldon, eds. 1996. *Ideas and Think Tanks in Contemporary Britain*. Vol. 1. London: Frank Cass.

Katzenstein, P. J. 1985. *Small States in World Markets: Industrial Policy in Europe*. Ithaca: Cornell University Press.

Kavanagh, D. 2001. New Labour, New Millennium, New Premiership. In *The Blair Effect: The Blair Government 1997–2001*, ed. A. Seldon, 3–20. London: Little, Brown.

Keating, M. 1998. *The New Regionalism in Western Europe: Territorial Restructuring and Political Change*. Cheltenham: Edward Elgar.

Keating, M., and J. Loughlin. 2002. *Territorial Policy Communities and Devolution in the United Kingdom.* Vol. 2002/1. Florence: European University Institute Working Papers.

Kellas, J. G. 1989. *The Scottish Political System.* 4th edn. Cambridge: Cambridge University Press.

Key, V. O. 1950. *Southern Politics in State and Nation.* New York: A. A. Knopf.

Kingdon, J. W. 1995. *Agendas, Alternatives, and Public Policies.* New York: HarperCollins.

Kirkpatrick, I., and R. Pyper. 2001. The Early Impact of Devolution on Civil Service Accountability in Scotland. *Public Policy and Administration* 16 (3):68–84.

Kitschelt, H. 2001. Partisan Competition and Welfare State Retrenchment: When Do Politicians Choose Unpopular Policies? In *The New Politics of the Welfare State,* ed. P. Pierson, 265–303. Oxford: Oxford University Press.

Klein, R. 1990. The State and the Profession: The Politics of the Double Bed. *British Medical Journal* 301 (3 October):700–2.

———. 2000. *The New Politics of the NHS.* 4th edn. London: Longman.

Klein, R., P. Day, and S. Redmayne. 1996. *Managing Scarcity: Priority Setting and Rationing in the National Health Service.* Milton Keynes: Open University Press.

Knox, W. W. 1999. *Industrial Nation: Work, Culture and Society in Scotland, 1800–Present.* Edinburgh: Edinburgh University Press.

Kumar, K. 2003. *The Making of English National Identity.* Cambridge: Cambridge University Press.

Lane, J.-E. 2000. *New Public Management.* London: Routledge.

Lawrence, R. J. 1965. *The Government of Northern Ireland: Public Finance and Public Services 1921–1964.* Oxford: Clarendon.

Lazar, H. 1997. Non-constitutional Renewal: Toward a New Equilibrium in the Federation. In *Non-Constitutional Renewal: Canada: The State of the Federation 1997,* ed. H. Lazar, 3–25. Kingston, Ontario: Queens University Institute of Intergovernmental Relations.

Le Grand, J., N. Mays, and J. Mulligan, eds. 1998. *Learning from the NHS Internal Market.* London: King's Fund.

Leichter, H. M., ed. 1992. *Health Policy Reform in America: Innovations from the States.* Armonk, New York: M. E. Sharpe.

Lewis, R. 2000. Political Culture and Ideology, 1900–1918. In *The Labour Party in Wales, 1900–2000,* ed. D. Tanner, C. Williams, and D. Hopkin, 86–109. Cardiff: University of Wales Press.

Lijphart, A. 1969. Consociational Democracy. *World Politics* 21 (January):207–25.

Lipset, S. M., and S. Rokkan. 1967. Cleavage Structures, Party Systems, and Voter Alignments: An Introduction. In *Party Systems and Voter Alignments,* ed. S. M. Lipset and S. Rokkan, 1–64. New York: Free Press.

Longley, M., and M. Warner. 1999. Health and Health Delivery in Wales. In *Wales Today,* ed. D. Dunkerly and A. Thompson, 199–212. Cardiff: University of Wales Press.

López-Casanovas, G. 2003. La descentralización sanitaria. Lecciones desde la experiencia española. In *Federalismo y políticas de salud: Descentralización y relaciones intergubermentales desde una perspectiva comparada,* ed. C. Auclair and C. Gadsden, 112–37. Ottawa/Mexico City: Forum of Federations/Instituto nacional para el federalismo y el desarrollo municipal.

Loughlin, M. 2000. The Restructuring of Central-Local Government Relations. In *The Changing Constitution*, 4th edn., ed. J. Jowell and D. Oliver, 137–66. Oxford: Oxford University Press.

Lustick, I. S. 1997. Lijphart, Lakatos, and Consociationalism. *World Politics* 50 (October):88–117.

MacMahon, P. 2002. How McLeish Made Up his Policies on the Hoof. *The Scotsman* (26 January).

Maioni, A. 1998. *Parting at the Crossroads: The Emergence of Health Insurance in the United States and Canada.* Princeton, NJ: Princeton University Press.

——.2002. Health Care in the New Millennium. In *Canadian Federalism: Performance, Effectiveness, and Legitimacy*, ed. H. Bakvis and G. Skogstad, 87–104. Toronto: Oxford University Press.

Mandelson, P. 1996. *The Blair Revolution: Can New Labour Deliver?* London: Faber and Faber.

March, J. G., and J. P. Olsen. 1989. *Rediscovering Institutions: The Organizational Basis of Politics.* New York: Free Press.

Marmor, T. 1999. The Rage for Reform: Sense and Nonsense in Health Policy. In *Health Reform: Public Success, Private Failure*, ed. D. Drache and T. Sullivan, 260–71. London: Routledge.

——.Fads in Medical Care Management and Policy. London: Nuffield Trust (Rock Carling Fellowship Lecture).

Marsh, P. T. 1994. *Joseph Chamberlain: Entrepreneur in Politics.* New Haven: Yale University Press.

Masterman, R., and J. Mitchell. 2001. Devolution and the Centre. In *The State of the Nations 2001: The Second Year of Devolution in the United Kingdom*, ed. A. Trench, 175–96. Thorverton: Imprint Academic.

McAllister, L. 2001. *Plaid Cymru: The Emergence of a Political Party.* Bridgend: Seren.

McCrae, M. 2003. *The National Health Service in Scotland: Origins and Ideals, 1900–1950.* East Linton: Tuckwell.

McCrone, D. 1992. *Understanding Scotland: The Sociology of a Stateless Nation.* London: Routledge.

McDonald, R. 2002. *Using Health Economics in Health Services: Rationing Rationally?* Milton Keynes: Open University Press.

McIntyre, A. 2001. Modern Irish Republicanism and the Belfast Agreement: Chickens Coming Home to Roost, or Turkeys Celebrating Christmas? In *Aspects of the Belfast Agreement*, ed. R. Wilford, 202–22. Oxford: Oxford University Press.

McKenzie, R. T. 1964. *British Political Parties: The Distribution of Power within the Conservative and Labour Parties.* 2nd edn. New York: Praeger.

McKeown, T. 1979. *The Role of Medicine: Dream, Mirage, or Nemesis?* Princeton, NJ: Princeton University Press.

McKittrick, D. 2002. Ulster 'Driven to Tranquilisers by Lingering War Psychology'. *The Independent* (8 August).

McLean, I. 2003. The Purse Strings Tighten. In *Second Term Challenge: Can the Welsh Assembly Government Hold Its Course?*, ed. J. Osmond, 82–98. Cardiff: Institute of Welsh Affairs.

McLellan, A. 2003. Milburn Secured Three stars for PM's Trust. *Health Services Journal* 113 (18 December):3–5.

McRoberts, K. 1997. *Misconceiving Canada: The Struggle for National Unity.* Toronto: Oxford University Press.

Mechanic, D. 1989. *Painful Choices: Research and Essays on Health Care.* New Brunswick, NJ: Transaction.

Meisel, J. 1992 [1963]. The Stalled Omnibus: Canadian Parties in the 1960s. In *Canadian Political Party Systems,* ed. R. K. Carty, 328–50. Peterborough, Ontario: Broadview. (First published in *Social Research,* 30(3).)

Midwinter, A., M. Keating, and J. Mitchell. 1991. *Politics and Public Policy in Scotland.* Basingstoke: Macmillan.

Midwinter, A., and N. McGarvey. 2001. The New Accountability? Devolution and Expenditure Politics in Scotland. *Public Money and Management:* 47–55.

Miguel, J. M. de, and M. F. Guillén. 1989. The Health System in Spain. In *Success and Crisis in National Health Systems: A Comparative Approach,* ed. M. G. Field, 128–64. London: Routledge.

Milne, S. D. 1957. *The Scottish Office.* London: Allen and Unwin.

Mitchell, J. 1990. *Conservatives and the Union: A Study of Conservative Party Attitudes to Scotland.* Edinburgh: Edinburgh University Press.

———. 1996. *Strategies for Self-Government: The Campaigns for a Scottish Parliament.* Edinburgh: Polygon.

———. 1998. Contemporary Unionism. In *Unionist Scotland 1800–1997,* ed. C. M. M. Macdonald, 117–39. Edinburgh: John Donald.

———. 2003. *Governing Scotland.* Basingstoke: Palgrave.

Mitchell, J., and Scottish Monitoring Team. 2001. Scotland: Maturing Devolution. In *The State of the Nations 2001: The Second Year of Devolution in the United Kingdom,* ed. A. Trench, 45–76. Thorverton: Imprint Academic.

———. 2003. Third Year, Third First Minister. In *The State of the Nations 2003: The Third Year of Devolution in the United Kingdom,* ed. R. Hazell, 119–41. Exeter: Imprint Academic.

Mohan, J. 2002. *Planning, Markets, and Hospitals.* London: Routledge.

Molas, I., and O. Bartomeus. 1998. *Estructura de la competència política a Catalunya.* Barcelona: ICPS.

Monaghan, S., J. Davidson, and D. Bainton. 1999. *Freeing the Dragon: New Opportunities to Improve the Health of the Welsh People.* London: Nuffield Trust.

Moran, M. 1999. *Governing the Health Care State: A Comparative Study of the United Kingdom, the United States, and Germany.* Manchester: Manchester University Press.

Morata, F. 1995. Spanish Regions in the European Community. In *The European Union and the Regions,* ed. B. Jones and M. Keating, 115–34. Oxford: Oxford University Press.

Moreno, L. 2001. Spain, a Via Media of Welfare Development. In *Welfare States Under Pressure,* ed. P. Taylor-Goodby, 100–22. London: Sage.

———. 2002. Decentralization in Spain. *Regional Studies* 36 (4):399–408.

Morgan, K. 2003. How Objective 1 Arrived in Wales: The Political Origins of a Coup. In *Contemporary Wales,* ed. R. Wyn Jones. Vol. 15. Cardiff: University of Wales Press.

Morgan, K., and G. Mungham. 2000. *Redesigning Democracy: The Making of the Welsh Assembly.* Bridgend: Seren.

Morgan, K. O. 1981. *Rebirth of a Nation: A History of Modern Wales.* Oxford: Oxford University Press.

——. 1984. *Labour in Power 1945–1951*. Oxford: Oxford University Press.

——. 1995. *Modern Wales: Politics, Places, and People*. Cardiff: University of Wales Press.

Morrison, J. 2001. *Reforming Britain: New Labour, New Constitution?* London: Reuters.

Mungham, G. 2001. Labour Pains. In *Contemporary Wales*, ed. R. Wyn Jones, 104–8. Vol. 14. Cardiff: University of Wales Press.

Myles, J., and P. Pierson. 2001. The Comparative Political Economy of Pension Reform. In *The New Politics of the Welfare State*, ed. P. Pierson, 305–34. Oxford: Oxford University Press.

Norton, P. 1996. Conservative Politics and the Abolition of Stormont. In *The Northern Ireland Question in British Politics*, ed. P. Catterall and S. McDougall, 129–42. Basingstoke: Macmillan.

Nottingham, C., ed. 2000. *The NHS in Scotland: The Legacy of the Past and the Prospect of the Future*. Aldershot: Ashgate.

Oates, W. E. 1999. An Essay on Fiscal Federalism. *Journal of Economic Literature* 37 (September):1120–49.

O'Connor, J. S., and G. Olsen, eds. 1998. *Power Resources Theory and the Welfare State*. Toronto: University of Toronto Press.

O'Leary, B., and J. McGarry. 1993. *The Politics of Antagonism: Understanding Northern Ireland*. London: Althone.

Omnium Cultural, ed. 1998. *Catalunya i Espanya: Una relació econòmica i fiscal a revisar*. Barcelona: Proa.

Osmond, J. 2000. A Constitutional Convention by Other Means: The First Year of the National Assembly for Wales. In *The State and the Nations*, ed. R. Hazell, 37–78. Thorverton: Imprint Academic.

——. 2003. From Corporate Body to Virtual Parliament: The Metamorphosis of the National Assembly for Wales. In *The State of the Nations 2003: The Third Year of Devolution in the United Kingdom*, ed. R. Hazell, 13–48. Exeter: Imprint Academic.

Parry, R. 1987. The Centralization of the Scottish Office. In *Ministers and Ministries: A Functional Analysis*, ed. R. Rose, 97–141. Oxford: Clarendon.

——. 2001. Devolution, Integration, and Modernisation in the United Kingdom Civil Service. *Public Policy and Administration* 16 (3):53–67.

Patchett, K. 2000. The New Welsh Constitution: The Government of Wales Act 1998. In *The Road to the National Assembly*, ed. J. B. Jones and D. Balsom, 229–64. Cardiff: University of Wales Press.

——. 2002. The Central Relationship: The Assembly's Engagement with Westminster and Whitehall. In *Building a Civic Culture: Institutional Change, Policy Development and Political Dynamics in the National Assembly for Wales*, ed. J. B. Jones and J. Osmond, 17–32. Cardiff: Welsh Governance Centre/Institute for Welsh Affairs.

Paterson, L. 1994. *The Autonomy of Modern Scotland*. Edinburgh: Edinburgh University Press.

——. 1998. Scottish Home Rule: Radical Break or Pragmatic Adjustment? In *Remaking the Union: Devolution and British Politics in the 1990s*, ed. H. Elcock and M. Keating, 53–67. London: Frank Cass.

Paton, C. 2000. New Labour, New Health Policy? In *Analysing Health Policy*, ed. A. Hann, 10–31. Aldershot: Ashgate.

Peters, B. G. 2003. Policy Reform: Is Uniformity the Answer? *Political Quarterly* 74 (4):421–8.

Peterson, M. J. 1978. *The Medical Profession in Victorian London*. Berkeley and Los Angeles: University of California Press.

Peterson, P. 1981. *City Limits*. Chicago: University of Chicago Press.

——.1994. *The Price of Federalism*. Washington: Brookings Institution.

Pierson, P. 1995. Fragmented Welfare States: Federal Institutions and the Development of Social Policy. *Governance* 8 (4):449–78.

——.2001. Post-industrial Pressures on the Mature Welfare States. In *The New Politics of the Welfare State*, ed. P. Pierson, 80–105. Oxford: Oxford University Press.

Poirier, J. 2001. Pouvoir normatif et protection sociale dans les fédérations multi-nationales. *Canadian Journal of Law and Society/Revue Canadienne Droit et Societé* 16 (2):137–71.

Pollitt, C. 1993. *Managerialism and the Public Services*. 2nd edn. Oxford: Blackwell.

Pollock, A.M. 2004. NHS PLC: The privatisation of our health care. London: Verso.

Porter, D. 1999. *Health, Civilization, and the State: A History of Public Health from Ancient to Modern Times*. London: Routledge.

Powell, J. E. 1966. *A New Look at Medicine and Politics*. London: Pitman Medical.

Powell, M. A. 1997. *Evaluating the National Health Service*. Milton Keynes: Open University Press.

Powell, W. W., and P. J. DiMaggio, eds. 1991. *The New Institutionalism in Organizational Analysis*. Chicago: University of Chicago Press.

Prats i Català, J. 1988. Una reflexión sobre las alternativas planteadas al centralismo español y su significación política diversa. In *Federalismo y Estado de las Autonomías*, 51–74. Barcelona: Planeta.

Ragin, C. 1987. *The Comparative Method: Moving Beyond Qualitative and Quantitative Strategies*. Berkeley: University of California Press.

Ragin, C., D. Berg-Schlosser, and G. de Meur. 1996. Political Methodology: Qualitiative Methods. In *A New Handbook of Political Science*, ed. R. E. Goodin and H.-D. Klingemann, 749–68. Oxford: Oxford University Press.

Rawlings, R. 1999. The New Model Wales. *Journal of Law and Society* 25:461–509.

——.2003. Towards a Parliament: Three Faces of the National Assembly for Wales. In *Contemporary Wales*, ed. R. Wyn Jones. Vol. 15. Cardiff: University of Wales Press. (O'Donnell Lecture, University of Wales).

Rhodes, R. A. W. 1981. *Control and Power in Central-Local Government Relations*. Westmead: Gower/Social Sciences Research Council.

Richardson, J. J., and G. Jordan. 1979. *Governing Under Pressure: The Policy Process in a Post-parliamentary Democracy*. Oxford: Robertson.

Rico Gómez, A. 1998. Descentralización y reforma sanitaria en España (1976–1996): Intensidad de preferencias y autonomía política como condiciones para el buen gobierno. Ph.D. dissertation, Instituto Juan March de Estudios e Investigaciones, Centro de Estudios Avanzados en Ciencias Sociales.

Rivett, G. 1986. *The Development of the London Hospital System 1823–1982*. London: King Edward's Hospital Fund for London.

——.1998. *From Cradle to Grave: Fifty Years of the NHS*. London: King's Fund.

Robinson, R., and J. Le Grand, eds. 1993. *Evaluating the NHS Reforms*. London: King's Fund.

Rodríguez, J. A., and J. M. de Miguel. 1990. *Salud y Poder.* Madrid: Centro de Investigaciones Sociológicas/Siglo Veintiuno.

Rodríguez-Zapata, J. 1996. *Teoría y Práctica del Derecho Constitucional.* Madrid: Tecnos.

Rose, P. 2000. *How the Troubles Came to Northern Ireland.* Basingstoke: Palgrave.

Rose, R. 1971. *Governing without Consensus: An Irish Perspective.* London: Faber and Faber.

——, ed. 1987. *Ministers and Ministries: A Functional Analysis.* Oxford: Clarendon.

——.1989. *Politics in England: Change and Persistence.* Basingstoke: Macmillan.

Ruane, J., and J. Todd. 1996. *The Dynamics of Conflict in Northern Ireland: Power, Conflict, and Emancipation.* Cambridge: Cambridge University Press.

——, eds. 1999. *After the Good Friday Agreement: Analysing Political Change in Northern Ireland.* Dublin: University College Dublin Press.

Ruohomaki, J. 2001. *Two Elections, Two Contests: the June 2001 Elections in Northern Ireland.* Belfast: Democratic Dialogue.

Russell, M. 2000. *Reforming the House of Lords: Lessons from Abroad.* Oxford: Oxford University Press.

Russell, M., and M. Sandford. 2002. Why are Second Chambers so Difficult to Reform? *Journal of Legislative Studies* 8 (3):79–89.

Russell, P. H. 1993. *Constitutional Odyssey: Can Canadians Become a Sovereign People?* Toronto: University of Toronto Press.

Sabatier, P. A. 1998. The Advocacy Coalition Framework: Revisions and Relevance for Europe. *Journal of European Public Policy* 5 (1):98–130.

Saltman, R. B., and C. van Otter, eds. 1995. *Implementing Planned Markets in Health Care.* Milton Keynes: Open University Press.

Sandford, M. 2002. *A Commentary on the Regional Government White Paper "Your Region, Your Choice: Revitalising the English Regions".* London: The Constitution Unit.

Sandford, M., and P. McQuail. 2001. *Unexplored Territory: Elected Regional Assemblies in England.* London: The Constitution Unit.

Sartori, G. 1999 [1986]. *Partidos y Sistemas de Partidos.* Madrid: Alianza Editorial.

Schmidt, V. A. 2002. *The Futures of European Capitalism.* Oxford: Oxford University Press.

Schulz, R., and S. Harrison. 1984. Consensus Management in the British National Health Service: Implications for the United States. *Milbank Quarterly* 62:657–81.

Seawright, D. 2002. The Scottish Conservative and Unionist Party: 'The Lesser Spotted Tory'? Paper presented at the Annual Conference of the Political Studies Association, Aberdeen, 5–7 April 2002. Forthcoming in *Tomorrow's Scotland*, ed. G. Hassan.

Seyd, P. 1987. *The Rise and Fall of the Labour Left.* Basingstoke: Macmillan.

Sharpe, L. J., ed. 1993. The Rise of Meso-Level Government in Europe. London: Sage.

Shonfield, A. 1965. *Modern Capitalism: The Changing Balance of Public and Private Power.* New York: Oxford University Press.

Simeon, Rachel. 2003. The Long-term Care Decision: Social Rights and Democratic Diversity. In *The State and the Nations: The Third Year of Devolution in the United Kingdom*, ed. R. Hazell, 215–32. Exeter: Imprint Academic.

Simeon, Richard. 1972. *Federal-Provincial Diplomacy: The Making of Recent Policy in Canada*. Toronto: University of Toronto Press.

——. 2002. *Political Science and Canadian Federalism: Seven Decades of Scholarly Engagement*. Kingston, Ontario: Institute of Intergovernmental Relations, Queens University.

——. forthcoming. Federalism and Social Justice: Thinking through the Jungle. In *Territory, Justice and Democracy*, ed. S. L. Greer. London: The Constitution Unit.

Simeon, R., and D. Cameron. 2002. Intergovernmental Relations and Democracy: An Oxymoron If There Ever Was One? In *Canadian Federalism: Performance, Effectiveness, and Legitimacy*, ed. H. Bakvis and G. Skogstad, 278–95. Toronto: Oxford University Press.

Simeon, R., and I. Robinson. 1990. *State, Society, and the Development of Canadian Federalism*. Toronto: University of Toronto Press.

Skocpol, T., and M. Somers. 1994. The Uses of Comparative History in Macrosocial Inquiry. In *Social Revolutions in the Modern World*, ed. T. Skocpol, 72–98. Cambridge: Cambridge University Press.

Smith, D. 1984. *Wales! Wales?* London: Allen and Unwin.

Smith, D. E. 1981. *The Regional Decline of a National Party: Liberals on the Prairies*. Toronto: University of Toronto Press.

Smith, R. 2003. The Failures of Two Contracts. *British Medical Journal* 326 (24 May):1097–8.

Smout, T. C. 1987. *A Century of the Scottish People 1830–1950*. London: Fontana.

Solé Tura, J. 1986. *Nacionalidades y Nacionalismos en España: Autonomías, Federalismo, Autodeterminación*. Madrid: Alianza Editorial.

Sparer, M. 1996. *Medicaid and the Limits of State Health Reform*. Philadelphia: Temple University Press.

——. 2003. Leading the Health Policy Orchestra: The Need for an Intergovernmental Partnership. *Journal of Health Politics, Policy and Law* 28 (2–3):245–70.

Sparer, M., and L. D. Brown. 1996. States and the Health Care Crisis: The Limits and Lessons of Laboratory Federalism. In *Health Policy, Federalism, and the American States*, ed. R. F. Rich and W. D. White, 181–202. Washington, DC: Urban Institute Press.

Stephens, P. 2001. The Treasury Under Labour. In *The Blair Effect: The Blair Government, 1997–2001*, ed. A. Seldon, 185–208. London: Little, Brown.

Subirats, J. 2003. Asymmetry and its Consequences. In *Territory, Justice and Democracy* ed. S. L. Greer. London: The Constitution Unit.

Subirats, J., and R. Gallego, eds. 2002. *Veinte años de autonomías en España*. Madrid: Alianza Editorial/CIS.

Swank, D. 2001. Political Institutions and Welfare State Restructuring: The Impact of Institutions on Social Policy Change in Developed Democracies. In *The New Politics of the Welfare State*, ed. P. Pierson, 197–236. Oxford: Oxford University Press.

Syett, K. 2003. A Technocratic Fix to the "Legitimacy Problem"? The Blair Government and Health Care Rationing in the United Kingdom. *Journal of Health Politics, Policy and Law* 28 (4):715–46.

Tanner, D., C. Williams, and D. Hopkin, eds. 2000. *The Labour Party in Wales, 1900–2000*. Cardiff: University of Wales Press.

Taylor, B. 2002. *Scotland's Parliament: Triumph and Disaster*. Edinburgh: Edinburgh University Press.

Templeton, S.-K. 2003. Health Minister Chisholm: NHS Treats 'Patients' not 'Consumers'. *The Sunday Herald* (Glasgow) (28 September).

Thelen, K. 1999. Historical Institutionalism in Comparative Politics. *Annual Review of Political Science* 2:369–404.

Thelen, K., and S. Steinmo. 1992. Historical Institutionalism in Comparative Politics. In *Structuring Politics: Historical Institutionalism in Comparative Analysis*, ed. S. Steinmo, K. Thelen, and F. Longstreth, 1–32. Cambridge: Cambridge University Press.

Thomas, I. C. 1987. Giving Direction to the Welsh Office. In *Ministers and Ministries: A Functional Analysis*, ed. R. Rose, 142–88. Oxford: Oxford University Press.

Thompson, S. 2003. A Proletarian Public Sphere: Working-Class Provision of Medical Services and Care in South Wales, *c.* 1900–1948. In *Medicine in Wales c. 1800–2000: Public Service or Private Commodity?*, ed. A. Borsay, 86–107. Cardiff: University of Wales Press.

Tiebout, C. M. 1956. A Pure Theory of Local Expenditure. *Journal of Political Economy* 74:416–25.

Timmins, N. 1995. *The Five Giants: A Biography of the Welfare State*. London: Fontana Press.

Trench, A. 2001a. Intergovernmental Relations a Year On: Whitehall Still Rules OK? In *The State of the Nations 2001: The Second Year of Devolution in the United Kingdom*, ed. A. Trench, 153–74. Thorverton: Imprint Academic.

——, ed. 2001b. *The State of the Nations 2001: The First Year of Devolution in the United Kingdom*. Thorverton: Imprint Academic.

——. 2003. *Intergovernmental Relations in Canada: Lessons for the UK?* London: The Constitution Unit.

——, ed. 2004. *Has Devolution Made a Difference? The State of the Nations 2004*. Exeter: Imprint Academic.

Trystan, D., R. Scully, and R. W. Jones. 2004. Explaining the 'Quiet Earthquake': Voting Behaviour in the First Election to the National Assembly for Wales. Manuscript, Institute of Welsh Politics, University of Wales Aberystwyth.

Tuohy, C. H. 1992. *Policy and Politics in Canada: Institutionalized Ambivalence*. Philadelphia: Temple University Press.

——. 1999. *Accidental Logics: The Dynamics of Change in the Health Care Arena in the United States, Britain, and Canada*. Oxford: Oxford University Press.

Viver i Pi-Sunyer, C. 1990. Conflictes de competències entre l'Estat i la Generalitat de Catalunya. *Autonomies: Revista Catalana de Dret Públic* 12:43–9.

Walker, J. L., Jr. 1989. Policy Communities as Global Phenomena. *Governance* 2:1–5.

Wall, A. 2001. *Being a Health Service Manager—Expectations and Experience: A Study of Four Generations of Managers in the NHS*. London: Nuffield Trust (Maureen Dixon Essay Series).

Walshe. 2003. *Regulating Healthcare: A Prescription for Improvement?* Milton Keynes: Open University Press.

Ward, S. 2001. Celtic Catch-Up. *Public Finance* (4 May).

Watts, R. L. 2000. *The Spending Power in Federal Systems: A Comparative Analysis*. Kingston, Ontario: Queens University Institute of Intergovernmental Relations.

Webster, C. 1998. *The National Health Service: A Political History*. Oxford: Oxford University Press.

Weir, M., A. S. Orloff, and T. Skocpol, eds. 1988. *The Politics of Social Policy in the United States*. Princeton, NJ: Princeton University Press.

Weissert, C. S., and W. G. Weissert. 1996. *Governing Health: The Politics of Health Policy*. Baltimore: Johns Hopkins University Press.

White, B. 1994. Training Medical Policemen: Forensic Medicine and Public Health in Nineteenth-century Scotland. In *Legal Medicine in History*, ed. M. Clark and C. Crawford, 145–65. Cambridge: Cambridge University Press.

White, J. 2003. Three Meanings of Capacity; Or, Why the Federal Government is Most Likely to Lead on Insurance Access Issues. *Journal of Health Politics, Policy and Law* 28 (2–3):217–44.

Whyte, J. 1990. *Interpreting Northern Ireland*. Oxford: Clarendon.

Whyte, T. 1983. How much Discrimination Was There under the Unionist Regime, 1921–1968? In *Contemporary Irish Studies*, ed. T. Gallagher and J. O'Connell, 1–35. Manchester: Manchester University Press.

Wilford, R., ed. 2001. *Aspects of the Belfast Agreement*. Oxford: Oxford University Press.

Wilford, R., and R. Wilson. 2000. 'A Bare Knuckle Ride': Northern Ireland. In *The State and the Nations: The First Year of Devolution in the United Kingdom*, ed. R. Hazell, 79–116. Thorverton: Imprint Academic.

——.2001. *Devolution and Health Quarterly Report (March)*. London: The Constitution Unit.

——.2003. Northern Ireland: Valedictory? In *The State of the Nations 2003: The Third Year of Devolution in the United Kingdom*, ed. R. Hazell, 79–118. Exeter: Imprint Academic.

Wilkins, R., and S. L. Greer. 2003. Decentralisation: Promise and Problems. In *Federalism, Financing, and Public Health*, ed. Australian Government Department of Health and Aging. Canberra: Commonwealth of Australia.

Wilkinson, R. G. 1996. *Unhealthy Societies*. London: Routledge.

Williams, C. 2000. Labour and the Challenge of Local Government, 1919–1939. In *The Labour Party in Wales, 1900–2000*, ed. D. Tanner, C. Williams, and D. Hopkin, 140–65. Cardiff: University of Wales Press.

Williams, G. A. 1985. *When Was Wales? A History of the Welsh*. London: Penguin.

Williamson, A., and G. Room, eds. 1983. *Health and Welfare States of Britain: An Inter-country Comparison*. London: Heinemann.

Wilson, R. 2003. *Northern Ireland: What's Going Wrong*. London: The Constitution Unit.

Wilson, R., and R. Wilford. 2001. Northern Ireland: Endgame. In *The State of the Nations 2001*, ed. A. Trench, 77–106. Thorverton: Imprint Academic.

Wilson, T. 1955a. Conclusion: Devolution and Partition. In *Ulster Under Home Rule*, ed. T. Wilson, 183–211. Oxford: Oxford University Press.

——, ed. 1955b. *Ulster Under Home Rule: A Study of the Political and Economic Problems of Northern Ireland*. Oxford: Oxford University Press.

Lord Windlesham. 1973. Ministers in Ulster: The Machinery of Direct Rule. *Public Administration* 51 (Autumn).

Winetrobe, B. 2001. *Realising the Vision: A Parliament with a Purpose: An Audit of the First Year of the Scottish Parliament*. London: The Constitution Unit.

Woods, K. J. 2002. Health Policy and the NHS in the UK 1997–2002. In *Devolution in Practice: Public Policy Differences within the UK*, ed. J. Adams and P. Robinson, 25–59. London: IPPR.

Woods, K. J. and D. Carter, eds. 2003. *Scotland's Health and Health Services.* London: HMSO.

Wright, K. 1997. *The People Say Yes: The Making of Scotland's Parliament.* Glendaruel, Argyll: Argyll.

Wyn Owen, J. 2000. Change the Welsh Way: Health and the NHS 1984–1994. Talk at the University of Wales, March.

Zahariadis, N. 1995. *Markets, States, and Public Policy: Privatization in Britain and France.* Ann Arbor: University of Michigan Press.

Zysman, J. 1983. *Governments, Markets, and Growth.* Ithaca: Cornell University Press.

Government documents

Audit Commission. 2002. *Public Services in Wales: Delivering a Better Wales.* London: HMSO.

Black Report. 1992. *Inequalities in Health: The Black Report and the Health Divide.* London: Penguin.

Commission appointed by the Governor of Northern Ireland (Cameron Commission). 1969. *Disturbances in Northern Ireland.* Belfast: HMSO.

Commission for Health Improvement. 2002. *Emerging Themes from 175 Clinical Governance Reviews.* London: CHI.

Commission on the Future of Health Care in Canada (Romanow Commission). 2002. *Building on Values: The Future of Health Care in Canada.* Ottawa: Government of Canada.

Committee of Enquiry into the Cost of the National Health Service (Guillebaud Committee). 1956. *Report of the Committee of Enquiry into the Cost of the National Health Service.* London: HMSO.

Department of Health. 1996. *The National Health Service: A Service with Ambitions.* London: HMSO.

——. 1998a. *A First Class Service: Quality in the New NHS.* London: Department of Health.

——. 1998b. *The New NHS: Modern-Dependable.* London: HMSO.

——. 2000a. *For the Benefit of Patients: A Concordat with the Private and Voluntary Health Care Provider Sector.* London: Department of Health.

——. 2000b. *The NHS Plan: A Plan for Investment, a Plan for Reform.* London: HMSO.

——. 2000c. *The NHS Plan: The Government's Response to the Royal Commission on Long Term Care.* London: HMSO.

——. 2001a. *From Vision to Reality.* London: Department of Health.

——. 2001b. *Shifting the Balance within the NHS: Securing Delivery.* London: Department of Health.

——. 2002. *Getting Ahead of the Curve: A Strategy for Combating Infectious Diseases (Including Other Aspects of Health Protection).* London: HMSO.

——. 2003a. *Annual Report.* London: HMSO.

——. 2003b. *Building on the Best: Choice, Responsiveness, and Equity in the NHS.* London: HMSO.

DHSSNI (Northern Ireland Department of Health and Social Services). 1998. *Fit for the Future: A Consultation Document on the Government's Proposals for the Future of the Health and Personal Social Services in Northern Ireland.* London: HMSO.

DHSSPS (Northern Ireland Department of Health Social Services and Public Safety). 2000. *Building the Way Forward in Primary Care.* Belfast: HMSO.

——. 2001a. *Best Practice, Best Care: A Framework for Setting Standards, Delivering Services, and Improving Monitoring and Regulation in the HPSS.* Belfast: HMSO.

——. 2001b. *Report of the Acute Hospitals Review Group.* Belfast: HMSO.

Government of Northern Ireland. 1969. *The Administrative Structure of the Health and Personal Social Services in Northern Ireland.* Belfast: HMSO.

House of Lords Select Committee on the Constitution. 2002a. *Devolution: Inter-Institutional Relations in the United Kingdom.* London: HMSO.

——. 2002b. *Devolution: Inter-institutional relations in the United Kingdom: Evidence.* London: HMSO.

Independent Inquiry into Inequalities. 1988. *Report of the Independent Inquiry into Inequalities in Health (Acheson Report).* London: HMSO.

Lloyd, A. 2002. NHS Wales News Bulletin: Structural Review in the NHS: Summary of Decisions (January); (www.wales.gov/healthplanonline).

Milburn, A. 2001. Shifting the Balance of Power in the NHS. Speech given at the launch of the NHS Modernisation Agency, 25 April.

National Assembly for Wales. 2001a. *Improving Health in Wales: A Plan for the NHS with its Partners.* Cardiff: National Assembly of Wales.

——. 2001b. *Structural Change in the NHS in Wales.* Cardiff: National Assembly of Wales.

National Audit Office. 1996. *Improving Health in Wales: Report by the Comptroller and Auditor General.* London: HMSO/NAO.

National Review of Resource Allocation (Arbuthnott Committee). 1999. *Fair Shares for All: The Report of the National Review of Resource Allocation for the NHS in Scotland.* Edinburgh: HMSO.

NHS Management Inquiry. 1983. Letter to the Rt. Hon. Normal Fowler MP, Secretary of State for Social Services, 6 October.

Office of the First Minister and the Deputy First Minister. 2001. *Programme for Government: Making a Difference 2002–2005.* Belfast: HMSO.

Public Inquiry into Children's Heart Surgery at the Bristol Royal Infirmary 1984–1995 (Kennedy Report). 2001. *Learning from Bristol.* London: HMSO

Review Body on Local Government in Northern Ireland. 1970. *Report (Macrory Report).* Belfast: HMSO.

Review of Health and Social Care in Wales. 2003. *The Review of Health and Social Care in Wales: The Report of the Project Team Advised by Derek Wanless.* Cardiff: National Assembly of Wales.

Scottish Executive Health Department. 2000. *Our National Health: A Plan for Action, a Plan for Change.* Edinburgh: HMSO.

——. 2003. *Partnership for Care: Scotland's Health White Paper.* Edinburgh: HMSO.

Scottish Office. 1997. *Designed to Care: Renewing the National Health Service in Scotland.* Edinburgh: HMSO.

——. 1998. *Toward a Healthier Scotland.* Edinburgh: HMSO.

Secretaries of State for Health; Wales; Northern Ireland; and Scotland. 1989. *Working for Patients.* London: HMSO.

Wanless, D. 2002. *Securing our Future Health: Taking a Long-Term View*. London: HM Treasury.

Welsh Assembly National Steering Group on the Allocation of NHS Resources. 2001. *NHS Resource Allocation Review: Targeting Poor Health: Professor Townsend's Report of the Welsh Assembly's National Steering Group on the Allocation of NHS Resources*. Cardiff: National Assembly for Wales.

Welsh Office. 1998a. *Better Health, Better Wales*. Cardiff: HMSO.

——. 1998b. *NHS Wales: Putting Patients First*. Cardiff: HMSO.

Welsh Office, Welsh Health Planning Forum. 1989. *Strategic Intent and Direction for the NHS in Wales*. Cardiff: HMSO.

Index

Lightning Source UK Ltd.
Milton Keynes UK
UKHW051805280219
337986UK00007B/136/P